The World This Century

Working with Evidence

Neil De Marco

Collins Educational

An imprint of HarperCollins*Publishers*

Published by
Collins Educational
An imprint of HarperCollins*Publishers*
77–85 Fulham Palace Road
London W6 8JB

First published 1987 by Unwin Hyman Ltd.
Reprinted 1988, 1989, 1990
Reprinted by Collins Educational 1991, 1993, 1994 (twice)

British Library Cataloguing in Publication Data
DeMarco, Neil
   The world this century: working with evidence
   1. History, Modern—20th century—
   Sources
   I. Title
   909 82′07   D421

ISBN 0-00-322217-9

Cover by Colin Lewis
Typeset by August Filmsetting,
Haydock, St Helens
Printed in Great Britain by
HarperCollinsManufacturing, Glasgow

Contents

Acknowledgements

The author and publisher are indebted to the following:

For permission to reproduce extracts:

The BBC for an extract from *From Our Own Correspondent* Ed. R. Lazar; Benn for an extract from the *Hungarian Revolution* by D. Pryce-Jones; J. Cape for extracts from *Face of Battle* by J. Keegan, 1976, and *China Phoenix* by P. Townsend; Cassell Ltd. for an extract from W.S. Churchill's *The Second World War*. Vol 4 *The Hinge of Fate*; William Collins and Sons Ltd for an extract from *Duce! the Rise and Fall of Benito Mussolini* by R.H. Collier, 1971; Collins Harvill for an extract from *Into the Whirlwind* by E. Ginzburg, 1967; Croom Helm Ltd for an extract from *Eye Deep in Hell* by J. Ellis, 1976; Curtis Brown Ltd on behalf of C & T Publications Ltd for an extract from *Finest Hour* by Martin Gilbert, © 1983 C & T Publications; Andre Deutsch for extracts from *Khrushchev Remembers, the Last Testament* by N. Khrushchev; Doubleday and Company Inc. for an extract from *Adolf Hitler* by J. Toland; Guardian Newspapers Ltd for an extract from *The Guardian* 10.8.56; Hamish Hamilton for an extract from *The Origins of the Second World War*; by A.J.P. Taylor; Hamlyn Publishing Group for an extract from *Hausfrau at War* by Else Wendel; Robert Hale Ltd for an extract from *The War Walk* by Nigel Jones 1983; David Higham Associates, on behalf of the author, for extracts from *The Rise and Fall of Stalin* by Robert Payne 1966; Longman Group UK Ltd for material from *Dreams, Plans and Nightmares* by Tony Howarth; Macmillan for an extract from *Knaves, Fools and Heroes* by J.W. Wheeler Bennett and an extract from *20th Century World History in Focus* by Harry Mills; Methuen & Co for a table from *Post Victorian Britain* by L.C.B. Seaman; Novosti Press for an extract from *The True Face of Maoism* by F. Burlatsky 1969; Oxford University Press for extracts from *European History 1815–1951* by J. Watson et al, *The Russian Revolution: A Personal Record* by N.N. Sukhanov, *Mao and the Chinese Revolution* by J. Che'en, 1949; *The Struggle for Mastery in Europe* by A.J.P. Taylor; A.D. Peters and Co Ltd on behalf of the author for an extract from *The Red Guard* by Ken Ling; Simulations and Design Corporation for an extract from *Conflict*; Thornton Butterworth for an extract from *Hitler Speaks* by H. Rauschning, 1939; Weidenfeld and Nicolson for material from *Recent History Atlas 1860–1960* by Martin Gilbert and *Chinese Communism* by R. North; Lois Wheeler Smith for an extract from *The Other Side of The River* by E. Snow, 1963; John Mueller for material from *War Presidents and Public Opinion* (University Press of America, 1985).

For permission to reproduce illustrations:
(a-above, c-centre, b-below, l-left, r-right)

The author 15(a)   British Museum 65   Bundesarchiv 86, 96(b), 99   Camera Press Ltd 163, 194,(a), 248   Edimedia 181   Evening Standard 96(a), 108, 140   Express Newspapers 129   Fulgur, Paris 123   Imperial War Museum 35, 128, 135, 139, 146   Institute of Social History, Amsterdam 82(a)   KAL, *The Economist* 168 (right)   Les Gibbard 222, 251   Library of Congress 198   Mail Newspapers 156, 227(b), 244   Mundi, Amsterdam 32   Musée Royal de l'Armée, Brussels 23   The New Statesman 227(a)   Novosti 61, 150   Peter Newark's Western Americana 197   Photosource 17(a), 70, 84, 91, 94, 109, 110(left), 121, 125, 155(b), 158, 169, 190, 209, 220(b), 238   *Punch* 47, 54, 72, 78, 107(a & b), 111, 124, 160, 161, 170, 178, 220(a), 223(a)   Popperfoto 15(c), 17, 29, 39, 44, 46, 56, 63, 98, 110(r), 126, 138(a & b), 143, 145, 155(a), 168(l), 173, 174, 176(a & b), 182, 187, 208(a), 210, 215, 218, 221, 223, 224(l & r), 225, 231, 234, 235, 236(a & b), 243(a & b), 246,(a & b), 250, 252 Süddeutscher Verlag 82(b)   Syndication International Ltd 131, 240   UPI/Bettmann Newsphotos 113, 115, 116(b), 201, 237   The Weiner Library 100   Zoke, courtesy of the *Sunday People* 211   Fort Worth Star-Telegram 194 (r)

Front cover:
BBC Hulton Picture Library (Listening to Churchill)
BBC Hulton Picture Library (1930s depression)
BBC Hulton Picture Library (Winston Churchill)
Popperfoto (Gorbachev and Reagan)
Photosource (Nazi rally)
Photosource (Red Guard)

The publisher and author are also indebted to:

Heinemann Educational Books Ltd for the maps on pages 245 and 249 based on maps in *A Map History of the Modern World* by Brian Catchpole; Arnold Wheaton for the illustrations on pages 133 and 134 based on illustrations appearing in *A Course Book in Modern World History* by P. Speed; Times Newspapers Ltd for the diagram on page 217 based on an illustration appearing in the *Sunday Times Magazine* of 31 March 1985.

Source Seven and Eight on page 91 are from *The German Economy* by G. Stolper. Source Nine on page 91 is from *Nazi Culture* by G. Mosse.

Every effort has been made to contact copyright-holders, but this has not proved possible in every case. The publishers would be pleased to hear from any copyright-holders not acknowledged.

Preface

Notes for pupils

This textbook is based on two types of historical evidence. Much of the evidence dates from the time of the events it describes. These cartoons, photographs or eye-witness accounts are called **primary sources**. Primary sources make for very vivid and exciting history because they are 'first-hand' but often they give only a personal and fragmented view of the past. To get a more balanced and overall picture of the past it is often necessary to write about past events decades or even centuries later. These sources are called **secondary**. They are written by people who did not witness the events they describe and quite often were not even alive at that time. All sources are valuable to historians because any source about the past gives us some information. What makes some sources more valuable than others is the skill of the people who interpret them. This book will try to help you develop this skill.

Important words are explained in the glossary and are emphasised the first time that they appear in each chapter.

Notes for the teacher

This textbook contains over 170 exercises based on a wide variety of primary and secondary sources. The exercises adopt a stepped approach, with the later questions of each exercise encouraging a more free-ranging response. As a skills based book, the exercises seek to bring out the ability to compare and contrast different types of evidence, to recognise the limitations of evidence and to deploy evidence in support of a particular argument. There are many exercises designed to develop empathetic skills. Most chapters also contain what I have termed **assignment units**.

Most of them concentrate on encouraging pupils to produce work which looks at 'events and issues from the perspective of people in the past' (SEG assessment objective 3). These assignment units are intended to produce work of roughly 500 words in length from information in the text and from the sources. Some of the units are more structured than others so that teachers can suggest topics more appropriate for the differing abilities of particular pupils.

Unlike many evidence based texts, this book also provides a substantial element of narrative on which the pupil is tested through text based exercises. The source material is continually integrated with the narrative to encourage cross-referencing skills. *The World this Century: Working with Evidence* is a book designed to elicit the kind of skills which are at the heart of the assessment objectives of the GCSE syllabuses of the major boards.

Introduction

The world in 1900

The nineteenth century had seen a tremendous growth in the power of the nations of Europe. The industries of Britain and Germany had dominated the world. Germany's army and Britain's navy stood supreme. The other European countries had also made their mark on the world scene. The French and the Dutch had conquered large parts of the Far East and had sizeable empires in the area. The French, along with the Italians, Belgians, Germans, Portuguese and Spanish had taken over almost all of the continent of Africa between 1880 and 1914. A quarter of the world's population of 1600 million lived in Europe. Another 500 million lived in the empires of European countries. It seemed as though the twentieth century was set to see another one hundred years of European power and supremacy. However, 87 years into that century we can see that things were going to turn out rather differently. Why this happened is one of the themes of this book.

Imperialism

With the benefit of hindsight – looking back into the past and being wise after the event – we can see that already in 1900 there were forces at work which were to lead to the end of Europe's supremacy. We can see the importance of the forces now, after 87 years, quite clearly but no one could really tell then how important they would be. Imperialism, the conquest of territory and peoples by other nations, has already been mentioned. Generally speaking, the European powers had rarely come to blows over quarrels about which European power had the right to take over which area of Africa or the Far East. Wars between European states were costly and arguments were usually settled peacefully by negotiation and diplomacy. The reasons behind the growth of **empires** by the beginning of this century were varied. One important reason was the search for profits. The areas conquered by the European powers offered large stocks of vital raw materials, like raw cotton, nickel, copper and rubber. These were essential for the growth of Europe's industries. By conquering the areas where these raw materials were found, European powers made sure that they would always have a good supply of them. These powers also had the added bonus of having somewhere to sell their own products since the colonies they acquired were forced to buy goods from the 'mother' country. The rivalries between the European powers became serious, however, when they could no longer be settled peacefully. One reason for the outbreak of the First World War in 1914 was imperial rivalry, and this war left the nations of Europe in a much weaker position.

Nationalism

Imperialism helped to bring about a devastating war in 1914 among the European powers. It also helped to create another force which was to have an even greater role in weakening the domination of Europe throughout the world: **nationalism**. As European influence, technology and knowledge spread among the European colonies of the world so the peoples in these

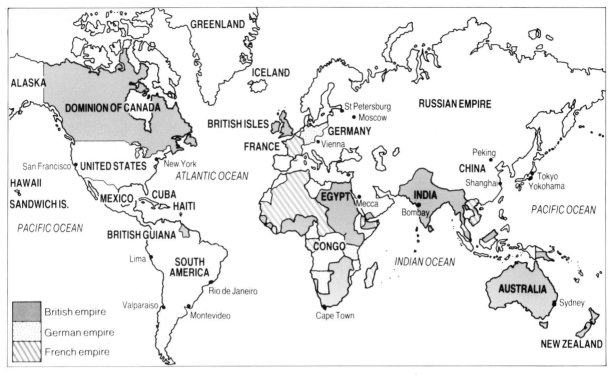

The empires of Britain, Germany and France in 1900

colonies became better educated. They resented the domination of their countries by their European masters. Many of these better educated people began to organise campaigns and movements to free their countries of foreign control. Nationalism was a world-wide movement whose aim was to rid the colonised nations of foreign, imperial control. For the first half of the twentieth century the Europeans were able to keep these nationalists in check with force. It was another war, the Second World War, which was to bring about the rapid collapse of the European empires in the decade-and-a-half after 1945.

The emergence of the non-European powers

Even if the European powers had not fought two massive wars against each other in the first half of the century it is unlikely that Europe would have dominated this century in the way it dominated the last. China, Japan and the United States have all emerged as major world powers. Nationalism grew strongly in China from the beginning of the century. The Europeans – Britain, Germany and France – came to early agreement about which parts of China they would each control. The Chinese were unable to resist the occupation of parts of their country but occasionally their anger exploded in events such as the Boxer Rising of 1900. Generally, the Europeans preferred to keep as little of China under their occupation as they could. They were essentially interested in trade and commercial activity and not in adding to their empires. One power which threatened this stable situation was Russia. The Russians actually occupied large areas of China. This brought them into conflict with Japan, who also had ambitions in China.

Japan

Britain had recognised the importance

of Japan as an ally against the Russians and signed a treaty with the Japanese in 1902. It was the first time a European power had made an alliance with an Asiatic power against a European one – Russia. In a sense it meant the end of the idea that it was the responsibility of the Europeans to bring their civilisation to the non-European world. Britain's new ally quickly showed just how powerful she was during the Russo–Japanese war of 1904–5. The Russians were decisively defeated. In fact, the British came to the conclusion that Russia was not such a threat to their empire in the Middle East after all, so feeble was the performance of the Russians in the war. In 1907 the British signed an agreement with Russia which pointed at Germany as the new enemy. The Japanese found that with the Russian threat now gone they faced another: the United States.

The United States

By 1900 the United States had made themselves the world's greatest economic power. They already produced more coal, steel and pig-iron than any other nation. Despite the fact that US military power at this time was slight, the United States became active in eastern Asia and the Pacific. In 1898 the Americans occupied the Pacific island of Hawaii and the Far Eastern Philippine islands. This expansion of US interest in the area was eventually to bring about the entry of the United States into the Second World War against Japan.

The Americans were also active in the Caribbean, much closer to home. The Monroe Doctrine of 1823, laid down by President Monroe, entitled the United States to resist the expansion of European control in the Americas. The Americans believed that the influence of aggressive imperial powers like Britain and France in the Americas threatened US security. With this in mind, Theodore Roosevelt, US President from 1901–8, brought about American control of Cuba, Puerto Rico and Panama. These were weak states and could have fallen into hostile European hands. To make it even clearer that the US had adopted a more active role for itself in the area Roosevelt sent the US fleet on a world tour in 1907. The US fleet though, at this time was still, in the words of one Congressman, a collection of old 'washtubs'. By 1920 it was a match for the British fleet.

United, the nations of Europe were overwhelmingly powerful. As the century moved on, it became clear that this unity was crumbling fast. With the crumbling of that sense of unity, tumbled the empires and the era of European supremacy in the affairs of the world.

Chapter 1

The First World War: 'an August Bank Holiday lark'

It was a fine sunny Sunday morning on 28 June 1914 in the town of Sarajevo. Sarajevo is in Bosnia, which was then part of the Habsburg **Empire** of Austria-Hungary. The Archduke Franz Ferdinand, heir to the throne of Austria-Hungary, was in Sarajevo to inspect a military parade. At around ten o'clock that morning a young Serbian nationalist, Gavrilo Princip, shot the Archduke in the throat. Fifteen minutes later he was dead. Within a month the First World War had started.

What were the causes of the war?

The quarrel between Austria and Serbia

Questions about the causes of the war cannot be answered in simple terms. History is rarely a matter of 'black' and 'white'. There were many causes of the war – the problem lies in trying to decide which of the causes were most important. For example, why should a Serbian nationalist want to assassinate the heir to the throne of the Austro-Hungarian Empire? This reveals one cause: the quarrel between Austria and Serbia. Serbia had become an independent state in 1878. There were many Serbs, though, that still lived inside the Habsburg Empire. They wanted to become part of a free Serbia. The Austrian government had always accused the Serbian government of stirring up trouble inside the Serbian region of Bosnia. Austria knew that the loss of 8 million Serbs to Serbia would spell the break-up of her empire (see map, page 28, Chapter 2). The assassination of Franz Ferdinand provided Austria with an ideal excuse to crush Serbia before it was too late. Austria blamed the Serbian government for organising the murder – though it is very unlikely that Serbia had anything to do with it. On 28 July 1914 Austria declared war on Serbia. The Austrians expected it to be a short war just between the two of them. Why were they wrong?

Serbia, though a small country, had a powerful ally – Russia. The Russians belonged to the same Slav race as the Serbs and felt obliged to assist them. At least, that is what the Russians claimed. But Russia also wanted to extend her influence in the Balkans, as this area of south-east Europe is known. She was especially keen to get hold of a Mediterranean port for her navy. Russia also had an alliance with France which dated back to 1893. In 1907 Russia had also signed an agreement with Britain – and three years before that Britain and France had signed a 'friendly understanding' or '**entente cordiale**'.

Austria-Hungary also had a powerful friend – Germany. In 1879 Germany and Austria had signed the Dual Alliance which Italy joined in 1882 to form the Triple Alliance. The Russians mobilised their huge army on 30 July. Two days later, the Germans, keeping to their agreement with the Austrians, decided to strike first and declared war on Russia. The Germans had been

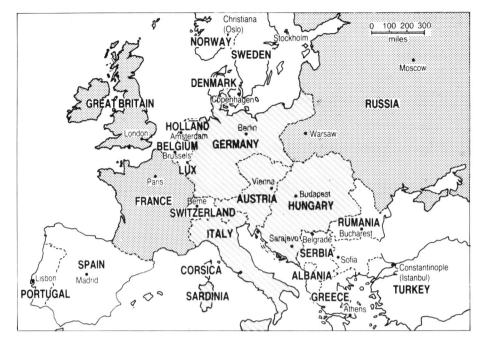

The European Alliance System 1914 (diagonal shading = Triple Alliance; speckled shading = Entente Powers).

planning for war for a long time and knew that the French would help the Russians as a result of their alliance of 1893. So, on 3 August, Germany declared war on France and invaded Belgium. Britain was not really bound to help France but she feared the growth of Germany. Germany's invasion of Belgium also gave Britain another reason to act. Britain had promised in 1839 to defend Belgium should she ever be invaded. On 4 August Britain declared war on Germany. In London, as in Paris, Berlin, Vienna and Moscow there was tremendous excitement. One poet, Philip Larkin, later described the long queues of young men waiting patiently to enlist, 'grinning as if it were all an August Bank Holiday lark'.

Imperial rivalries

All this helps to explain why the Russians, French and British were on one side and the Austrians and Germans on the other – Italy stayed neutral until May 1915 and then joined the 'Entente Powers', as the French, British and Russian forces were called. But it does not explain why these countries made alliances in the first place, decades earlier. One factor which brought together some of these countries was imperialism – the policy of controlling other countries by military or economic means. Britain had the biggest empire in the world. A big empire is a source of wealth and that empire was safe because Britain had the biggest navy in the world to protect it. But from about 1900 onwards the Germans had begun expanding their navy at a rapid rate. They already had the largest and best equipped army in Europe. Britain saw all this as a threat to her empire and position. The French were also afraid of Germany and they wanted revenge for their humiliating defeat in 1871 which had cost France the provinces of Alsace and Lorraine. Russia and Austria had long been rivals in the Balkans. Russia knew that if the Habsburg Empire were to break up then they would have a chance to establish their leadership in the area instead. All this helps to explain why the major European states were divided in the way they were, but did this division have to lead to war?

Austria's 'blank cheque'

It has already been said that the Austrians were not expecting a major conflict over Serbia. Germany has often been blamed for encouraging the Austrians to be tough with Serbia and so provoke a wider conflict. The Austrians believed, rightly, that Kaiser William II would commit Germany to Austria's aid if Russia became involved. Indeed, the Germans had backed Austria in 1908 when she took over Bosnia and so the Austrians believed they had a 'blank cheque' for German support. Why did Germany not hold back the Austrians and make it clear that she would not get involved in a major war? It is possible that Germany believed that the Russians would back down when faced with the possibility of war with Germany and Austria and so stay out of any war involving Serbia. If so, then it was a serious miscalculation.

Exercise
■■■■■■ **1**

a What was the aim of the 8 million Serbs living in the Habsburg Empire?
b How did the Austrians use the assassination as an excuse for war with Serbia?
c Why was Russia likely to get involved in any conflict in the area?
d In what ways did Britain feel threatened by Germany?
e What evidence is there in the text that the war may have been started by miscalculations?

The Schlieffen Plan

In 1905 the German Chief of Staff, General Schlieffen, drew up a detailed plan for the event of war with France and Russia. The Germans believed that they could not win a war on two fronts – against Russia in the east and France in the west – at the same time. So Schlieffen drew up a plan which would knock France out of the war very quickly. After France's defeat Germany could concentrate on dealing with the Russian army, which stood at 1 300 000 men – though it was quickly to rise to an effective strength of some 4 million. The bulk of Germany's armies – $1\frac{1}{2}$ million men – was allocated to the war in the west. The rest, some 400 000, were ordered to hold the Russians until reserves could be moved across from the Western Front after the defeat of the French.

Schlieffen had planned that the vast majority of the German army in the west should attack through Belgium and northern France while a small force should attack in the south along the Franco-German border. The actual ratio was about 10 to 1. Schlieffen knew the small southern wing would be driven back because of its weakness. As it retreated he expected it to draw more French armies after it and so weaken their strength further north. Then the huge northern wing would come crashing down on the French, smashing them like a hammer pounding on a blacksmith's anvil. But as we shall see, Count Schlieffen's successor, Count von Moltke, altered the balance of the two forces so that the southern wing was four times the original strength (10 to 4). This had two effects. First the northern force was now much smaller and made much slower progress when it attacked. Second, the southern army was so much stronger that when it attacked it did not get driven back.

The Battle of the Marne

The British quickly sent over their entire army of just 100 000 men – the British Expeditionary Force. Though small, the BEF was a well trained and professional army. Combined with

Belgium's similar sized army, the BEF held off the Germans at Mons on 21 August. The delay in Belgium enabled the French to continue using the Channel ports to ship in further British reinforcements. Worse news was arriving from the Eastern Front for Moltke. The Russians had mobilised unexpectedly quickly and had launched an attack on East Prussia. Moltke panicked and sent two army corps to assist General Ludendorff who commanded Germany's forces on the Eastern Front. Ludendorff told Moltke they were not needed but the decision further weakened the northern armies. Nonetheless, von Kluck's First Army of some 320 000 men advanced to within 20 miles of Paris. In the process, though, von Kluck had become separated from the German Second Army. Joffre, the French commander, decided to drive a wedge between the two armies and launch a counter-offensive against the tired German Troops. The Battle of the Marne (6–11 September) that followed drove back the Germans to the river Aisne where they dug in. From then on until March 1918 the front line was not to move more than 10 miles either way.

The Battle of the Marne not only wrecked the Schlieffen Plan but it also ruined Germany's chances of winning the war, as she would now be forced to fight a war on two fronts. Outnumbered in terms of men and material, the longer the war went on the less chance the Germans had of winning it. Moltke's frank honesty to the Kaiser ('Your Majesty, we have lost the war') was little consolation. Besides, the Kaiser was far from admitting defeat. Moltke was sacked and replaced by Falkenhayn. It was to take another four years and 8 500 000 dead to convince their High Command that the war had been lost.

Exercise 2

These two maps show the original plan devised by Count Schlieffen and the plan that was put into effect by von Moltke. Using the two maps and information in the text describe what the Germans had planned and contrast it with what actually happened. Explain the reasons for the failure of the plan and the consequences of the defeat.

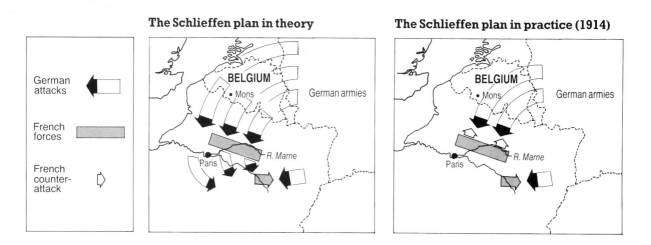

The Schlieffen plan in theory

The Schlieffen plan in practice (1914)

Exercise 3

The strengths of the major powers in January 1914

Carefully study the following statistical information and then answer the questions which follow:

	GB & Emp.	France	Russia	Italy	Germany	Aust-Hun.	Turkey
Population	45m (+390m)	40m	164m	35m	65m	50m	20m
Soldiers on mobilisation	0.71m (volunteers)	1.25m	1.3m	0.75m	2.2m	0.8m	0.36m
Military expenditure 1913–14	£50m	£37m	£67m	£10m	£60m	£22m	£8m
Battleships built (and being built)	64	28	16	14	40	16	–
Submarines	64	73	29	12	23	6	–
Tonnage of merchant ships	20m	2m	0.75m	1.75m	5m	1m	–

Note: *Turkey joined Germany and Austria-Hungary in November 1914*
(From: M. Gilbert, *Recent History Atlas 1860–1960*, 1977)

    a Which country
      i   spent the most money 1913–14?
      ii had the biggest army?
      iii had the most battleships?
      iv had the most submarines?
    b Why do you think merchant shipping is included as an important factor?
    c Which weapon also listed was likely to be most effective against merchant shipping?
    d Add up the relative strengths of the Entente Powers and the Central Powers in each of the areas listed. (Exclude Britain's Empire population of 390 million.) Which country was best prepared for war and why?

Assignment unit 1

Assessing the powers, August 1914

This assignment unit is in two parts. The second follows later in the chapter. In this unit you are to write a secret report to Kaiser Wilhelm assessing the strengths of Germany and her allies as against the Entente Powers. The statistics in Exercise 3 will help you here. In addition, suggest the best strategies to be adopted by Germany as regards:

a the war on land; how best to go about establishing strong defensive positions on enemy soil (read the section on page 14, 'Bullet, spade and wire', first).

b the war at sea; note Germany's relatively weak naval strength compared to Britain; given this weakness, what strategy do you recommend as regards a full-scale surface battle with the British fleet and why?

c Since Britain is the heart of the Entente Powers, suggest a method of striking at Britain's merchant fleet without risking a major surface battle, i.e. submarine warfare. What would be the effect of such a policy on Britain's food supplies and how long would it take to have any effect?

The Western Front 1914–17

'Bullet, spade and wire'

By the end of 1914 it was clear that the old fashioned warfare of dashing cavalry charges and rapid movements of troops was over. As one military historian, J.F.C. Fuller, put it: success 'depended on overcoming the defensive trinity of bullet, spade and wire'. The Germans, occupying French and Belgium soil, were perfectly happy to stay where they were. They dug in and dug deep. German trenches were therefore much sturdier and their dug-outs set deeper, with concrete and iron girders in the roofs. Both sides protected their trenches with layers of barbed wire and the devastating fire of the machine gun. Most World War One machine guns could, in theory, fire 500 rounds or bullets a minute. Front line trenches had support trenches behind them and finally reserve trenches in the rear. Between these were communication trenches which linked them. The trenches were zig-zagged to make it harder for enemy artillery to destroy them and to prevent enemy soldiers from firing down the length of the trench if one section was captured.

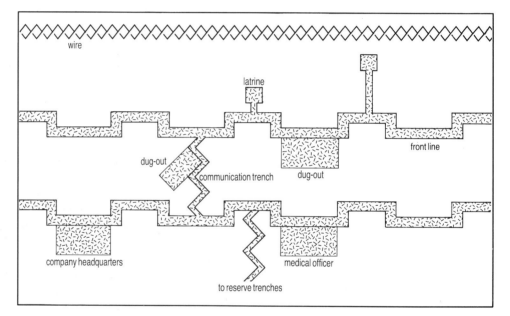

Front-line trenches

Occasionally, running out at right-angles from the front line trench were narrow passages thirty yards or so long, called saps. These led to isolated positions in which sat two or three men whose job was to listen for the slightest enemy movement. Shell craters proved ideal listening posts and were often fought over for that reason. One noise which was especially listened for was the sound of shovels and picks underground. Enemy mining parties often tried to burrow beneath the front line to plant a huge bomb to blow the trenches and the men in them to pieces. In June 1917 the British placed 19 huge mines under the German lines at Messines – a million pounds of high explosive. At 3.10 am on 7 June they went off and between 10 000 and 20 000 Germans were buried alive. (Two mines, though in place, were not used. Their exact position was lost. One went off in a rainstorm in 1955. The other, containing 40 000 pounds of explosive, has yet to make itself heard).

A section of preserved trenches in the Ypres Salient. Even 70 years later the zig-zagged layout of the trenches is clearly visible

British sappers digging a mine tunnel. Many of these men were recruited from the coal-fields of Britain

The Battles of Verdun and the Somme: 1916

On the Western Front in 1915 no significant advances were achieved by either side – though the Germans did use poison gas for the first time at Ypres. The year 1916 was to see two huge battles at Verdun and on the Somme. The German commander on the Western Front, Falkenhayn, decided to launch an offensive against the fortress town of Verdun. He knew that the French would defend the town and its surrounding forts to the last, since defeat there would open the road to Paris. The offensive began on 21 February with a barrage of 1400 guns and a million shells. The defence of Verdun was in the hands of General Petain who promised that the Germans 'shall not pass'. Falkenhayn's plan was brutally simple: as the French rushed to defend Verdun they would be smashed by heavy artillery and repeated attacks. France would be 'bled white'. To an extent it worked. The Germans launched offensive after offensive until July by which time the Germans were exhausted. Then in October Petain ordered a counter-offensive to recapture lost ground. The battle finally ended in December. The Germans had inflicted 380 000 casualties on the French but had themselves lost 340 000. Neither had Verdun fallen.

France's allies had not been idle during this great battle. In July on the Eastern Front the Russians had launched the Brusilov Offensive which had forced the Germans to take 15 **divisions** from their Verdun campaign. Another offensive was launched by the British to force the Germans to take troops away from Verdun. On 1 July, after a week-long bombardment of the German lines, the assault along the Somme was launched. It was the worst day in the history of the British army: 57 000 casualties were suffered – 20 000 of them dead. When General Haig's offensive finally ground to a halt in the November mud along the 30 mile front, the furthest advance was seven miles. German casualties totalled 650 000, British 410 000 and the French 195 000. But these two battles had greatly worn down the Germans – though Haig was also criticised for the losses. British Prime Minister Asquith paid the penalty and resigned in December, to be replaced by David Lloyd-George.

Exercise 4

a Why were trenches 'zig-zagged'?
b What was the job of the listening posts?
c Why were the Germans' happy to stay where they were'?
d What was Falkenhayn's strategy for the Verdun offensive?
e How did France's allies come to her aid during this battle?
f Why was Verdun really a defeat for the Germans?
g A German soldier of the war described the British troops as 'lions led by donkeys'. What do you think he meant by this and was he right?

Exercise 5

The Verdun offensive

Study the map of the battle and then answer the following questions:
a How many French forts were there protecting Verdun?
b On what sort of ground were these forts built?
c How many of these forts were captured by the Germans?
d What evidence is there in the map that the river Meuse helped to hold up the German advance?

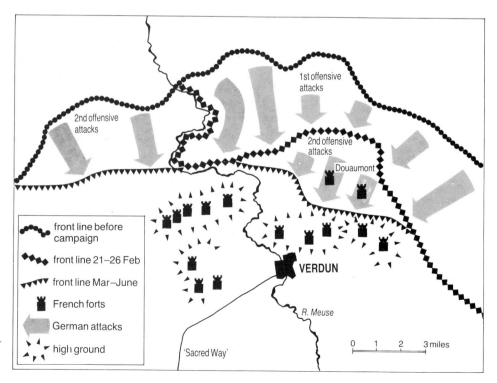

The Battle of Verdun. February–June 1916: The German attacks

e Using the scale of the map estimate the closest distance the Germans came to the city of Verdun.

f Using information provided by the map and the text write a 20 line summary of the strategy, course and outcome of the battle.

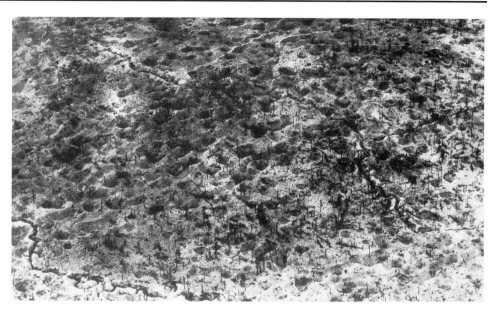

An aerial view of the Verdun sector in 1916 showing the thousands of shell craters. Trench lines are visible – especially in the bottom left-hand corner

The Eastern Front 1914–17

Tsar Nicholas II hoped that the war would rally public opinion behind his increasingly unpopular rule. For a while it seemed he may have been right, as the outbreak of the war was greeted with the same outburst of patriotic fervour in St Petersburg as in London or Berlin. ('St Petersburg' was later changed to 'Petrograd' as the old name sounded too 'German'). However, two crushing defeats at Tannenberg in late August and the Masurian Lakes in early September at the hands of General Hindenburg and his Chief of Staff, Ludendorff, revealed just how weak the Russian army was. In June 1916, though, the Russians launched their only really successful campaign of the war: the Brusilov Offensive. The Russian army, then under General Brusilov's leadership, launched a surprise offensive along a 300 mile front. Within two weeks over 200 000 Austrian prisoners were taken, but gradually German counter-attacks forced back the Russians who had, in some places, advanced 100 miles. The most important reason for the successful secrecy of the Brusilov Offensive was that there had been no big troop build-up or artillery barrage before. It was a lesson that should have been noted on the Western Front.

Russia's collapse

In March 1917 the Tsar paid the price for the poor quality of the Russian leadership and the defeats. He was overthrown and replaced by a Provisional (or temporary) Government. Despite obvious evidence that the war was now extremely unpopular the new government decided to carry on with the war. In July Brusilov launched another offensive. It failed and he was replaced, but by now the Russian war

The Eastern Front 1914–17

effort was crumbling, with desertions numbering some 40 000 a month. In November the government was itself overthrown by the **Bolshevik (Communist) revolution**. The Bolsheviks immediately started negotiations with the Germans for an end to the war. In December an **armistice**, or cease-fire, was signed. Russia's First World War was over.

The war on other fronts

The entry of Turkey into the war in November 1914 on the side of the Central Powers (Germany and her allies) opened up another front. Some British war leaders, notably Winston Churchill, then First Lord of the Admiralty, believed that a decisive blow against the Central Powers could be struck in the Balkans. A naval bombardment followed by a landing at Gallipoli in the Dardanelles was planned. The aim was to capture Constantinople, the Turkish capital, knock Turkey out of the war and open another front against Austria-Hungary. Churchill believed that a decisive breakthrough could not be made on the Western Front because of

Germany's strong defensive position. He argued that a new front in the Balkans would lead Germany to weaken herself in the west to come to the aid of her Habsburg ally. The preliminary naval bombardment in February 1915 served only to warn the Turks that a major attack was planned. When the eventual landings did take place only 75 000 troops were used and it was over two months after the naval campaign had started. By this time, 25 April, the Turks were ready and reinforced. The British, Australian and New Zealand forces (ANZACs) made no progress of any significance. By November, when the troops were withdrawn, 252 000 Allied casualties led to the triumph of the 'Westerners' – those that believed that the war could only be won in the west. The battles of Verdun and the Somme were the consequence.

The Italian Front: 1915–18

Another front was created in May 1915 with the entry of Italy into the war against the Central Powers. The fighting, high up in the mountains for much of the time, was bitter. The Italians made repeated efforts to drive the Austrians beyond the river Isonzo. Not until the Eleventh Battle of the Isonzo in August and September 1917 did Italy finally force the Habsburg forces back. Germany rushed in reinforcements and the advance was halted. In October the Austro-German forces were ready for a counter-offensive – the Twelfth Battle of the Isonzo which is better known as *Caporetto*. The Italians were sent into headlong retreat. Eventually a defensive line was established with the enemy some twenty miles from Venice. There were 40 000 Italians killed or wounded but the numbers of prisoners and deserters, 275 000, reveal how close to collapse Italian morale came. Only in the following September, 1918, were the Italians able to mount another offensive. By this time the Habsburg

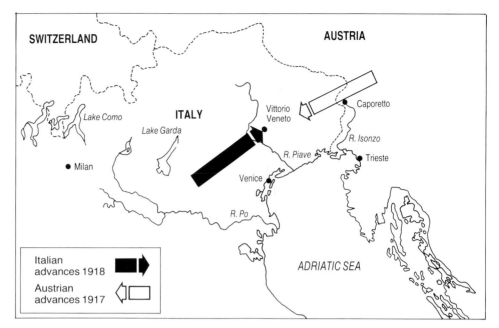

*The Italian Front
1917–18*

Empire was disintegrating as various subject races declared their independence. On 24 October General Diaz launched the final attack at Vittorio Veneto. Six days later the Austrian army had been beaten: 30 000 killed and 427 000 taken prisoner. Austria-Hungary surrendered on 3 November.

Exercise 6

a Why was the Brusilov Offensive of June 1916 such a success at first?
b What serious error did the Provisional Government of Russia make after the Tsar's overthrow?
c What was the basic strategy of those 'Easterners' like Churchill who planned the Gallipoli campaign?
d What indication is there in the text that much of the fighting on the Italian Front took place in the same area?
e What have you learnt so far that tells you that neither the Germans nor the Entente Powers had learnt the lesson of the Brusilov offensive of 1916?

Exercise 7

Historians and the Somme

Read the following extracts from recent books on the Battle of the Somme and then answer the questions which follow:

Extract One

> The British themselves often simplified the Germans' task. To allow the troops to get into no mans' land it was necessary to cut gaps in the wire just before the attack. As one soldier who was there remarked: "The advertisement of the attack on our front was absurd. Paths were cut and marked ... days before ... Small wonder the machine gun fire was directed with such fatal precision.
> (J. Ellis, *Eye Deep in Hell*, 1976)

5

Extract Two

But all this immense weight of shellfire had not fatally damaged the enemy as the Allied Commanders had fondly hoped; far from it. The Germans were now past masters in the arts of fortification and digging in ... Their defences consisted of a vast network of dug-outs, trenches, dormitories dug ... to depths of forty feet.

5

The Germans had plenty of warning about the coming attack – from their eyrie-like lines they had watched as the New Armies were brought up into the Somme sector ... When the barrage opened, the Germans obediently scuttled below and sat out the storm, secure in the knowledge that even

10

the heaviest shells could not penetrate their subterranean fastnesses. This fundamental failure by the British Command to realise the strength of the enemy defences, coupled with the imperfectly cut wire and the rigid parade-ground manner in which the infantry attacked were the main reasons for the horrible failure of the attack ...
(N. Jones, *The War Walk*, 1983)

Extract Three

However, about a million (of the 1.5 million shells fired by the British artillery barrage) of the shells were shrapnel ... and these could do very little damage to earthworks, since they were filled only with light steel balls, and only a little more to wire, though it was their alleged wire-

5

cutting capability which justified the firing of the enormous number used.
(J. Keegan, *Face of Battle*, 1976)

a Why do you think it was necessary 'to cut gaps in the wire just before the attack'. (Extract One.)

b How did the Germans know in advance of the attack? (Extract Two.)

c Why were so many of the British shells fired ineffective? (Extract Three.)

d How did the Germans know where to direct their machine gun fire? (Extract One.)

e Are the three sources **primary** or **secondary** accounts? Explain your answer.

f Which of the three accounts includes a primary source? How do you know it is a primary source?

g From the three extracts find evidence to support each of the following statements concerning the battle:

    i   the Germans knew in advance of the attack;

    ii   the German defences were very strong;

    iii   the artillery bombardment was ineffective;

    iv   the British method of attack led to high casualties.

The war at sea

Jutland 1916

Both Germany and Great Britain knew that naval power was vitally important in deciding the war. Should either side gain control of the seas it could starve the other into defeat by cutting off food supplies or it could even use the fleet to launch an invasion. For this reason both Admiral Jellicoe of the British Grand Fleet and Admiral Tirpitz of the German High Seas Fleet spent the first two years of the war avoiding a major battle. The only large scale sea battle of the war, at

Jutland, 31 May 1916, took place by accident. Tirpitz had been replaced in March by Admiral Scheer who decided to try to lure a small part of the Grand Fleet into battle.

Admiral Jellicoe sent a small squadron under Admiral Beatty as bait to try and lure the Germans into a trap. Neither knew that each other's main fleet was nearby. The two decoy squadrons came face to face off the coast of Jutland in the North Sea. Within 30 minutes two British battleships were blown to pieces – destroyed by direct hits to their magazines. This weakness, which left the magazine area so vulnerable had been noted after an earlier battle at Dogger Bank in January 1915 but nothing had been done to strengthen the armour protection. German gunnery was much better and their ships better constructed. Within a few hours both fleets had been drawn into the battle – 250 ships including 44 Dreadnoughts, the most modern and heavily armed type of battleship. Scheer soon realised the danger he was in and, aided by the misty darkness, managed to escape. Fourteen British ships had been sunk, including three battle cruisers, and over 6000 sailors killed. German losses were lighter: 11 smaller ships and 2500 men. In Germany there was jubilation – technically they had won a victory. In Britain there was some embarrassment but the Germans, with a much smaller fleet, could not afford their losses. They lost their nerve and stayed safely inside their harbour at Kiel for the rest of the war. This meant that the Grand Fleet had the run of the sea and could enforce its blockade of Germany with ruthless effectiveness.

The U-boat campaign

The effectiveness of the blockade was a key factor in bringing Germany to her knees. It has been estimated that as many as 800 000 Germans died as a result of the British blockade. The widespread hunger in Germany towards the end of 1918 and the civil rioting that took place forced the German High Command to surrender. However, Britain also came close to defeat through starvation. Although the Germans had only 30 U-boats (submarines) when the war began and only 130 at its end they took a heavy toll of British merchant shipping. In April 1917 they came close to victory when Britain had only six weeks' supply of corn left and 430 ships had been sunk. The introduction of the convoy system by Lloyd-George, which meant that supply ships now had destroyer escorts, cut down the effectiveness of the U-boats. Mines also accounted for large numbers of U-boat sinkings – 20 in 1917 out of a total of 63. 'Q'-ships (warships disguised as merchant ships) sank six and made U-boat commanders approach merchant ships more cautiously. Rationing also ensured that Britain's food supply stretched that bit further. Perhaps the most important result of Germany's U-boat campaign was that it brought the United States into the war in April 1917 as a result of the loss of American shipping sunk by the Germans in a desperate bid to starve Britain before the USA could play a major role in the war.

Exercise
8

a Why was control of the seas so important in the war?
b In what ways was the German High Seas Fleet superior to the British Grand Fleet?
c Why could both sides claim a victory at Jutland?
d Why was the blockade so important in bringing about Germany's defeat?
e How did Britain also come close to defeat through starvation?

Exercise  9

The defeat of the U-boats

The following information concerns the number of German submarines sunk by the British during the war and the methods used to sink them:

Method	Number sunk	
1914–16		
By warships – rammed	2	
By patrol vessels	15	
By 'Q'-ships	5	
By merchant ships	0	
By convoy escorts	0	
By mines	10	
By accidents	7	
By unknown causes	7	*Total:* 46
1917		
By warships – rammed	0	
By patrol vessels	16	
By 'Q'-ships	6	
By merchant ships	3	
By convoy escorts	6	
By mines	20	
By accidents	10	
By unknown causes	2	*Total:* 63
1918		
By warships – rammed	1	
By patrol vessels	24	
By 'Q'-ships	0	
By merchant ships	4	
By convoy escorts	10	
By mines	18	
By accidents	2	
By unknown causes	10	*Total:* 69

(From: *Purnell's History of the 20th Century*)

a How many U-boats were sunk in total? Which of the eight methods proved the most successful?

b Can you give a reason why no submarines were sunk by convoy escorts between 1914 and 1916?

c Can you suggest a possible reason for the fact that no U-boats were sunk by 'Q'-ships in 1918?

d What other figure would you need to know to assess whether the Allies were winning the campaign against the U-boats?

e The U-boats sank 11 millions tons of shipping out of a total loss of 13 million tons of merchant shipping. Given the number of U-boats lost do you think the Germans considered it a small or heavy price to pay? Give reasons for your answer.

f Translate the statistics in the table into a graph.

Exercise ▮▮▮10

a Why do you think not wasting bread would help 'defeat the U-boat'?

b Which particular cereal was the poster asking the British to economise on?

c In which month and year do you think this appeal would have been most needed? Why?

d What method is being used to sink the U-boat in the poster?

e Look back at your graph. Why is the method in the poster an unlikely one?

f If the poster had tried to be statistically accurate which method of U-boat sinking should it have showed? Can you suggest any reason why the method in the poster was chosen instead?

Source One *British poster*

Assignment unit 2 ████████

Assessing the assessment

In Assignment unit 1 you suggested some military strategies for the Kaiser to follow as regards the war on land and at sea. Now it is time for you to judge how good your advice was to the Kaiser in another secret report, dated December 1917. You will need to comment on:

a the war on land, 1914–17. How well has it gone? Have the forces of the Imperial German Army managed to establish themselves firmly on enemy soil? Discuss the importance of the major battles (the Marne, Gallipoli, the Somme and Verdun) on the course of the war.

b the war at sea; some honest comment on the battle of Jutland is needed here. Was it really the success the German papers claimed? What has been the major strategic result of the battle? Who controls the seas? Was your advice in your earlier report acted on or was it ignored?

c the U-boat campaign; how successful has it been (the section on the U-boat campaign earlier will help you here)? What methods have the British taken against the U-boats and how successful are they?

d future strategies and developments; here you will have to comment on the entry of the USA to the war and its likely effect in 1918 as well as the defeat of Russia and how best the Kaiser can make use of the troops no longer needed on the Eastern Front. Finally, can the war still be won or should Germany consider some kind of settlement now while she is still strong?

The last year of the war

1917 had seen no end to the stalemate on the Western Front. The new commander of the French armies, General Nivelle, tried a new offensive in April which failed. He was replaced by the hero of Verdun, Petain. The biggest battle of the year was the Third Battle of Ypres, also called Passchendaele in which the British attempted to break through and seize the U-boat bases on the Belgian coast. The campaign from July to November cost 324 000 British casualties for a four mile advance. Many thousands of the dead had drowned in mud-filled shell craters. The final British offensive of 1917 at Cambrai is mainly noted for the large-scale use of tanks – over 400 of them. They had first been used at the Somme but the surprise effect of the terrifying weapon had been wasted then because only 50 were used and most of them broke down. The collapse of Russia at the end of the year, though, was made up for by the entry of the USA on the side of the Entente in April.

'Operation Michael'

Hindenburg and Ludendorff had replaced Falkenhayn on the Western Front in August 1916. Both knew that if the war was going to be won it had to be won before the Americans could intervene in large numbers. Ludendorff drew up 'Operation Michael'. Its strategy was simple. The Germans, strengthened by 400 000 troops from the Eastern Front, planned to drive a wedge between the Allies at the Somme. Ludendorff expected the British to fall back towards the Channel ports and the French towards Paris. The Germans would pour into the gap, using new 'infiltration' tactics. Enemy strong-points would be avoided and Ludendorff's highly trained storm-troopers headed for the weakest parts of the enemy line. It was the basis of the '**blitzkrieg**' tactics that Hitler was to use with such success in the early years of World War Two. It almost succeeded. The British Fifth Army was routed and began to fall back towards the Channel ports. The Somme was crossed two days after the attack began, on 23 March, and Paris was bombarded. Marshall Foch was given command of the Allied forces and ordered a general withdrawal of the French armies towards Paris. By the end of May the Germans were once again within 40 miles of Paris. But this was a different German army to the one of 1914. It was short of

supplies, having advanced too quickly for the supplies to keep pace. It was hungry, and discipline began to break down. On 8 August, the Allies, led by Foch, launched their massed counter-attack at Amiens. The exhausted and now demoralised Germans were driven back, beyond the heavily defended Hindenburg Line. Germany's allies were also collapsing. Bulgaria surrendered on 30 September, Turkey on 30 October and the Austro-Hungarian Empire simply fell apart. On 11 November at 11 am the war ended when the armistice signed with Germany came into effect. Britain and the Empire had lost 947 000 dead; France 1 360 000; Russia 1 700 000; Italy 460 000; USA 114 000. The Central Powers' war dead were: Germany 2 000 000; Austria-Hungary 1 100 000; Turkey 375 000.

a What was the idea behind the Ypres offensive of 1917?
b How had the British wasted the potential of the tank in 1916?
c How did Ludendorff plan to split the Allies in 1918?
d Why did 'Operation Michael' eventually fail?
e How did the Allies ensure that their counter-offensive was a united one?

Map study of the Western Front

a Look at the list of offensives for 1914–17 in Source Two. Rewrite them in the order in which they took place, giving the year and month in which they began and where possible the month the offensive ended.

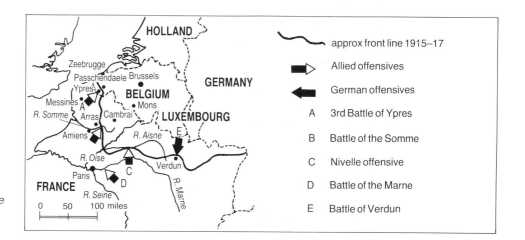

Source Two *The Western Front 1914–17*

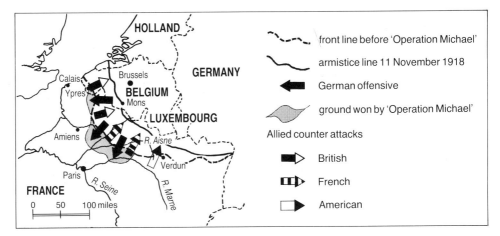

Source Three

The Western Front 1918

b What evidence is there in Source Two that the Germans during 1914–17 were content to maintain a defensive position?

c What effect was this likely to have on
(i) German casualties; (ii) British and French casualties?

d Explain the reasons behind your answer to question c.

e The thick black line in Source Two shows how little change there was in the front line between 1914–17. Now look at the gains of 'Operation Michael' in Source Three. How happy do you think Ludendorff would have been with the progress of his attack? Explain your reasons.

f What evidence is there in Source Three that the United States played a fairly small part in the final victory?

g Despite the eventual defeat of their last offensive, can you see any reason in Source Three to justify the view of many Germans that they never really lost the war in military terms?

Chapter 2

The Paris Peace Treaties: 1919–20

Wilson's 14 Points

In January 1919 the leaders of the victorious powers met in Versailles to decide what the terms of the new peace treaties should be. In addition to the 'Big Three' of the United States, Great Britain and France, Italy and Japan were also represented. The Japanese played little part and the Italian leader, Orlando, soon walked out in anger at the way his country was being ignored by the 'Big Three'. Orlando did return to the conference but the Italians were to remain angry, convinced that the promises made by Britain and France to Italy at the Treaty of London in 1915 were not kept. At this secret treaty Britain, France, and Russia had promised Italy large areas of Austrian territory if the Italians joined the war on their side. At the end of the war Italy did in fact gain a lot less than had been promised. So, the real decisions at the Versailles Peace Conference were made by Woodrow Wilson, the United States' President, David Lloyd George for Great Britain and Georges Clemenceau for France.

America had joined the war, Wilson claimed, 'to make the world safe for **democracy**'. It was an ambitious aim. In 1918 he had drawn up a list of '14 Points' which he believed promised a fair settlement and end to the war. This was in January and the Germans rejected Wilson's proposals because they believed they could still win the war. Wilson's 14 Points contained four basic ideas. Perhaps the most important was that of 'national **self-determination**'.

This meant that every nation or people had the right to govern themselves and not be ruled by a foreign power. This particularly affected the **empire** of Austria-Hungary which governed many different races such as the Czechs and Slovaks. A glance at the map on page 28 will show the large number of different peoples within the Austro-Hungarian Empire. Wilson also believed that no nation had the right to stop other countries from trading with its colonies or closing off waterways to international shipping. Thirdly, every nation should begin to reduce its stocks of weapons so that the risk of war would be lessened. Finally, Wilson's most ambitious point of all, the fourteenth, was that an international body should be set up, a League of Nations, which would settle disputes between nations peacefully. Wilson's other points concerned particular details about how these principles should be carried out.

Wilson was determined that these ideas should form the basis of the peace settlement. He wanted to see that Germany was not harshly punished so that good relations between the defeated powers and the Allies could be quickly established. It was easy for Wilson to take this view. United States' war dead totalled 115 000. France had lost 1 360 000 and Britain and the Empire 947 000 men. Clemenceau, nicknamed 'the Tiger', was determined to see Germany punished heavily for the suffering and destruction in France. French memories of the defeat and humiliation of 1870 in the Franco-Prussian War had lingered. The return of Alsace-Lorraine, ceded to the Germans

The peoples of the Habsburg Empire 1867–1918

then, was only the first of many demands that Clemenceau was to make. British public opinion was as keen on revenge against Germany as France. Lloyd-George had promised that the pockets of the Germans would be searched for 'the uttermost farthing'. But Lloyd-George knew that a Germany stripped of her economic resources such as coal and iron would be unable to help European trade expand. Furthermore, they would be too poor to buy British goods.

A **Communist** rebellion in Berlin in January also reminded the peacemakers that too harsh a settlement could easily push Germany into the arms of '**Bolshevism**' and perhaps spark off further Communist revolutions elsewhere in Europe.

Exercise 1

a Why were the Italians angry with the 'Big Three'?

b Why did the principle of 'self-determination' especially affect Austria-Hungary?

c Why were both Britain and France likely to take a harsher view of how Germany should be treated than the United States?

d What other reasons did Lloyd-George have for not wanting to see Germany too harshly dealt with?

e The United States was especially keen that free trade across the seas be established. How had the USA defended that principle in April 1917?

The Treaty of Versailles

In June 1919 the Big Three had finished their drafting of the terms of the treaty which the Germans were to sign. The terms were not for negotiation. Germany's new civilian government was given the option of either signing the treaty or facing an Allied invasion

German delegates outside the Palace of Versailles, June 1919

and a continued naval blockade. The German Chancellor (Prime Minister) called the treaty a '*Diktat*' – an imposed settlement – and so Scheidemann, the German Chancellor, resigned rather than sign. However, a new government reluctantly accepted the terms on 23 June – four hours before the Allied deadline.

The terms can be divided into three main categories: territorial losses; military clauses; **reparations** (compensation in money and goods to the Allies).

1 *Territorial losses*
   a Germany lost all her colonies in Africa (e.g. Togoland and the Cameroons) and the Pacific. These areas became '**mandates**' which meant that they were to be run by different Allied powers until they were ready for self rule. East Africa was mandated to Britain while Britain and France divided the Cameroons and Togoland between them. New Guinea in the Pacific went to Australia.
   b Alsace-Lorraine was returned to France.
   c Eupen-Malmedy went to Belgium after a **plebiscite** (a vote on a

single issue by the people) in 1920.
   d North Schleswig went to Denmark, also after a plebiscite, in 1920. (South Schleswig voted to remain part of Germany.)
   e Posen and West Prussia were given to the new state of Poland to provide the Poles with a 'corridor' (the 'Polish Corridor') to the sea.
   f Poland also acquired Upper Silesia after a plebiscite in 1921.
   g The League of Nations took control of the Saar and the port of Danzig.
   h The city of Memel went to the newly created Baltic state of Lithuania.

2 *Military clauses*
   a The Rhineland was demilitarised. This meant that the Germans were forbidden to place troops or carry out any military activities in the area.
   b Allied troops were stationed there instead.
   c The German army was cut to 100 000 men. Conscription was abolished so the army was to consist only of volunteers who had to serve at least twelve years.
   d The navy was to be handed over to the British – in fact the Germans sank or scuttled their own fleet before it could be handed over. Germany was to have a maximum of six battleships in its new navy. (In 1914 she had 23.)
   e Germany was not allowed to build any submarines, planes or tanks.

3 *Reparations*
The Allied Reparations Commission finally decided in 1921 that Germany should pay £6600 million in gold and goods. All the coal produced in the Saar was to go to France for five years.

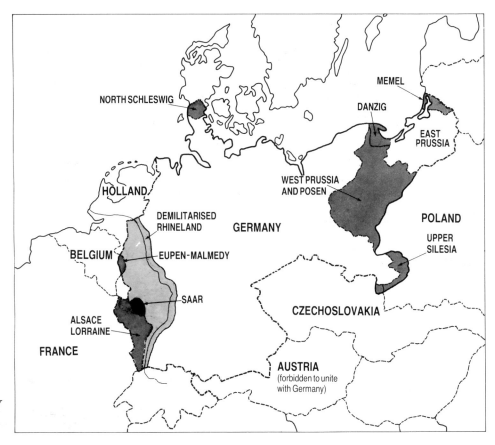

Germany's losses by the Treaty of Versailles

'The first roll of drums' – the German reaction

The Germans were shocked by the harshness of the terms. They were especially angered by the 'War Guilt' clause (Article 231) which laid the blame for starting the war on Germany. Having signed the clause, of course, the Germans knew they were agreeing to pay for the damage caused. The territory lost by Germany came to 13% of her total and about 6 million subjects. With that territory went 48% of her iron production and 16% of coal production. Agricultural output dropped by 15% and industry's output by 10%. The loss of Germany's colonies and their establishment as Allied mandates led many Germans to suspect that empires were a bad thing only for beaten powers. At the same time, the Germans claimed, they were expected to be able to pay reparations of £6600 million! The German concern at the high level of reparations was also shared by an economic adviser to the British at the time, John Maynard Keynes. He had recommended a maximum of £2000 million. The terms of the military clauses left the Germans feeling both humiliated and bitter – a bitterness that nationalist politicians in Germany were quick to exploit. One of these later wrote that peace treaties which are a burden to a nation often 'strike the first roll of drums of the uprising to come'. That man was Adolf Hitler.

Was the treaty a mistake?

There is no real answer to this question. There are as many opinions on the treaty as there are historians. As long as each opinion is backed up by solid evidence it is a valid one. We can look back and say that it is obvious that such a harsh treaty would only store up trouble for the future. Was it fair to make Germany's first democratically elected government take the responsibility for a war started by the Kaiser? Did it make sense to take away so much of Germany's industrial resources which would be needed to produce the wealth to pay the reparations? On the other hand put yourself in the place of the Allied leaders. The most terrible war in history had just ended. The desire for revenge was very strong and understandable. Besides, there is much evidence that the Germans, had they won, would have imposed an even harsher treaty – like the one they forced defeated Russia to sign at Brest-Litovsk in March 1918. (See Chapter 3, page 48, for further details.)

Exercise 2

a Why did the Germans have to sign the treaty?

b Why was it important for the Allies that Germany signed Article 231?

c What evidence do you think the Germans would use to prove that they could not pay the reparations?

d What argument could be used to support the view that Germany deserved a harsh treaty?

e What do you think Hitler meant by the sentence quoted in the text.

Assignment unit

Examining the evidence

This unit contains some statistics about the cost of the war for the French and the United States. These facts are 'neutral'. They do not support any point of view unless you make them do so.

Using the information provided in the statistics and any other details you can find in the text your task is to draft the proposal of the French delegation at the negotiations in Versailles concerning the terms to be imposed on Germany. Present your proposal under the following headings:

Germany's responsibility for the war
Make out a case from the French point of view justifying the 'War Guilt' clause.

The demands of France
Outline the terms the French want imposed on Germany with particular reference to territorial changes, reparations, demilitarisation, disarmament; at the same time use the statistics on US and French losses and costs during the war to explain why the French are right to make these demands while the Americans can afford to take a more lenient and less harsh view.

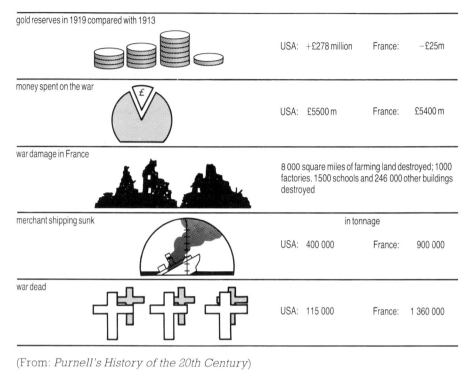

The future security of Europe

In this final section state how important it is to keep Germany in a condition of weakness – both economically and militarily. Refer to German aggression in 1870 and the threat to future peace if Germany is not kept under control.

gold reserves in 1919 compared with 1913

USA: +£278 million   France: −£25m

money spent on the war

USA: £5500 m   France: £5400 m

war damage in France

8 000 square miles of farming land destroyed; 1000 factories. 1500 schools and 246 000 other buildings destroyed

merchant shipping sunk   in tonnage

USA: 400 000   France: 900 000

war dead

USA: 115 000   France: 1 360 000

(From: *Purnell's History of the 20th Century*)

Ruins of the French city of Cambrai after a heavy bombardment in 1915. Just a few of the 246000 buildings destroyed in the war

Exercise 3

Extract

Read this account adapted from an American book published in 1946, '*Germany Tried Democracy*'.

The Allies made a tragic mistake in agreeing to a truce at a moment when the German armies, though in retreat, were still intact and when all the fighting was taking place on Allied soil. They should have marched to Berlin to make clear to the Germans the decisiveness of their defeat on the field of battle, in order to
5   uproot the legend ... nurtured in the minds of Germans that their armies were unconquerable ...
    This error was made worse by Wilson's refusal to negotiate with the 'military masters' of Germany ... The humiliation of accepting responsibility for the surrender fell not on the Supreme Command but on a civilian, Erzberger, and
10 on the newly formed republic.
    Almost immediately German militarists spread the theory that the armies of the Reich had never been defeated on the battlefield, that they had been stabbed in the back by ... pacifists, liberals, socialists, communists, Jews.

(S. W. Halperin, *Germany Tried Democracy*, 1946)

a On what date was the truce referred to in line 1 signed?
b Name one of the 'military masters' in lines 7–8.
c Who was the civilian Chancellor who signed the truce?
d What is the author claiming was the serious result of the 'tragic mistake' referred to in line 1?
e In what way is the author making use of hindsight – the ability to look back in time and be wise after the event? (Clue: Hitler's rise to power: refer back to the section 'The first roll of drums'.)

The other treaties

Versailles was only one of five treaties that were signed during 1919 and 1920. Together they are known as the Treaties of Paris as they are named after various suburbs of the city. Two treaties were concerned with the old empire of Austria-Hungary which was now split up. The treaty of Saint Germain dealt with Austria; Trianon with Hungary. The other defeated Central Powers signed the Treaties of Neuilly (Bulgaria) and Sevres (Turkey). All the defeated powers lost territory and agreed to pay some small reparations. Austria, like Hungary, became a republic. '*Anschluss*' or union with Germany was forbidden by the treaty, and Austria's armed forces were also limited. Two completely new states were created out of the old Habsburg Empire's lands: both Czechoslovakia and Jugoslavia. Further territory was lost to Rumania, Poland and Italy. (See the map, page 34). Wilson had tried hard to make sure that the various peoples of the Austro-Hungarian Empire were given self-determination. The Serbs, Croats and Slovenes now had their own state – Jugoslavia. The Czechs and Slovaks had their own nation too. The Austrians complained, though, that Czechoslovakia now contained some 3 million Germans living in the Sudetenland area and Italy some 250 000 Germans in the South Tyrol. Where were the rights to self-determination of the German people? In Istria 400 000 Slavs said

Included in Poland
Included in Rumania
Included in Jugoslavia
Included in Italy
Boundary of the Austro-Hungarian Empire, 1914

The former Austro–Hungarian Empire: the treaties of St Germain and Trianon

Sevres demolished the empire of the Sultan. Greece acquired Eastern Thrace; Britain, Cyprus; and Italy, Rhodes and the Dodecanese islands. In the Middle East Turkey gave up all her Arab lands. Britain received as 'mandates' Palestine, Iraq and Transjordan. Another mandated territory was Syria which went to France. (See the map on page 35). This treaty, signed in 1920, proved too much of a humiliation for some Turks – especially the loss of land to their former slaves, the Greeks. Kemal organised a nationalist movement both to overthrow the Sultan and negotiate a new treaty. The Sultan was overthrown in November 1922 and a revised treaty, the Treaty of Lausanne, was signed in July 1923. Eastern Thrace was returned to the Turks and Turkey was not required to limit her armed forces or pay any reparations. The mandated settlement of the Arab lands was not changed. The Allied powers had shown, however, that they could be persuaded by force to alter a treaty. Neither had they come to the aid of their ally, Greece, when Kemal had attacked the Greeks in 1922. These were bad omens for the future security of the Paris settlement.

much the same thing as they now became part of Italy as well. It was a feeling echoed by 3 million Hungarians, now part of Rumania, Jugoslavia and Czechoslovakia.

Another empire which perished along with the Habsburgs was the Ottoman Empire of Turkey. The Treaty of

Exercise 4

a Which two completely new states were created from the Austro-Hungarian Empire?
b In which two areas were the inhabitants denied the right to self-determination?
c Which part of the Treaty of Sevres was an especially bitter blow to Turkish pride?
d What were the 'bad omens' referred to in the last sentence of the passage above?
e In what way could they prove a threat 'to the future security of the Paris settlement'?

Problems for the future

In some respects the Allies themselves admitted that the treaty had been too harsh on Germany. In 1929, for example, the Young Plan set a new reparation figure for Germany of £2000 million. But Germany was not the only country with a sense of bitterness.

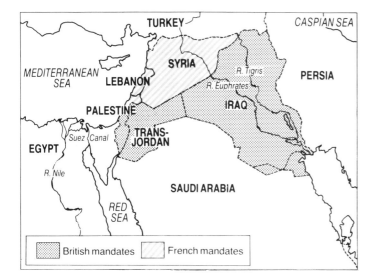

League of Nations mandates in the Middle East

to join the League of Nations until 1926. The Italians felt cheated when they failed to get the town of Fiume and a stretch of Dalmatian coast, as they had been promised by the secret Treaty of London in 1915 by the Allied Powers. None of these countries survived to the outbreak of war in 1939 as democracies. All of these powers had a grievance against the **status quo**.

Equally determined to keep the treaties unaltered were the French. Unfortunately for them the British and the Americans did not share France's determination. The United States Congress refused to give its approval to the treaties and turned its back on European affairs until 1941. Britain made fine statements about making sure the treaties were honoured but often fell short when it came to taking action to defend them. The French knew their security depended on making the treaties stick but Britain felt no such threat to herself. In the end everyone was to pay the penalty for the failure of '**collective security**' – the policy of international agreement to keep the peace.

Austria, its population reduced from 22 million to just 6.5 million, lost its key industrial areas to Czechoslovakia. Hungary suffered similar economic problems with the loss of her richest corn land to Rumania, and her population was cut by two-thirds to 7 million. These three countries felt themselves excluded from the international community. This sense of rejection was not helped when Germany was forbidden

Source One
Demobilised German troops, 1918

Exercise 5

Study the photograph on page 35 of German soldiers returning to their homes at the end of the war and answer the following questions:

a Why is it likely that this photograph was taken after 11 November, 1918?

b What evidence is there that the local population had treated the troops as heroes?

c How would you describe the general condition and attitude of these soldiers?

d In what way does this photograph support the theory of the German militarists referred to in lines 11–13 of Extract One, page 33?

Exercise 6

Below is a copy of an imagined front page of a German nationalist newspaper of June 1919. It shows one possible reaction to the terms of the Treaty of Versailles. Copy it on to a full page of your exercise book. (You may, of course, think up your own title and headline.) Complete the rest of the page in your own words, describing the anger that was felt in many areas of Germany. Comment on those terms that caused the most bitterness and also include an interview with General Hindenburg, putting across the army's point of view – Extract One will help you here.

THE BERLINER

June 28 1919

GERMANY'S DAY OF SHAME

Bauer signs treaty

The new map of Germany

Interview with Hindenburg

(*Footnote:* the *Deutsche Zeitung* – the 'German Times' – ran this headline on 28 June, 1919: 'VENGEANCE! GERMAN NATION – Today in the Hall of Mirrors, the disgraceful Treaty is being signed. Do not forget it. The German people will with unceasing labour press forward to reconquer the place among nations to which it is entitled. Then will come vengeance for the shame of 1919.'

Chapter 3

Russia 1917–24: Lenin's revolution

Russia before the revolution

For 300 years the Romanovs had ruled Russia. The **Tsars** or Emperors had ruled as **autocrats** – rulers with absolute power who made laws as they pleased. In 1894 Nicholas II succeeded to the throne and intended to govern as ruthlessly as his father, Alexander III. He and his wife, Alexandra, had an income of some £12 million a year – an incredible sum even by today's values. They lived a life of luxury and ease, assisted by their 15 000 servants. Nicholas' father had governed with a firm hand and made no concessions to calls for reform. Nicholas, however, faced two serious difficulties in trying to rule

like his father. Firstly, he did not possess Alexander's strength of character. Nicholas was a weak man whose opinion was easily swayed. His father said of him: 'he is still absolutely a child, he has infantile judgements'. The other difficulty was that Russia was changing rapidly. Its industries were beginning to spread and the number of people living in towns and working in factories was increasing all the time. Much of this new industry, though, was owned by foreigners investing in Russia. This was to have a serious effect because it meant that there were fewer Russian factory owners and middle class businessmen. So when it came to leading a challenge to the Tsar, the challenge had to come from the workers and the peasants. By 1913 Russia had 2.3 million industrial workers and they were not as prepared

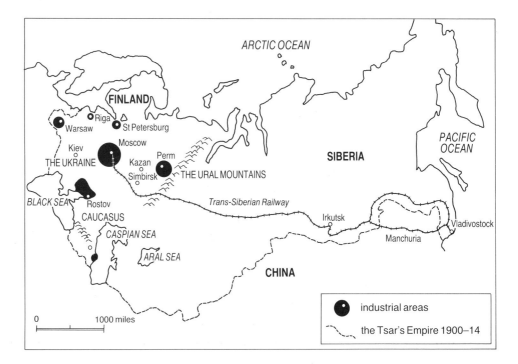

Industrial Russia

to accept poor wages and conditions as the peasants were.

When forced to do so, Nicholas would make changes. After an unsuccessful **revolution** in 1905 Nicholas paid attention to some of his more sensible advisers. He allowed a Parliament, or *Duma*, to be elected in 1906. But as soon as it began to criticise the lack of freedom Nicholas shut it down. However, Nicholas did allow one man, Peter Stolypin, to make some important changes. Between 1906 and 1911 Stolypin introduced a series of reforms which made it easier for peasants to own their own land. But even by 1916 only 24% of peasants owned any land – the rest still worked for wealthy landowners. Stolypin was assassinated in 1911. Some historians suspect that the Tsar may have been involved because the assassin was later discovered to be a police agent who was posing as a revolutionary.

Exercise 1

Russia's industrial growth

Study the following groups of statistics about Russia in the years before the revolution:

SOURCE A: Population 1900 (in millions)

Russia	103	France	39
Germany	56	Great Britain	41
Austria-Hungary	45	Italy	32

SOURCE B: Railways – kilometres of track in 1900 (in thousands)

Russia	53	France	38
Germany	52	Great Britain	35
Austria-Hungary	36	Italy	16

SOURCE C: Coal production in 1900 (in million tonnes); figures in brackets refer to percentage increase in production since 1890

Russia	16 (170%)	France	33 (28%)
Germany	149 (67%)	Great Britain	225 (24%)
Austria-Hungary	39 (50%)	Italy	(0.5%)

SOURCE D: Steel production (in million tonnes)

	1890	1900		1890	1900
Russia	0.4	1.5	France	0.7	1.6
Germany	2.3	6.7	Great Britain	3.6	4.9
Austria-Hungary	0.5	1.2			

(Sources A, C and D from A.J.P. Taylor, *Struggle for Mastery in Europe, 1848–1918*, 1971)

a Which two countries, on the basis of Sources C and D, had the biggest industrial output?

b Of the five countries listed in both Sources C and D where would you rank Russia in terms of output?

c Which of the nations listed in Sources C and D was growing the most quickly in terms of output? Support your answer with evidence from the statistics.

d Source B shows Russia as having the largest railway network.
   i Why is this a misleading statistic?
   ii How does Source A put Source B and the other sources concerning Russia
      in a more accurate position?
e What do you think this exercise tells you about the dangers for historians of
   using statistics?

Russia and the First World War

The military aspects of Russia's involvement in the First World War are dealt with in the first chapter. What concerns us here is how that war affected the country and made certain that there would be a revolution. There is enough evidence to suggest that there would have been a revolution in Russia to overthrow the Tsar sooner or later. The First World War simply made it happen sooner. Stolypin's intelligent reforms to improve the lot of the peasants had not gone far enough and made little impression on the sense of anger and frustration felt by most of Russia's peasants. Russia's industrial workers were becoming more and more involved in confrontations with the government over wages and conditions. In 1912 there were over 2000 separate strikes – ten times as many as in 1910. In the seven months before the outbreak of war in 1914 this number had risen to 4000. In 1912, 270 miners had been shot dead during a strike in the Lena goldfields. But the lack of freedom also affected and angered middle class people in Russia, who found that because they did not belong to the wealthy nobility their chances of rising to important posts in the government and civil service were very slim. There was also little work for lawyers in a legal system in which the decision of a policeman was enough to send a man or woman to imprisonment in Siberia.

These problems were all made worse by the war. In the first place, after a few minor victories at the very start of the war, the Russian armies suffered terrible casualties in a series of defeats. Those that survived had to put up with hunger and lack of equipment. This demoralisation soon filtered back to the villages and towns where anti-war feeling steadily grew. Russia's economy

Tsar Nicholas blesses his troops as they kneel in respect. Within a few months they were to help overthrow him

was a long way behind her enemies. **Industrial output** actually fell by 50% as peasants were brought into the factories lacking the right skills to work the machinery. At the same time there were fewer labourers to work the land – some 15 million peasants were conscripted during the war. Agricultural production dropped. The shortages of food led to rapid **inflation**: prices rose by some 700% between 1914 and 1917. The Tsar foolishly made himself supreme commander of the armed forces (August 1915) and therefore became responsible for the string of defeats. Nicholas and his family were further criticised because of their strange relationship with an unpleasant 'monk' named Rasputin. This man had a powerful influence over the Tsar's wife, the Tsarina, because of his ability to ease the suffering of her sick son. Rasputin's influence soon extended to government affairs – which greatly angered the court nobility. Eventually he was murdered in December 1916 but by then the damage to the Tsar's image had been done.

Exercise 2

a What is an autocrat?
b How had Stolypin tried to modernise Russian agriculture?
c What evidence is there in the text that industrial workers were becoming increasingly discontented?
d Why were middle-class people also angry?
e Which two issues brought personal criticism for the Tsar?

The March Revolution 1917

In Russia the events which led to the overthrow of the Tsar are called the February Revolution. The old Russian calendar ran 13 days behind the calendar used by the rest of Europe. For us the revolution began on 8 March (23 February in the Old Style). It began with a strike by 90 000 textile workers, protesting about the shortage of bread and fuel. Soon they were joined by other workers. The banners became more political: 'Down with the War' and later 'Down with the Tsar'. By the end of the week 400 000 workers were on strike in Petrograd. Troops sent by the Tsar to put down the demonstrations mutinied, shot their officers and joined in. On 15 March the Tsar abdicated and gave up the throne in favour of his brother who refused the throne. The Romanov dynasty was at an end. The Duma stepped in. The Duma, the Russian Parliament, was elected by a small minority of wealthy Russians. However, it was the closest Russia had to a voice for the people. Several leading members of the Duma were chosen to become a 'Provisional Government' to run the country until new and more democratic elections could be held to decide on a proper government. The Provisional Government was led by a **liberal** aristocrat, Prince Lvov.

The **revolution** had not been planned by anybody. Nobody had expected it. Yet within a week one of the world's most repressive governments had been swept aside and replaced by a government that soon introduced wide, democratic freedoms. But the Provisional Government was not the only source of power in Petrograd. From the very start of the revolution another body had been set up – the Petrograd Soviet of Workers' and Soldiers' Deputies. *Soviet* is Russian for council; the Petrograd Soviet had first appeared in 1905. It represented the views of the city's workers and tried to direct the course of the unsuccessful re-volution then. As soon as the events of March began it set itself up and soon established the total support of key workers in the transport, railway and communication industries. Nothing could happen in the city without the permission of the Soviet. However, there was no conflict between the Soviet, led by moderate socialists called Mensheviks, and the Provisional Government. They quickly agreed on two issues: to make Russia a **democracy** and to carry on with the war.

Exercise
■ 3

An eyewitness account:

Extract One

This is taken from an account by N.N. Sukhanov, a Menshevik, who became a member of the Petrograd Soviet.

Tuesday March 6 [New Style dates are given]. I was sitting in my office. Behind a partition two typists were gossiping about food difficulties, rows in shopping queues ... 'Do you know', suddenly declared one of these young ladies, 'if you ask me, it's the beginning of the Revolution' ...

5   On Friday, the 9th, the movement swept over St. Petersburg (Petrograd) like a great flood. Fugitive meetings were held in the main streets and were dispersed by Cossacks and mounted police – but without any real energy ... A few of the biggest factories had been occupied, others were besieged by troops. Here and there the attackers had met with some resistance – some pistol
10 shots from young workers ...

The unforgettable 12th of March came. There were no officers visible at all with the patrols ...; they were disorderly groups of grey greatcoats, mingling and openly fraternising with the working class crowd ... willingly giving up their rifles ...

15 I elbowed my way through to the rooms occupied by the Soviet ... standing on stools ... one after another the soldiers' delegates told of what was happening in their companies ... 'They told us not to serve against the people any more, to defend the people's cause' ... 'Long live the Revolution' ...

(Adapted from N.N. Sukhanov, *The Russian Revolution, 1917: A personal record*, 1955)

An eyewitness account:

Extract Two

This is taken from an account by Alexander Kerensky – at that time a socialist deputy in the Duma. He was later to become leader of the Provisional Government.

The stage had been set for the final crash, but as is usually the case in such events, no one expected it to come precisely on the morning of March twelfth. How could I ... have guessed as I rushed out of my apartment in what a different position I would be when I returned to it? ... We had one common inspiration –
5   Russia! Russia in peril ... Russia betrayed by the old regime, Russia prey to the blind raging mob ...

I learned that Rodzianko, President of the Duma, had received an order from Nicholas II dissolving the Duma at midnight ... I rushed to the telephone and urged some friends to go to the barracks of the insurgent regiments and direct

10   the troops to the Duma ... I addressed the troops and asked them to follow me into the Duma and take over the defence of the building from the Tsarist troops ...

(A.F. Kerensky, *The Catastrophe*, 1927)

a Why do you think there are so many references to soldiers in the text of Extract One?

b Explain why 'rows in shopping queues' (line 2, Extract One) would have been quite common at this time.

c What evidence is there in Extract One that the soldiers were not with the revolution from the very start?

d Explain the reference to 'the Soviet' (line 15, Extract One). Why do you suppose Sukhanov made his way to the Soviet rather than the Duma to find out about the events of the revolution?

e What date do both these extracts agree on as being very important?

f What evidence is there that Kerensky in Extract Two was not especially sympathetic to the people involved in the revolution?

g What impression does Kerensky give of his role in the events of the revolution?

h Which of these two accounts do you think historians would consider more reliable and why?

Exercise ▮ 4

Source One is a German cartoon of July 1917. It shows an imprisoned Tsar and, from left to right, Lloyd-George, Wilson and Ribot (prime minister of France). The three are saying:

'We never deal with autocratic government, never.' Nicholas thinks to himself: 'Once these rascals were like brothers to me.'

a Who is the Tsar shown imprisoned?

b Why do you think the three were 'once like brothers' to the Tsar?

c Why are these three men now turning their backs on the Tsar?

d What do Lloyd-George, Wilson and Ribot all have in common as government leaders which the Tsar did not share?

e Give two reasons why these three leaders were likely to get on well with the Provisional Government.

f Explain in a paragraph of 20 lines how the Tsar came to be no longer the ruler of Russia.

Source One *German cartoon*

Enter the Bolsheviks

So far only one political party has been mentioned – the Mensheviks. The term *Menshevik* means minority and it dates from 1903 when the Russian Social Democrat Party split into two groups. The Mensheviks believed that the party should have an open membership which would allow anyone to join as long as they sympathised with the party's ideas. They also wanted co-operation with wealthy factory owners and other middle-class groups to overthrow the Tsar. The other, **Bolshevik**, group (the majority), led by Lenin, wanted the party membership to consist only of dedicated, professional revolutionaries. He did not see the point of co-operating with the wealthy groups (or **bourgeoisie** as the Bolsheviks called them) against the Tsar.

Lenin was forty-seven at the time of the March Revolution. He came from a comfortable middle-class background and had been well educated. Vladimir Ilyich Ulyanov, Lenin's real name, was seventeen when his brother, Alexander, was hung for his part in a plot to assassinate Tsar Alexander III. Lenin was as fiercely opposed to the Tsar as his brother but he believed that terrorism could never be a permanent solution to Russia's problems. Lenin wanted the workers in alliance with the peasants to seize power and establish **socialism**. Both Mensheviks and Bolsheviks claimed that their policies were those of the nineteenth century German revolutionary, Karl Marx. But after the Social Democrat Party split in 1903 these two groups were bitterly hostile to each other. By 1917 the Mensheviks, despite the origin of their name, were a much bigger party than the Bolsheviks.

There was another left wing party called the Socialist Revolutionaries. Their basic policy was that the peasants should own the land. This gave them a great deal of support from the biggest group in Russia – the peasants. Kerensky was a member of the SRs. Wealthy business and professional people also had a party known as the Cadets – short for Constitutional Democrats. They were not socialists but they did want to see an end to the Tsar's autocratic rule and the setting up of a parliamentary system like the one in Britain.

None of these parties played a major role in the March Revolution but the Mensheviks and the SRs quickly won a majority of the delegates to the Petrograd Soviet. Of the 1500 soldiers' and workers' delegates in the Soviet the Bolsheviks had only about 40. They were a tiny, rather unimportant revolutionary organisation with perhaps only 23 000 members in the whole of Russia. At first, the Bolsheviks, led by Stalin because the other leading Bolsheviks such as Lenin were still in exile and had not returned to Russia, followed the policies of the Mensheviks and supported the Provisional Government which was led by Cadets. When Lenin, who was in Switzerland when the Tsar was overthrown, heard what Stalin was doing he was furious. But how could he get to Russia across Germany, a country still at war with Russia? The German government knew Lenin was against the war and would, if he came to power, pull Russia out of the war. This would be a great help to Germany. So the Germans provided Lenin and about 100 other Bolsheviks with a special train to take them across Germany. It was an unlikely alliance and Lenin was later accused by his enemies of being in the pay of the **Kaiser** and of being a German spy.

Lenin arrived in Petrograd early in April, 1917. Straight away he told the cheering crowd that the Bolsheviks should organise to overthrow the Provisional Government, end the war and hand over the land to the peasants.

Trotsky

'Peace, Land and Bread' and 'All Power to the Soviets' were his simple and very effective slogans. Most people thought he was mad and paid him little attention. Russia had just had a revolution and now she was a democracy – why have another? Another Marxist revolutionary arrived in Russia shortly after Lenin. He was Leon Trotsky (real name Bronstein). Trotsky had also been a member of the Social Democratic Party and had opposed Lenin after the split in 1903. Despite an often very bitter quarrel about the best way to bring about a revolution in Russia, Trotsky quickly settled his differences and joined the Bolsheviks in 1917. Lenin was very pleased to have a man of Trotsky's ability in the party. He was to prove an invaluable asset.

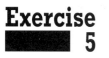

Exercise 5

a Into what two groups did the Russian Social Democrat Party split in 1903?

b What policies did the Bolshevik group call for?

c What were the policies of the other three major political parties in Russia?

d Why was Lenin so angry when he learned of the policies Stalin was following while he was in Switzerland?

e Do you think the Germans' decision to help Lenin get to Russia was a shrewd one? Explain your reason.

f Explain how Lenin's policies were designed to appeal to (i) the soldiers; (ii) the workers; (iii) the peasants.

The Provisional Government's mistakes

The Provisional Government made some popular decisions to begin with. It released all political prisoners, legalised political parties, introduced the right to strike and an eight-hour working day. It also called for the election of a Constituent Assembly to decide Russia's new **constitution**. All the Tsar's estates were confiscated, but because many wealthy landowners supported the new government nothing was done to provide the peasantry with any other land. That was to prove a fatal error. The decision to continue the war against Germany was another mistake which was to lead to the end of the Provisional Government. Prince Lvov, and later Kerensky, made the mistake of thinking that the Russian people would be willing to fight for a free and democratic Russia now that the Tsar had gone. Furthermore, Kerensky believed that, by continuing to fight with democratic nations such as Britain and France, Russia had a better chance of surviving as a democracy herself. But the Russian people wanted only peace, bread and land. One man – Lenin – was prepared to promise them these.

A new offensive was launched at the end of June. It went the way of most other Russian offensives and failed. But it was a serious setback for the government. In June alone there were 30 000 desertions and numbers were increasing all the time. As Lenin put it, they were 'voting with their feet'. Once these peasants in uniform made their way back to the villages they began seizing the land which they believed rightfully belonged to them. Kerensky became Prime Minister in July. Criticism of the government increased as the war went on and the government still stalled on transferring land to the peasants. The promised election for a Constituent Assembly was continually put off. The Mensheviks and SRs began to lose support in the Petrograd Soviet, as they had from the start supported the increasingly unpopular Provisional Government. Support for the Bolsheviks, on the other hand, who had constantly condemned the government, rapidly began to increase. Before the March Revolution the Bolsheviks numbered only 2000 in Petrograd and 600 in Moscow. By the end of July the membership had grown to 36 000 for the capital and 15 000 for Moscow.

In July Lenin nearly suffered a fatal blow to his hopes of another revolution. In that month the 'July Days' occurred in which massive demonstrations against the government took place. Many of the 500 000 demonstrators were armed sailors from the Kronstadt naval base. They marched on the government but Kerensky had enough support to crush them and 400 were killed. Lenin had argued that the time was not right for a revolution but Kerensky seized his chance to order the arrest of the leading Bolsheviks. Trotsky was arrested and Lenin forced into hiding. That might have been the end of the Bolsheviks but events soon turned in their favour again.

At the beginning of September, General Kornilov, commander-in-chief of the Russian armies, ordered his troops to march on Petrograd, crush the Soviet and cleanse the government of socialists. It seemed a serious threat. Kerensky released the Bolsheviks from gaol when they offered to help defend the government. Over 20 000 Bolshevik Red Guards ('Reds') organised the defence of the city and infiltrated Kornilov's army, urging the men to desert. They did just that and the march fizzled out. The popularity of Lenin and his party received a massive boost. In September Bolsheviks won a majority of delegates in both the Moscow and Petrograd Soviets. With the support of Russia's workers and soldiers behind him, Lenin decided that the time to move against Kerensky had come.

The November Revolution

On 20 October 1917 the Bolshevik Central Committee supported Lenin's call to plan for a seizure of power. Trotsky, now chairman of the Soviet, was given the job of working out the details for the take-over. The revolution was planned for the night before the All Russian Congress of Soviets was to meet in Petrograd. This meeting was to have present all the delegates from all of the city and village soviets in Russia. On the night of 6–7 November the Red Guards in Petrograd seized control of the stations, telegraph office, bridges and government buildings. Kerensky fled the city. The Provisional Government crumbled away. Five people were killed in Petrograd – all Bolsheviks. In Moscow it took a week's bitter fighting, with 200 killed before the city was taken. By the end of it Lenin controlled the heartland of Russia – but little else. The ease with which Kerensky's government was toppled showed how little real support the Provisional Govern-

Red Guards in St Petersburg, November 1917

ment had and how well Lenin had judged the moment to seize power. Kerensky had known that the Bolsheviks were planning against him. In October he ordered the Bolshevik-dominated Petrograd garrison to the front, hoping to weaken the Bolsheviks' armed support. The garrison simply refused to go and there was nothing Kerensky could do about it.

Exercise 6

a Why did the Provisional Government not decide to hand over all land to the peasants?

b What do you think Lenin meant by the phrase that the soliders were 'voting with their feet'?

c What evidence is there in the text that support for the Bolsheviks increased rapidly after the March Revolution?

d How did General Kornilov's attempted march on Petrograd help the Bolsheviks?

e What evidence is there in the text that Kerensky had little real support in Petrograd?

f What evidence is there in the photograph above of the Red Guards that many were former soliders?

g How would you describe the Red Guards' means of transport in the photograph? Can you suggest a reason for the fact that although many of the Red Guards had joined the Bolsheviks already equipped with weapons they seemed unable to use more military types of transport?

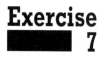

Exercise 7

City council elections

The following are the election results to the Moscow city council in 1917. Study them and then answer the questions which follow:

Parties	Councillors elected	June votes	%	Councillors elected	September votes	%
Cadets	17	109 000	17	30	101 000	26
SRs	58	375 000	58	14	54 000	14
Mensheviks	12	76 000	12	4	16 000	4
Bolsheviks	11	75 000	11	47	198 000	51

(From: J. Reed, *Ten Days that Shook the World*)

a Which parties (i) lost the most votes; (ii) gained the most votes; (iii) kept more or less the same number of votes?

b What sort of people would have voted for the Cadets? Were there likely to be more or less of these people in a big city like Moscow than in the countryside?

c Large numbers of peasants had been drafted into the cities to work in the factories. Which party was most likely to benefit from this? Do the voting figures for June confirm this?

e How do you explain the tremendous drop in popularity of the Mensheviks and SRs?

f Which party picked up many of these votes? How do you explain this large increase in votes won? (Note the date for the second election and remember an important event early in that month).

Exercise 8

BETRAYED.

THE PANDER. "COME ON; COME AND BE KISSED BY HIM."

Source Two **Punch**
cartoon, 12 December 1917

a Identify the figure rubbing his hands, standing in the doorway.

b Which person would best represent the Bolshevik dragging the woman?

c Explain the reference to 'German Gold' on the bag around the Bolshevik's waist.

d Why was this figure in the drawing rubbing his hands and were his hopes proved justified?

e This is a British cartoon, published in December 1917. Why do you think the cartoonist is so obviously hostile to both the Bolsheviks and the figure in the doorway?

f A 'pander' is somebody who helps another person carry out an immoral or low act. Why is the Bolshevik shown by the cartoonist as a 'pander'? Who or what is being 'betrayed' as it says in the title?

Lenin in power 1917–24

Few people expected Lenin's government to last long. Seizing control of the capital and major cities did not make the Bolsheviks masters of all Russia. However, in contrast to Kerensky's dithering, Lenin moved very quickly to issue new laws. The first decree was a peace offer and called for immediate negotiations to end the war. Secondly, Lenin announced that all of Russia's 540 million acres now belonged to the peasants of Russia. At a stroke the Bolsheviks had won over the support of 80% of the population – though Lenin knew that the private ownership of land, even by peasants, went against **Communist** principles. But one of Lenin's most important qualities as a leader was his ability to compromise when necessary. One of the severest difficulties faced by 300 000 Bolsheviks trying to run a huge country was lack of skilled and experienced administrators. The Commissar (or minister) for Finance for example, was given the job simply because he had worked in a French bank – as a clerk!

The Constituent Assembly

The elections for the long delayed Constituent Assembly went ahead – as promised by Lenin. The results, though, were a big disappointment for the Bolsheviks. The Socialist Revolutionaries won a decisive majority with nearly 17 million votes out of 41 million cast. This gave them 370 seats out of the 707 available in the Assembly. The Bolsheviks came second with 10 million votes and 175 seats (25%). The Mensheviks managed only 16 seats and the Cadets 17. A small minority of SRs was willing to support Lenin but the vast majority was hostile. When the Constituent Assembly met in January it bitterly criticised the Bolsheviks and their revolution. On its second day Lenin shut it down. The Bolsheviks decided that the new Soviet Government could not permit such opposition. A new secret police force was set up, the **Cheka**, to deal with any serious opponents – although Lenin, unlike Stalin, his successor, was prepared to allow criticism and argument *inside* the Communist Party (the new official title of the Bolsheviks).

Brest–Litovsk, March 1918

There was plenty of argument over the next big issue that faced the Soviet Government: the treaty of Brest–Litovsk with Germany. The terms demanded by the Germans were very harsh. The Russians were to lose 26% of their population, 27% of farm land and 74% of their iron ore and coal. Trotsky, the Commissar for Foreign Affairs, argued against the terms. Some Communists called for a 'revolutionary war' against Germany. But Lenin knew that the army could not fight any more and that to carry on with the war would lead to defeat and the overthrow of the Soviet Government. Lenin won the vote and the peace was signed in March 1918. Fortunately for the Communist Government when Germany lost the war the treaty was cancelled and Russia got most of her territory back, except for Finland and the Baltic states which remained independent.

No sooner had one problem been dealt with than another faced Lenin. Anti-Bolshevik forces, the Whites backed by troops and weapons from the **Entente** powers still fighting Germany, were beginning their campaign against the Reds. The Civil War thus began in the spring of 1918 and lasted until the end of 1920. The first important victims were the Tsar and his family who were shot by the Reds in May, 1918. The Cheka, which in the first six months of its existence, from

The Treaty of Brest–Litovsk 1918

December 1917 to June 1918, had shot only 22 people, now began a serious policy of terror against the Whites. By the end of the year 6000 'counter-revolutionaries' had been shot. The Whites, backed by a confused mixture of supporters of the Tsar and the Provisional Government, launched an even more vicious terror campaign of their own. The Cheka, in these early days, was not as ruthlessly efficient as it was later. In January 1919, for instance, Lenin was held up by bandits on his way to work and robbed of his car and possessions!

Map labels: FINLAND, BALTIC SEA, Petrograd, RUSSIA, POLAND, Brest-Litovski, Moscow, THE UKRAINE, RUMANIA, CASPIAN SEA, BLACK SEA, GEORGIA, TURKEY

0   300

- - - boundary of Russia in 1914

territory lost at Brest-Litovsk but re-gained after the war

territory lost at Brest-Litovsk and not returned after the war

---

Exercise 9

a How did Lenin immediately make sure of peasant support for the revolution?
b What was Lenin's response to the disappointing election results for the Constituent Assembly?
c What was Lenin's attitude to debate and criticism from within the Communist Party?
d What evidence is there that the Cheka only began to terrorise opponents once the Civil War began?

Assignment unit

Write a confidential report from the British ambassador, Sir George Buchanan, in Petrograd to the British Prime Minister, Lloyd-George, about the Bolshevik seizure of power. Include the following points in your report:

a the reasons for the success of the November Revolution;
b the policies of the new Soviet Government – the likely response to them of the Russian people and how they might affect Britain (especially the war policy of Lenin).

> **c** Assess the problems facing Lenin and his prospects of survival.
>
> **d** Make a recommendation to Lloyd-George on whether the British government should recognise the new Soviet Government or give support to the White Russians organising opposition to Lenin. Outline the good and bad points of both courses of action, e.g. supporting the Whites might lead to Lenin's overthrow and the re-entry of Russia into the war (how much help would Russia be?) but if the Whites lost then Britain would make an enemy of the new government.

The Civil War: 1918–1920

Foreign powers, especially Britain, France, the USA and Japan, were keen to see the Bolsheviks overthrown but their troops played little part in the Civil War. Most of their support for the Whites was in the form of weapons. The United States gave the Whites 200 000 rifles and Britain gave a further 100 000. Though the Reds were outnumbered and less well-equipped they did have some advantages. The Communists controlled the industrial centres and the extensive railway network which enabled the Reds to rush supplies and troops to any part of their front under threat. This advantage is known as 'inner lines of communication'. In the east the Bolsheviks faced a twin threat from Admiral Kolchak's forces and from the Czech Legion. The Czech Legion consisted of 40 000 former soldiers in the Habsburg armies, taken prisoner by the Russians. Their basic aim was to make their way back to the new state of Czechoslovakia but they soon found themselves involved in fighting against the Red forces. In the south-west stood the armies of General Denikin and those of his successor, General Wrangel. In the north-west the forces of General Yudenich threatened Petrograd. The decisive year was 1919 when Kolchak's forces were crushed and their leader taken prisoner and later shot. That year also saw Denikin's advance on Moscow checked and, in March 1920, his forces finally destroyed – apart from a small portion later commanded by Wrangel. Yudenich came within a few miles of Petrograd and was only driven back after a personal appearance at the front by Trotsky, now the leader of the Red Army. Wrangel's forces in the Crimea were the last serious obstacle and these were overwhelmed in November 1920.

Amidst this civil war another war was being fought, this one against the new state of Poland. The Poles, anxious to seize further territory from their traditional enemy, had invaded Russia in the spring of 1920 led by General Pilsudski. Their plan to take advantage of the Soviet Republic's problems with the Whites went seriously wrong. The Poles were driven back to the gates of Warsaw and only a failure of planning and co-operation between two Red generals allowed the Poles to save their capital and drive the Red Army back. A military historian, J.F.C. Fuller, has described the Battle of Warsaw as one of the most important battles ever. If the Bolsheviks had won and conquered Poland they would have been in a position to come to the aid of German Communists and, perhaps, ensure the success of a soviet revolution in

Germany. The Treaty of Riga (March 1921) led to an expansion of Poland and the addition of some 6 million Ukrainian and Russian subjects.

Apart from having inner lines of communication, another decisive Red advantage was the superior morale and determination of their troops. This was largely due to Trotsky's skills as an organiser and motivator. The White Armies suffered from a total lack of unity. The White generals were jealous of each other and refused to co-ordinate their offensives and therefore the Reds never really had to face an attack by all of their enemies at the same time. Some White leaders, such as Kolchak, were brutal and established a harsh rule over their territories. Land-lords were always given back their land and this led more and more peasants to support the Bolsheviks. Denikin slaughtered 100 000 Jews in the Ukraine and such savagery made it hard for the Western powers to increase aid to the Whites.

Western support also had the effect of making the Whites appear as tools of foreign governments while the Red Army could claim to be fighting for a Russia free from foreign control. To begin with, the Red Army was desperately short of officers – most of these sided with the Whites. Trotsky's solution was to force some 30 000 former Tsarist officers to work for him by taking prisoner their families as 'insurance' for loyal service.

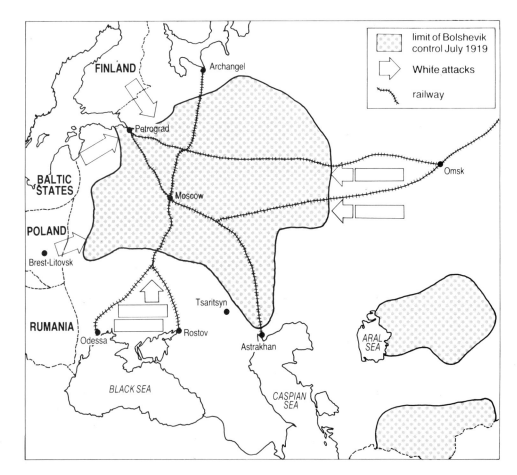

Russian Civil War: 1918–20

Exercise 10

Map work

a Copy the map on page 51 into your book. Read through the section on the Civil War and then mark inside the arrows, or the boxes next to the arrows, the names of the generals who led the attacks in that area.

b Explain the importance for the Bolsheviks of the railway network.

c Explain how Rostov and Odessa would have been useful to the White forces in the area for their campaign against the Reds.

d Can you think of any reason why the Bolshevik-controlled areas south and east of the Aral Sea were left alone by the Whites?

e How would the capture of Astrakhan by the Bolsheviks have put the Whites in an even more difficult position?

Lenin's economic policies

'War Communism' and the NEP

At first Lenin had intended to move slowly as regards the Russian economy, and only the big industries like the banks, railways, steel, iron and coal were **nationalised** or taken over by the State. But the urgent needs created by the Civil War led to a more drastic policy called 'War Communism'. Peasants were forced to give up all their surplus crops to the government to feed the Red Army. Workers were told where to work and often forcibly moved hundreds of miles to a new factory.

All firms employing more than 10 workers were nationalised but many workers seized control of firms with only one or two employees. Of the 37 000 taken over by the state in 1920, 5000 had only one employee. Industrial production fell sharply as the economy was plunged into chaos. In 1920 large-scale Russian industry was producing only 18% of its 1913 output. Some Bolsheviks, including Trotsky, argued that 'War Communism' should be continued after the Civil War was won because it meant a more equal Russia. But Lenin disagreed and the Kronstadt Mutiny in March 1921 convinced him it

had to be replaced. In March the sailors of the Kronstadt naval base rose up in revolt against the banning of all political parties except the Communist Party. They demanded the free election of soviets and an end to the harsh policies of 'War Communism'. The rising was crushed by Trotsky with great bloodshed. In the same month the new Economic Policy (NEP) was approved by the party. In this Lenin proposed that peasants should hand over a fixed proportion of their crops as a tax to the state. Anything above that they could keep and sell privately. Many small firms were returned to their former owners and incentive schemes set up to encourage more production. Agricultural output increased rapidly so that in 1925 the grain harvest yield was 72 million tonnes – 22 million tonnes up on the 1922 figure of 50 million.

The emergence of Stalin

The banning of political opposition during the Civil War seemed unavoidable but after the Red Army victory Mensheviks and SRs continued to be arrested by the OGPU (the successor to the Cheka). In 1921 opposition within the Communist Party itself was banned and the control of Lenin and the Party over the affairs of the Soviet Republic was complete. But Lenin himself was increasingly ill and played practically no role in political matters for the last year of his life. One man, Stalin, was already making sure he would be in a good position to become Lenin's successor. In 1922 he was appointed General Secretary of the Party and this gave him control of the appointment of people to key jobs inside Russia.

Lenin was well aware of the power Stalin was beginning to acquire and it worried him. In January 1923 he wrote an addition to his political will or testament. In it he advised the Central Committee to replace Stalin as General Secretary of the Party. He recommended they find someone 'more tolerant, more loyal, more polite and more considerate'. Earlier Lenin had written of Stalin that he had 'unlimited authority concentrated in his hands and I am not sure whether he will always be capable of using that authority with sufficient caution'. He also criticised Trotsky for his excessive 'self-confidence' but said that he was the 'most capable man in the present Central Committee'. If Lenin's Testament had been made public Stalin's chances of becoming leader would have been ruined, but the Bolshevik leaders only discussed it among themselves ... and did nothing.

When Lenin died on 21 January 1924 Stalin was already too powerful to be challenged by Trotsky. Within four years of Lenin's death Trotsky was expelled from the Party and Stalin was master of Russia. Lenin's death at the age of 53 was a blow to the Soviet Republic because it was now deprived of its most able and undisputed leader. Lenin had governed Russia firmly but without cruelty. He was a modest man who shunned public attention and had always been concerned with the welfare of ordinary Russians. He was replaced by a man who possessed none of these qualities.

Exercise 11

a What effect did 'War Communism' have on industrial production in Russia?
b Why did the NEP please the peasants so much?
c How was Stalin able to concentrate 'unlimited authority' in his hands?
d Whom do you think Lenin preferred as his successor and why?
e Other Bolsheviks at the time mocked Stalin, calling him ''Comrade Card-Index'' and a ''grey blur''. What do you think they meant?
f Write a 20 line statement from Trotsky to the Central Committee outlining why he ought to be the man to succeed Lenin in 1924, giving details of his role as a Bolshevik since joining the Party in May 1917.

Exercise 12

Study the cartoon on page 54 and then answer the following:
a Give the name of one possible 'Russian Bolshevist' mentioned in the cartoon.
b Who were the 'bourgeoisie' referred to by the Bolshevist?
c Name one political party in Russia which would have agreed with the view of this *Punch* cartoon.
d In what ways had the Bolsheviks dug 'a grave for the bourgeoisie' by the time this cartoon was published (November 1920)?
e What is the cartoonist implying about the chances of Russia recovering from her problems?
f To what extent, if at all, do you think the Bolsheviks had managed 'to get out' of the grave and put Russia back on its feet by the time of Lenin's death?

THE ABYSMALISTS.

BRITISH EXTREMIST. "WHAT ARE YOU DOING DOWN THERE?"
VOICE OF RUSSIAN BOLSHEVIST FROM BELOW. "DIGGING A GRAVE FOR THE BOURGEOISIE."
BRITISH EXTREMIST. "THAT'S WHAT I WANT TO DO; BUT HOW DO YOU GET OUT?"
VOICE FROM BELOW. "YOU DON'T."

Source
Three **Punch**
*cartoon, 17
November 1920*

Exercise
13

Copy this outline of the front page of the Communist party paper *Pravda* into
your exercise book. Although it is an imagined front page try and make it as
realistic as you can – you can of course change the headline and sub-headings.
Make some reference to the problems of who is to succeed Lenin and include
an interview with Trotsky or Stalin.

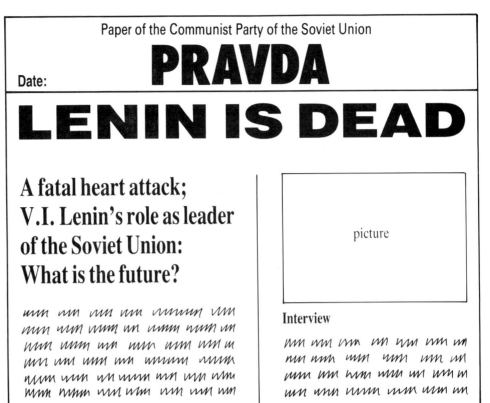

Paper of the Communist Party of the Soviet Union

PRAVDA

Date:

LENIN IS DEAD

A fatal heart attack; V.I. Lenin's role as leader of the Soviet Union: What is the future?

picture

Interview

Chapter 4

Stalin and the USSR: 1928–39

Stalin's rise to power

Joseph Stalin (real name, Djugashvili) was one of the few old **Bolshevik** leaders who did not come from a middle-class background. Stalin's father had been a shoe-maker. His poor background and the fact that he was not an intellectual, full of fine phrases and long words, made him popular with some **Communists**. Stalin played on this image as a man of the people, rough and ready. On the other hand, Leon Trotsky (real name, Bronstein) came across very differently. Trotsky came

Lenin and Stalin

from a middle-class family and had a brilliant mind. He was an intellectual, full of ideas on how to change the face of Russia. But he had only become a Bolshevik in 1917, after patching up a quarrel with Lenin that had gone on for years. Many old, established Bolsheviks resented his rapid promotion and success inside the Party. Stalin found willing allies in the form of Kamenev and Zinoviev who were also determined to keep Trotsky from power.

The three of them managed to persuade the Central Committee to shelve Lenin's Testament in which Lenin had recommended Stalin's removal from office. This alliance argued against Trotsky's proposals for the future of the Soviet Union. Trotsky's idea of 'World **Revolution**' was not really popular with most Party members. Trotsky believed that it was vital for the Russians to cause revolutions in advanced countries like Germany. Once **Communism** spread to industrialised nations they could then offer aid to the industrially backward Soviet Union. But most Party members were tired of revolutionary upheavals and, besides, revolutionary movements in various European countries had all been beaten by 1923. Stalin offered what seemed to many Bolsheviks a more attractive solution: '**Socialism** in one country'. It appealed to the patriotic feelings that many still had, whereas Trotsky offered only more struggle and hardship involved in spreading the revolution abroad. The Bolsheviks were only now beginning to realise the extent of the losses caused by the Civil War and just how much needed to be done. Russia could and should concentrate on building a socialist system on its own, Stalin argued, no matter what went on elsewhere in Europe or the world. Trotsky had always argued that this was impossible but his message was too bleak and demoralising. Stalin's idea offered some hope for the future.

First Trotsky was removed from the post of Commissar for War in 1925. The election of new supporters of Stalin to the Central Committee for 1926 meant that Stalin no longer needed the support of Zinoviev and Kamenev. By the end of 1926 they were all dismissed from the Central Committee and in 1927 Trotsky was forced to leave the Soviet Union for a life of exile. He was never to return. In 1940 a Stalinist agent split Trotsky's head in two with an ice-pick in Mexico. The last of the Revolution's children had been devoured.

Stalin's triumph by 1928 was as thorough as it was surprising. Even in 1924 most people would have backed Trotsky or Zinoviev for the leadership of the Party. The fact that Stalin was underestimated by many – especially by Trotsky and others like Zinoviev and Kamenev, was to his advantage. Trotsky arrogantly dismissed Stalin as a 'mediocrity' and another contemporary described him as a 'grey blur'. Unlike Trotsky, Stalin was a master schemer and tactician. Between 1924 and 1926 he sided with Zinoviev and Kamenev against Trotsky. With Trotsky out of the way by 1926, he sided with Bukharin against Zinoviev and Kamenev. When these last two had been expelled from the party he turned on Bukharin, who was expelled in 1929.

Once he was in total control, Stalin set about dealing with Russia's problems as ruthlessly as he dealt with his opponents.

Exercise 1

a Why was Stalin popular with some Communists?

b Why was Trotsky unpopular with some Communists?

c Why was Trotsky's theory of 'World Revolution' less attractive than Stalin's theory of 'Socialism in one country' to many Party members?

d What error did Trotsky make in his attitude to Stalin?

e Explain the point of the sentence 'The last of the Revolution's children had been devoured'?

Stalin's Five Year Plans: industry

As you already know Russia was far behind the Western **capitalist** nations like Britain, Germany and the USA in terms of industrial power. Stalin was convinced that Russia risked eventual invasion by the West to destroy Communism. In 1931 in a speech he made this perfectly clear: 'We are fifty or a hundred years behind the advanced countries. We must make good this distance in ten years. Either we do it or we shall be crushed.' Industry and agriculture had to be transformed and they had to be modernised quickly. The New Economic Policy, introduced by Lenin in 1921, had outlived its usefulness. It could not bring the needed changes rapidly enough. Russia had to undergo massive and forced industrialisation and the peasants would have to be brought together in huge **collective farms** and taken off their tiny, privately owned plots. When Trotsky had urged this very policy in the mid 1920s Stalin had opposed him. Now Stalin was to carry out his rival's policies – but in his own much harsher way.

The key to industrial power is heavy industry – coal, iron, steel, oil. Each of the heavy industries was set a tremendously high target in the Five Year Plans, beginning in 1928. Stalin increased the pressure on the factory managers and workers by not only expecting them to exceed the target but often expecting it to be done ahead of schedule. The penalties for failure were severe. Hundreds of new factories were built, new mines dug and oil wells sunk. Whole new industrial cities were created in remote mountain areas like Magnitogorsk in the Urals for iron and steel production. A huge dam was built on the Dnieper to generate hydro-electric power and oil fields developed in the Caucasus. These achievements were accomplished with a mixture of encouragement and force. Capitalist-style incentives were introduced such as piece-work in which workers were paid according to how much they produced. Differentials were restored between skilled and unskilled workers. Workers with high output were awarded medals, like Stakhanov, a miner who cut ten times the usual amount of coal in a shift. Pressure

was put on other workers to become 'Stakhanovites'. On the other hand, discipline was fierce. Absenteeism was punished by a term in a labour camp. Workers were forcibly uprooted and sent hundred of miles to live in cold and terrible conditions as in Siberia at Komsomolsk. Every worker had to carry a work record book which had to be shown if he applied for a job. A poor record meant no job. No job often meant starvation or a life of crime in order to survive.

The First Five Year Plan (1928–32) set out to triple production levels in heavy industry. The authorities claimed that the targets were reached a year ahead of schedule but, in fact, the targets were reached only by the oil industry. Nonetheless, there is no doubt that the Plans in general were a remarkable success. By 1940 the USSR had overtaken Britain in iron and steel production and was within 20% of Germany's output. The Second Five Year Plan (1933–37) concentrated, like the first, on heavy industry and set tar-

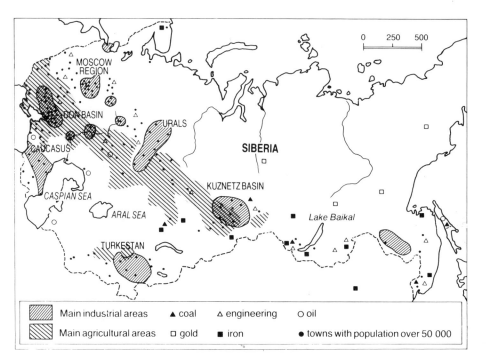

Economic development in the Soviet Union in 1939

▨ Main industrial areas	▲ coal △ engineering	○ oil
▧ Main agricultural areas	□ gold ■ iron	● towns with population over 50 000

gets which were double and triple the 1932 levels. The Third Plan switched the emphasis from heavy to light industry so that consumer goods could be produced to raise the standard of living. But the plans for consumer goods had to be dropped and production switched to armaments instead as the threat of war spread its shadow.

It is worth pointing out that from the mid 1930s onwards the quality of life for Russian industrial workers was improving gradually. Pension and sickness benefits were guaranteed by the new **constitution** of 1936. Free medical care was available more effectively – there were more doctors per 1000 people than in any of the major Western nations. Illiteracy was cut from 50% in 1924 to 19% in 1939. One American visitor to Russia later wrote 'I have seen the future, and it works'. However, most of these improvements only really concerned the industrial workers in the towns. As we shall see, for the peasants in the countryside life in the 1930s was to be much harsher and, in millions of cases, a lot shorter.

Exercise 2

a Why was Stalin so concerned to catch up with the West?
b What types of industry did Stalin concentrate on?
c How did Stalin encourage workers to work harder?
d Which sentence in the text indicates that the Five Year Plans were a success?
e What do you think the American visitor to Russia meant by the sentence quoted ('I have seen the future and it works')? Given that the visitor, a journalist, was on an official visit, how accurate a picture of life in Russia do you think he would have got? Explain your answer.

Exercise 3

Industrial production

The First Five Year Plan: 1928–32

		Output in 1927	Target	Actual output 1932
Coal		35.4	75	64
Oil	in million	11.7	22	21.4
Pig iron	tons	3.3	10	6.2
Steel		4.0	10.3	5.9

The Second Five Year Plan: 1933–37

		Output in 1932	Target	Actual output in 1937
Coal		64	152.5	128.0
Oil	in million	21.4	46.8	28.5
Pig iron	tons	6.2	16.0	14.5
Steel		5.9	17.0	17.7

(Quoted in T. Howarth, *Dreams, Plans and Nightmares*)

a Make up four graphs – one for each industry – which show the actual increases in production from 1927 to 1932 to 1937.
b Of the four industries which was (i) the most successful in terms of percentage increase over the period and (ii) the least successful?

c Which industry in the First Plan and which in the Second did best in terms of fulfilling the target set?

d Using the information in the table above and from the text write a 20 line report in 1937 for Comrade Stalin on the state of Russian industry. Comment on the methods used to achieve the changes and on whether any alterations might be needed in the next Plan, intended to boost consumer goods.

The Five Year Plans: agriculture

The NEP had succeeded in boosting Russia's agricultural output but the grain harvest of 1928 (73 million tons) was still 7 million tons below the 1913 figure. Every leading Communist agreed that the NEP could not go on indefinitely allowing peasants to own their own land and sell their produce for a profit. **Marxist** theory required that the land should be farmed in state or collective farms (called *kolkhoz*) with no private ownership of land at all. Some Communists, like Bukharin, believed that the peasants and the NEP should be left alone for the time being. But Stalin, who at first supported Bukharin, declared in 1929 that the farms must be collectivised and the class of wealthy landowning peasants, the **kulaks**, 'smashed'. The kulaks were peasants who owned medium-sized farms and employed landless peasants to work for them. They were determined not to give up their land to the collectives.

There were some 25 million peasant small-holdings in Russia in 1928. They were too small for efficient agriculture which required the use of tractors, combine-harvesters and fertilisers. The landless peasants, the vast majority of Russia's 100 million peasants, were only too happy to join the collective farms. But the kulaks refused to give up their land, sheep, cattle and barns to the government. They bitterly resisted, preferring to burn their buildings and crops and slaughter their animals rather than let the authorities take them. Kulaks that resisted in this way were arrested and sent on forced marches to remote and barren areas where they simply perished. As many as 5 million kulaks were killed in this way. At least another 5 million peasants starved to death during the terrible famine of 1932–33, caused, in part, by the destruction by the kulaks of their crops and by the poor levels of grain output. Nothing, though, was allowed to interfere with the progress of the Plan. By 1932 about three-quarters of Russian farmland had been collectivised and by 1937 it was well over 90%. However, it was not until 1953 that the numbers of cattle, horses and other livestock reached the 1928 figures. The state farms were now provided with new machinery. Before 1930 there were fewer than 25 000 tractors and 1000 combine-harvesters in use in Russia. By 1933 the numbers were 200 000 tractors and 25 000 harvesters. Despite the mechanisation, it was a long time before Russia's grain output recovered from the effects of collectivisation and the kulak resistance to it. The 1931 grain harvest yielded only 69.5 million tons – compared to 73 million in 1928. By 1937, though, output reached 97 million tons.

Though collectivisation was never the startling success that the Five Year Plans for industry were, it did modernise Soviet agriculture. Concessions were made to the peasants on the kolkhoz. They were allowed to own a small plot of land and rear a few farm animals. They were permitted to sell this produce privately in the local markets. Of the kolkhoz output 90% was sold to the state at a fixed price and what was left over the peasants shared among themselves in place of wages.

The number of livestock began to increase slowly as a result of the concessions. In 1928 there were 70 million cattle and 26 million pigs in Russia. In 1933 the respective figures were 41 million and 12 million. By 1937 these numbers had increased to 63 million cattle and 23 million pigs. Stalin is reported to have commented on the collectivisation process by saying that 'You can't make an omlette without breaking eggs'. Not all of the 'broken eggs', though belonged to the kulaks, as we shall soon find out.

Peasants joining a collective farm. While many landless peasants were content to join the collective farms, as the photograph indicates, several million wealthy peasants, the kulaks, were strongly opposed to them. 'We would like to work together' was the title for this government photograph of 1931

Exercise 4

a What did Marxist or Communist theory require should happen to Russia's land?
b How did the kulaks resist Stalin's collectivisation plans?
c Why do you think the grain output for 1931 was so low?
d In what way did Stalin compromise with the peasants?
e What do you think Stalin meant by the phrase 'You can't make an omlette without breaking eggs'?

Exercise 5

Extract One: Stalin on collectivisation

In 1943 Churchill and Stalin met. Churchill later wrote his version of one conversation in his book, *The Hinge of Fate*. The topic was the collectivisation of agriculture, described here by Stalin:

It was fearful. Four years it lasted. It was absolutely necessary for Russia if we were to avoid the periodic famines, to plough the land with tractors. We must mechanise our agriculture. We gave tractors to the peasants, they were all spoiled in a few months. Only collective farms with workshops could handle tractors. We took the greatest trouble to explain it to the peasants. It was no

5

use arguing with them . . . He always answers that he does not want the collective farm, and he would rather do without the tractors.'

'These were what you call kulaks?'

'Yes', he said, but he did not repeat the word. After a pause, 'It was all very
10 bad and difficult – but necessary'.

'What happened?' I asked.

'Oh, well,' he said, 'many of them agreed to come in with us. Some of them were given land of their own to cultivate in the province of Tomsk . . . but the great bulk were very unpopular and were wiped out by their labourers.'

15 There was a considerable pause. Then, 'Not only have we vastly increased the food supply, but we have improved the quality of the grain beyond measure'.

(Winston Churchill, *The Hinge of Fate*)

a How many tractors did Stalin's policy provide for the peasants by 1933?

b Can you suggest any reason why, according to Stalin, 'they were all spoiled in a few months'? (lines 3–4)

c Why did the kulaks 'not want the collective farm' (lines 6–7)?

d What sort of land do you think the kulaks were given 'to cultivate in the province of Tomsk' (in Siberia)?

e Earlier in the conversation Stalin admitted that 10 million kulaks were involved. To what does he attribute the cause of death of many of them?

f Identify two sentences from the text above which many historians would consider untruthful and explain your reasons for choosing them.

g In some respects, though, it was a frank conversation on Stalin's part. Which phrases support this view?

h What particular problems do you think the source for this conversation (i.e. Winston Churchill) might present to historians?

The mathematics of murder: the purges

'In the mathematics of murder', wrote one biographer of Stalin, '1000 = 1 000 000'. It will be clear from what has been said of Stalin so far that he was not a man to tolerate opposition. The elimination of millions of kulaks, though, could be justified on political and economic grounds as being necessary for the modernisation of Russia. No such excuse can be put forward to justify the murder of tens of thousands, probably as many as 3 million, people whose only crime was to seem a threat to Stalin's own position of absolute power. Before 1934 Stalin had been content to force fellow Communists who disagreed with his policies to serve prison terms. The murder in 1934 of the chief of the Leningrad Communist Party, Kirov, provided Stalin with the excuse to launch a campaign of murder of almost all of the old Bolsheviks of Lenin's days. Stalin's **purges** had begun.

'Show trials'

It is likely that Stalin had Kirov murdered anyway. Kirov was too popular. Bukharin, Kamenev and Zinoviev were all experienced Bolshevik leaders who had known Lenin well. Stalin saw them all as a threat. Kamenev and Zinoviev were put on public display in 'show trials' where they confessed to plotting with Trotsky to take over control of the Soviet Union. Why did these men confess to crimes they had not committed? In some cases it was to save the lives of their families or because of torture or because they believed their deaths were in the interest of the country. Kamenev and Zinoviev were shot in 1936. Zinoviev's death was described by one NKVD (Secret Police) officer: 'The lieutenant took him (Zinoviev) by the hair with his left hand, made him bow his head and, with his right hand, fired a bullet into his brain.' Two years later, after another show trial, Bukharin was executed. Of the 15 members of the first Bolshevik Government 10 had been executed or imprisoned, 4 had died; only Stalin remained.

The army purged

In the year that Zinoviev and Kamenev met their deaths Stalin published the new Soviet Constitution. It guaranteed all civil liberties: freedom of speech, assembly, even freedom to demonstrate. But no activities not approved by the Party could be carried out. 'We shall not give a scrap of paper nor an inch of room to those who think differently', said *Pravda*, the official Party paper. The only remaining source of danger to Stalin came from the armed forces. In 1937 another vicious purge of the army, air force and navy took place. Its most famous victim was Marshall Tukhachevsky, a hero of the Civil War, and Commander-in-Chief of the army. He was followed by two more of Russia's five full marshalls, three out of four full generals, all 12 lieutenant-generals, 60 out of 67 corps commanders and 136 out of 199 divisional commanders. About a third of the entire officer corps disappeared. What was left of the army was certainly loyal, and probably always had been, but it was so severely weakened that the Red Army was swept aside in the first months of the war against Germany. Just to make sure that nobody ever felt safe Stalin had also shot the head of the NKVD, Yagoda, and his senior staff.

Exercise ■ 6

a What do the men standing in the picture have in common?
b To what Bolshevik organisation do you suppose they belonged?
c What impression of Stalin's role in the Revolution is the artist trying to get across?

Source One This painting of 1935 shows Stalin with Lenin in 1917 organising the November Revolution. The painting places Stalin at the heart of the Revolution. His real role was less important but it was not prudent to say so in Stalin's time as ruler

d Does this view of Stalin's role agree with what you have read about how the Revolution was planned and carried out? Explain your answer.

e Suggest a reason why the artist painted the picture in the way that he did, exaggerating Stalin's importance in the events of November 1917.

'Double or triple the guard . . .'

Historians have been divided on Stalin – as they are on practically all other issues. Many claim that his policies, though brutal, were necessary to modernise Russia. There is no doubt that this modernisation was achieved, and in a remarkably short time. If it had not been for Stalin, they add, Russia would surely have perished in the war against Germany. Stalin's opponents among historians point to his record of mass murder and the fact that these purges deprived the Soviet Union of many of its most talented leaders. Even today Soviet agriculture is still grossly inefficient and this must be laid at Stalin's door as a result of the collectivisation programme. Stalin has also been criticised by some Marxist historians who support Marx's ideas of Communism. Nonetheless, they believe that Stalin created a system in which workers and peasants ended up being just as exploited as they had been under the Tsar. When Stalin died in 1953 the fears and sense of relief were later expressed by a poet, Yevtushenko:

'Double or triple the guard
beside his grave,
So that he will not rise again,
and with him – the past.'

(Quoted in Robert Payne, *The Rise and Fall of Stalin*, 1966.)

Exercise 7

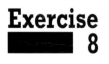

a What was the excuse Stalin used to launch his purges from 1934 to 1938?

b Who were the three most famous old Bolshevik victims of these purges?

c What sentence, quoted in the text, indicates that the 1936 Constitution offered no real liberties to the people?

d Why was the purge of the armed forces such a threat to Russia's future security?

e What do you think is meant by the phrase, 'In the mathematics of murder 1000 = 1 000 000'? In what way is it a fair comment on Stalin's rule in the 1930s?

Exercise 8

A Soviet poster in praise of Stalin (page 65)

a What groups of people are the two top figures on the left intended to represent?

b The bottom figure is waving a banner with the words 'Menshevik News' on it. What character do you think it is intended to represent?

c The banner in the top right corner claims that the Five Year Plan has been achieved in four years. From what you have read in the text is this claim justified? Explain your answer.

d How does the poster make it clear that one of Stalin's great achievements is industrial growth?

Source Two
Soviet poster

   e How would you describe the expression on Stalin's face? What does it appear
      is his attitude to the enemies of Soviet Russia on his right?
   f Contrast this view of Stalin's attitude to opponents with the treatment given
      out to them in the extract in Exercise 9.

Exercise

Extract Two: A political trial, 1937

This is taken from the account of Evgenia Ginzburg, a Communist teacher, put
on trial for being part of the plot to murder Kirov. Her 'trial' lasted seven
minutes. She ended up serving 18 years in labour camps.

       Now my hour had come. The military tribunal of the Supreme Court – three
officers and a secretary – sat facing me across the table . . .
      'You have read the charge sheet?' the chairman asked in a voice of
unutterable boredom. 'You plead guilty? No! But the evidence shows' . . .

5   Thumbing through the thick file, he muttered: 'Here's witness Kozlov, for
instance . . .'
      'Not Kozlov – Kozlova a woman. And a despicable woman at that.'
      'Kozlova yes. And there's Dyachenko.'
      'Dyakanov . . .'

10   'Yes. Well they both state . . .'
      But what it was they stated the judge was too pressed for time to say.
Breaking off, he asked me:
      'Any questions you wish to ask the court?'

15

'Yes I do. I am accused under Section 8 of Article 58. This is a charge of terrorism. Will you please name the political leader on whose life you believe I made an attempt? . . .'

'Don't you know that Comrade Kirov was killed in Leningrad?'

'Yes. But it wasn't I who killed him, it was someone called Nikolayev. And I've never been in Leningrad in my life . . .'

20

'Are you a lawyer or something?' snapped the judge.

'No I'm a teacher.'

'Then don't split hairs. All right, you've never been to Leningrad. But he was killed by people who shared your ideas, so you share the moral and criminal responsibility.'

(E. Ginzburg, *Into the Whirlwind*, 1967)

a With whose murder was Evgenia Ginzburg charged?

b On what grounds did she deny the charge?

c What evidence is there in the text that the judge knew little about the case?

d Why was the defendant found guilty? Do you think it was a fair verdict? Explain your reason.

e 'Are you a lawyer or something?' snapped the judge.' In what way might this comment be considered an unintentionally funny one?

f Do you think this case would have been fairly typical of trials in Russia at this time? Justify your answer. How is it different from trials in a country like Britain today?

Assignment unit

Write an autobiographical account of your activities as a young Bolshevik during the events of 1917 to your arrest and trial in 1936. The following points will help you:

a your reasons for joining the Bolsheviks; the return from exile to Russia with Lenin in April 1917;

b your role in the Revolution of November 1917 and the Civil War;

c the struggle for power after Lenin's death between Trotsky and Stalin (whose side were you on and why?);

d Stalin's policies towards agriculture, industry and opposition;

e your arrest in 1934 for 'anti-Soviet' activities and involvement in the murder of Kirov; what is your defence or do you plead guilty to save your family from attack?

Chapter 5

Mussolini's Italy: bombast and bluff

Benito Mussolini

Mussolini, like Hitler, liked to exaggerate the poverty of his youth. He was the son of a **socialist** blacksmith and a schoolmistress and they had a comfortable life. But he was an unruly child. He had a violent and bullying nature and was expelled from one school for stabbing a fellow pupil with a penknife. As a young man he became a revolutionary socialist and spent most of his time in Switzerland avoiding the Swiss police and hard work. In 1912, at the age of 29, he became editor of the socialist daily *Avanti*, but was later expelled from the Socialist Party for urging Italy to join the war against Italy's old enemy, Austria. He set up his own 'socialist' paper, *Il Popolo d'Italia* (*'the Italian People'*) and called for Italy's entry to the war. He was given money by big business and Allied governments who were anxious to get Italy into the war. When war was declared in May 1915 he described it as 'Italy's baptism as a great power'. He was conscripted in September and later invalided out of the army after a grenade explosion during a training exercise. The end of the war left Mussolini more determined than ever to make a name for himself. He hated Italy's parliamentary politicians and its **democratic** government and his mood became more and more violent.

Italy in 1919

The mood of Mussolini in 1919 matched that of Italy. The treaties with Germany and Austria left Italy angry and frustrated. Though Italy was given the South Tyrol, Istria and Trieste as promised by the **Entente** in 1915, President Wilson refused to allow the handing over of Dalmatia and several Aegean islands, as there were no Italians living there. Italy also laid claim to the town of Fiume – though she had not been promised that. Mussolini was quick to realise that this sense of angry **nationalism** could help him to power if he could control it. In September 1919 a poet and war hero, D'Annunzio, showed the way when he and his 2600 'legionaries' seized the town. It was not until 16 months later that the Italian government was able to drive him from the city. The treaty of Rapallo in 1922 between Italy and Yugoslavia led to the city being given international status – though it eventually became Italian in 1924.

Not all Italians were especially concerned about the fact that Italy had been 'cheated' of what she had considered rightfully hers. Most Italians, though, were very concerned about Italy's economic situation. In the south there was extreme poverty. Most of the population were landless peasants, scratching a living from its infertile soil. The north was more industrial but there was just as much anger. Prices had risen sharply (560% between 1914 and 1921) and unemployment was increasing. The socialists organised strikes (2000 in 1920) and factory occupations – 280 in Milan in 1919 alone. The socialists seemed about to launch a **Bolshevik** style **Communist** take-over of the country. Big firms like Fiat and Pirelli looked desperately for someone to crush this threat. In the south the pea-

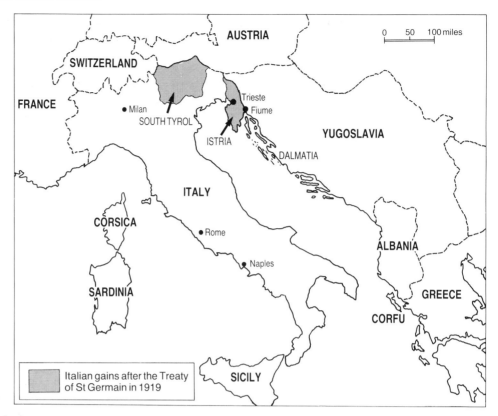

Italy after the First World War

Italian gains after the Treaty of St Germain in 1919

sants began seizing land and the land-owners were convinced that **revolution** was about to swamp the country.

The 'Combat Squads' in action

The government could do nothing. Italy's **proportional representation** system meant that no single party could ever govern on its own. Proportional representation meant that if, for example, a party got 5% of the votes then it would get 5% of the seats in parliament. This encouraged the setting up of many parties with the result that no one party could ever hope to win an outright majority of 51% of the seats. Governments had to be formed with groups of parties together, called **coalition governments**, to make sure they had the support of more than half of the MPs or deputies. The problem was that the parties in the coalition often

quarrelled, with the result that the government had to resign.

Between 1919 and 1922 Italy had five different coalition governments, none of which was able to make firm decisions. Mussolini saw his chance. Abandoning the last of his old socialist ideas he promised the bosses and the landowners to smash the socialist-organised land and factory seizures. He would provide disciplined law and order. In 1919 he had set up his own **Fascist Party**. It consisted of many angry former soldiers, spoiling for a fight. He let them loose on the workers and peasants. These 'Combat Squads' clubbed their victims – often to death – or forced them to drink castor oil which made them violently sick. The workers' movement was broken. Wealthy industrialists and landowners showed their gratitude with huge sums of money -- the banks alone handed over £1½ million. The **Liberal** Prime Minister, Giolitti, was also impressed and in 1921 he asked Mussolini to join the government's election group. This made the Fascists even more respectable among the wealthy and those anxious for law and order at any price. Mussolini won 35 seats as opposed to none in 1919. He also stopped making anti-Catholic speeches and gave up his anti-monarchy views.

The King, Victor Emmanuel III, became more sympathetic as did the Pope, Pius XI, to this new movement. Here, it seemed, was a man who would save Italy from the twin evils of Communism and Godlessness.

Exercise  1

a What kind of personality did Mussolini have as a child?
b What was the cause of Italy's 'angry nationalism' after the war?
c How did Italy's economic problems worsen after the war?
d How did proportional representation make Italy's position more difficult?
e Why were the wealthy so willing to back Mussolini?
f What do you think Mussolini meant by the phrase that the war would be 'Italy's baptism as a great power'? Did Italy's role in, and gains from, the war prove Mussolini right? Explain your answer.

Exercise 2

'The flower of fascism'

(On each of the petals of the flower are represented the interests of the bankers, the iron and steel industry and the landowners.)

a Why has the cartoonist included sums of money (millions of lire) on the petals?
b What reasons did these wealthy interests have for supporting Mussolini?
c What contribution did one of these interests make – in millions of pounds?
d Why have the stamens of the flower been drawn as clubs?
e Would you describe the cartoon as pro- or anti-Fascist? Give reasons for your view.
f Think of your own title for the cartoon and explain why you think it is a good one.

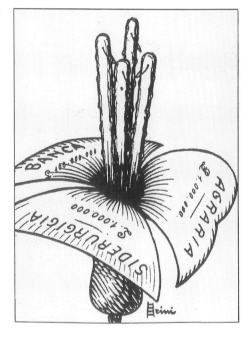

Source One

1922: 'The March on Rome'

The decisive year was to be 1922. Mussolini's party now had a membership of 320000 – at least 50000 of these were members of his terror gang of thugs: the Blackshirts. August provided them with another opportunity to exercise their 'talents' when the Socialists and the newly-formed Communist Party called a general strike. It was a disastrous failure – in Milan the Fascists took over the public services and made sure everything carried on as normal. The strike was later called 'the Caporetto of Italian Socialism'. Mussolini knew now was the time to strike. He demanded to be made Prime Minister and assembled 50 000 Blackshirts in Florence, ready to march on Rome and seize power if necessary. Facta, another new Prime Minister, asked the King for special powers to deal with the threat. Victor Emmanuel was a small and rather weak man. He knew the army could stop Mussolini's badly equipped and trained rabble but what if there were a civil war later? Already

Mussolini liked to be photographed in striking poses. This was one taken from a low angle to give an impression of height and power

reports were arriving that the Fascists had seized control of several cities. What if he were overthrown and replaced by his more dashing cousin, the Duke of Aosta, or a victorious Mussolini? He refused to give Facta the authority to use Rome's 12 000 regular troops against the Blackshirts. Instead, on 29 October 1922 he asked Mussolini to become Italy's new Prime Minister. Mussolini arrived in Rome by train to be followed by thousands of his joyous supporters. He had taken power quite legally, having only threatened to use force.

Fascist historians later pretended that the 'March on Rome' had been a glorious and revolutionary act of violence to seize power. The point was that Mussolini was now in control. He had built a party and inspired a large part of the nation with his stirring speeches of a return to the old glories of the Roman Empire. Italy would acquire the empire she deserved; national pride would be restored and the Mediterranean would become an Italian lake. Mussolini was anxious that Fascism be seen as a continuation of ancient Rome. The symbol of power in Rome had been a bundle of rods bound round an axe. The Fascists had adopted it as their symbol as well.

1922–25: prelude to dictatorship

The Matteotti Murder

Italy did not become a **dictatorship** straight away. Mussolini moved cautiously. His government contained politicians from all the main parties except the Socialists and Communists. In 1923 the Acerbo Law was passed. This allowed the party with most votes – provided it was more than 25% – to take 66% of the seats in the Parliament. New elections were called for April 1924. In the meantime the Blackshirts set about their acts of brutality against their opponents. Mussolini's promise of

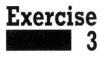

The Fasces – symbol of authority in ancient Rome and symbol of Fascism in Mussolini's Italy

strong but not extreme government won-over moderate middle-class people. The Fascists won 65% of the vote anyway and so the Acerbo Law was not really needed. But in June things began to go seriously wrong for the '*Duce*', or leader, as Mussolini now liked to be known. In that month the Socialist leader, Matteotti, a vigorous opponent of Mussolini, was kidnapped and murdered. There was an outburst of protest against the murder throughout Italy. Mussolini may not have actually ordered the murder but if he condemned it he risked losing the respect of his own more violent supporters. He could well have found himself overthrown. If he took responsibility for the assassination and refused to punish the murderers then he would make it clear what Fascism really stood for: thuggery and dictatorship.

Mussolini hesitated. Support for Fascism began to dwindle away. The opposition Socialist and Popular Party MPs withdrew from Parliament, leaving behind only the Fascists and a few conservatives. It has been estimated that the Fascist newspapers at this time had only 300 000 readers, compared to the 4 million readers of the opposition Liberal press. On 31 December 1924, 50 Blackshirts burst into Mussolini's office and told him to act decisively and set up a dictatorship or they would remove him from power. On 3 January 1925 Mussolini told Parliament that if Fascism was an association of thugs then he was its head. There was to be no apology or regret for Matteotti's death.

Exercise 3

a Why did the general strike of 1922 benefit the Fascists?
b What did Mussolini threaten to do with his 50 000 Blackshirts in Rome?
c Why did the King refuse to give Facta emergency powers?
d What emotions and feelings did Mussolini appeal to in his speeches?
e Why did the Matteotti crisis bring Mussolini close to defeat?
f Explain the point of the phrase that the general strike of 1922 was 'the Caporetto of Italian Socialism'. (Refer back to page 18 of Chapter One if you need to refresh your memory.)

Exercise 4

Extract: 'Duce'

The following account is adapted from a book on Mussolini, published in 1971. It concerns the occasion when Mussolini was confronted by his own supporters:

Unannounced they strode, not speaking, across the grained hardwood floor. Mussolini . . . raised his eyebrows in scowling interrogation . . . Tarabella lost no time in showing his teeth. 'We're tired of slowing down', he told Mussolini savagely, 'the prisons are full of Fascists – they're putting Fascism on trial
5 and you don't want to take responsibility for the revolution'. Hemmed in on all sides, Mussolini asked desperately, 'But what do the action squads want? Nowadays we need to normalise things, nothing else'. An angry chorus of jeers greeted his words . . . Mussolini burst out: 'The body they threw between my feet prevents me from walking'.
10 'What kind of revolutionary chief are you', Tarabella taunted him, 'to be frightened by a corpse. You're bending over backwards to please the opposition . . . You must make up your mind to shoot the chiefs of the opposition.'
. . . As if to further press home the point, one man drove his dagger into
15 Mussolini's polished rosewood desk . . . Mussolini glared round the circle,

striving to simulate the man of iron, reading the same message from every man's eyes: contempt for a wavering leader . . .'

(R.H. Collier: *Duce! the rise and fall of Benito Mussolini*, 1971.)

a On what date did this event take place?
b By what other name are the 'action squads' (line 6) known?
c To whom do 'the body' (line 8) and 'the corpse' (line 11) refer?
d Why was this man murdered and by whom?
e In what way had Mussolini bent 'over backwards to please the opposition' (lines 11–12) on becoming Prime Minister?
f In what ways does the author get over the threatening nature of Tarabella and his colleagues?
g What impression does this account give of Mussolini's character?

a In Source Two who are the 'all blacks' referred to by Mussolini?
b What was the crime committed by these 'all blacks' about which Mussolini seems concerned?

BLACK JERSEYS AND BLACK SHIRTS.

Signor Mussolini. "I SOMETIMES WISH *MY* 'ALL BLACKS' WERE ONLY FOOTBALLERS!"

Source Two
Punch *cartoon, 24 November 1924*

c Why has the cartoonist drawn the shadowy figure behind Mussolini?

d Why do the ancient Roman ruins make a suitable background?

e What point do you think the cartoonist is trying to make by having Mussolini say: 'I sometimes wish my 'all blacks' were only footballers'?

f Does your impression of Mussolini from this cartoon support or disagree with the view of him from Exercise 4? Explain your answer.

What was Fascism?

You have come across the word 'Fascist' a great deal in the text so far. From its use you will have realised that it stood for some principles like anti-Communism and for **nationalism**. You are unlikely to have grasped much more than this. In 1925, 35 million Italians knew little more about Fascism than you do because of the vagueness and lack of definite policies of Mussolini. But this vagueness was actually one reason for his success. Mussolini actually 'made up' Fascism as he went along, adopting those policies that seemed best in the circumstances. The basic elements of Fascism were as follows:

1 *extreme nationalism:* Mussolini wanted to restore Italy to what he believed was its former glories under the ancient Romans; he was determined to prove Italy's superiority to other 'inferior' races and establish an empire in Africa as a symbol of that greatness.

2 *dictatorship:* Mussolini believed that democracy made nations weak and soft; only a firm ruler in total control could provide the necessary leadership – that man was the 'Duce'.

3 *economic self-sufficiency* (*autarky*): the country had to develop its resources and depend as little as possible on imports; the economy although still owned by private individuals, had to be directed by the government in the interests of the nation.

4 *military strength and war:* Mussolini had declared that 'War is to the male what childbearing is to the female'; he believed that success in war was the only true test of a nation's greatness and so devoted much of Italy's slender resources to building up Italy's armed forces and making the Italians more 'warlike'.

Fascism had a wide appeal. Mussolini's plans of making Italy a great and respected power attracted all classes of Italians and the military in particular supported his imperial ambitions. His firm anti-Communism was a strong point with the wealthy landowners and businessmen. At the same time Mussolini appealed to the small shop keepers and businessmen by promising to protect them from the competition of the big firms.

Mussolini in power

Two features of the old democratic Italy were to disappear before the end of 1925: a free press and political parties. Some papers simply had their offices burnt down and presses destroyed – like the socialist *Avanti*. Others were simply told to change their editors and were told by Mussolini what to write. Political parties hostile to Fascism were abolished and a new secret police, the OVRA (a meaningless title!), was set up to harass political opponents. A few were beaten to death, others forced to leave the country and in all some 4000 were imprisoned. Many, like the Communist leader, Gramsci, were to die in gaol. It is true to say that Mussolini's rule was nowhere near as cruel and brutal as Hitler's Germany. There were no concentration camps and only 10 death sentences were actually carried out up to 1940. (Many more, though, died from beatings or were simply murdered both inside and outside Italy.)

The economy

One of the main aims of Fascism was to create a self-sufficient state that did not rely on imports. With this in mind, Mussolini launched the 'Battle for Wheat'. Agriculture was to expand wheat production and so cut down Italy's reliance on imports of wheat. In the 10 years after 1925 wheat imports were reduced by 75% – but only at the expense of other profitable crops that could have earned money in export sales. A similar 'battle' for births failed to increase the population as the birth rate dropped. Mussolini abolished trade unions and replaced them with 'Corporations'. These were organisations set up in each industry, representing both workers and employers. They were run by Fascists whose job it was to settle disputes between workers and their bosses without strikes – which were illegal anyway. In practice, the interests of the bosses always came out on top and so the living standards of workers fell sharply. In the meantime unemployment rose, reaching 1.1 million in 1932 – nearly ten times what it had been in 1925.

Serious economic problems

On the one occasion when Mussolini did have a capable Minister of Finance – as he did between 1922 and 1925 when De Stefani balanced the budget – Mussolini sacked him because powerful industrialists were angry that De Stefani had cut out large cash benefits or subsidies to their industries. Another and more serious reason was that '*Il Duce*' did not like to have about him men whose abilities might outshine his own. Mussolini insisted on a high value for the Italian currency, the lira. In 1926 he set the lira at 90 to the pound instead of 150. This made Italian exports very costly and demand abroad for Italian goods fell sharply causing a decline in orders. Unemployment increased and many factories went on a three-day week. Vast sums of money were squandered on reckless foreign adventures such as the invasion of Abyssinia in 1935 and the help given to Franco in the Spanish Civil War.

There were some advances, though. Public works schemes like motorway building and the draining of the Pontine Marshes did create work and help to modernise the country. A serious effort was made to excavate and display Italy's Ancient Roman heritage and this boosted tourism. By 1930 iron and steel production had doubled and by 1937 hydro-electric power had increased by the same margin. But despite Mussolini's frequent boasting, Italy was still a poor country and her resources had been squandered. Italy's serious economic problems had not been solved, as the Second World War was to prove. Mussolini's real crime was to take Italy into that war knowing that her country could not match the industrial might of her enemies and knowing that her armed forces were weak, badly equipped and badly led.

a How did Mussolini deal with Italy's free press from 1925?
b Why is the figure of 10 legal executions between 1925 and 1940 a misleading one?
c Why was the 'Battle for Wheat' both a success and a failure?

d What were the 'Corporations'?

e Why was De Stefani sacked and why was it such a serious issue for Italy's future?

f Why did Mussolini's high valuation of the lira cause more problems for Italy's economy?

The Lateran Treaty 1929

One of the worst problems affecting political life in Italy was the quarrel between the Pope and the Italian State. This began in 1870 when Italian forces seized Rome from the Pope at that time and made it into the capital of Italy. Since then successive Popes had forbidden Italian Catholics to play any part in Italy's politics. Mussolini was well aware of the prestige and new support that would result from an end to this dispute. In 1929 Mussolini reached just such an agreement with Pope Pius XI called the Lateran Treaty. The Pope now agreed to recognise the Kingdom of Italy and gave up his claim to the lost territories in and around Rome. In exchange, Mussolini, compensated the Church for the property seized by earlier governments and recognised Catholicism as Italy's official religion. The Vatican City also became an independent state in Rome with the Pope as its ruler. Catholics in Italy and throughout the world were delighted that the quarrel was at last over and Mussolini's popularity increased sharply. Once again Mussolini had shown his willingness to shed his old beliefs in order to strengthen his position.

However, relations with the Church gradually turned sour as the Fascist Youth organisation, the *Ballila*, found its popularity threatened by the rival Catholic youth groups. Matters grew still worse when, in 1938, Mussolini introduced anti-Jewish laws as a sign of Italy's closer relationship with Nazi Germany. These laws were widely ignored in Italy. Indeed, the Italian army in the occupied areas of Southern France and Greece saved the lives of at least 240 000 Jews by refusing to hand them over to the Germans during the Second World War. Pius XI firmly condemned these new laws but his successor in the following year, Pius XII, was less inclined to criticise Mussolini or Hitler.

Exercise 7

Study Source Three on page 76 (The writing on the monument reads: 'The founders of the new Roman Empire')

a What does the she-wolf symbolise?

b Explain the significance of the word 'Tirol' in the mouth of the wolf? Why would this be a sore point for Germans?

c Identify the King, at the foot of the monument. How does the cartoonist get across the small stature of the man?

d Apart from the presence of the suckling Mussolini, how else can we tell that this cartoon is referring to Fascist Italy?

e What contribution had D'Annunzio made to this new 'Empire'?

f Which of these words – and why– sums up the attitude of the cartoon:

   i aggressive;

   ii mocking;

   iii bitter;

   iv angry?

TIROL

MUSSOLINI   D'ANNUNZIO

DEN
BEGRÜNDERN
DES
NEUEN RÖMISCHEN
WELTREICHS

Source Three

*German cartoon of
1926*

Foreign Policy

The Bombardment of Corfu

Like much else that Mussolini did, his foreign policy lacked consistency. At first he was strongly anti-German but from 1936 onwards he came more and more under Hitler's domination. There is one theme, though, which runs through all his years as ruler of Italy: his obsession to make Italy feared and respected abroad. In his view only an aggressive Italy would earn this respect.

In 1923 some Italian soldiers were killed in an incident while mapping out

Albania's borders with Greece. Though the Greek government had had nothing to do with the incident Mussolini acted aggressively. He bombarded and then occupied the Greek island of Corfu. He refused to leave until he was paid compensation and received an apology from the Greeks. The Conference of Ambassadors (a body set up to make the detailed arrangements for the territorial changes of the treaties of 1919) sided with Italy. Mussolini was convinced that it proved his theory that 'might is right'. Up to 1936 he was increasingly worried by the strength of Germany and in 1925 he signed the Locarno Pacts with France and Britain in which Italy promised, along with Britain, to protect France's border with Germany.

The Dollfuss Murder

At first Mussolini tried to encourage good relations with Britain, supporting some British views on the Middle East. Winston Churchill was full of praise for Mussolini after a visit to Rome, impressed by '*Il Duce*'s' anti-Communism'. While pretending that Fascist Italy only wanted peace Mussolini secretly organised terror groups in countries like Yugoslavia and Greece which he wanted to conquer. Albania became totally dependent on Italy through trade and economic aid. But such a policy was not aggressive enough and in April 1939 Mussolini ordered the invasion of the country. In 1934 he acted rapidly and firmly when Hitler seemed about to launch an attack on Austria. In July Austrian Nazis, probably on Hitler's orders, murdered the Austrian Chancellor, Dollfuss. Mussolini knew that if Hitler took over the country Italy would face a powerful potential enemy on her border in place of a weak and easily dominated Austria. He sent three tank divisions to the Austrian border and threatened to use them to defend Austria's independence. For once

Hitler was out-bluffed and out-bullied. He backed down. The Italian leader confirmed his determination to make a stand against Hitler in the Stresa Front agreement of April 1935. At Stresa Italy, France and Great Britain had condemned Hitler's rearmament programme.

All this was soon to change. In October 1935 Mussolini invaded the only independent state in Africa – Abyssinia. A successful conquest would also erase the memory of Italy's humiliating defeat in 1896 by the Abyssinians. The invasion was an inevitable success with Mussolini introducing his new 'civilisation' with the benefit of poison gas and flame-throwers. Many Italians were probably impressed by the prestige it brought but they were soon to learn the true cost of the victory. The League of Nations, backed by Britain and France, had applied **sanctions** against Italy as the aggressor nation. The sanctions were feeble – they did not include oil and coal – but they angered Mussolini. Only Germany offered to trade normally and make up Italy's shortages. From then onwards Italy was drawn into a close alliance with Germany but it was an alliance which Hitler, not Mussolini, was to dominate. The alliance was not popular in Italy where most Italians still considered Germany as their traditional enemy.

The end of a dictator

Italy's entry and role in the Second World War are dealt with in a later chapter (Chapter 12). Her successive defeats at the hands of the Allies eventually led to a movement organised by some Fascists and the King. Mussolini was removed from power on 25 July 1943 without a struggle. He was confined to a mountain-top hotel under heavy guard. In September a daring rescue bid ordered by Hitler rescued him from captivity and he was taken to

CONSULTING THE ORACLE.

(As recorded by Mr. Punch's magic microphone.)

HERR HITLER. "WHAT IS YOUR MESSAGE FOR GERMANY?"

SIGNOR MUSSOLINI. "TELL HER SHE MUST BE CAREFUL TO KEEP ON THE RIGHT SIDE OF ITALY."

HERR HITLER. "AND HOW CAN SHE MAKE SURE OF DOING THAT?"

SIGNOR MUSSOLINI. "BY KEEPING ON THE OTHER SIDE OF AUSTRIA."

Source Four

Punch *Cartoon,*
20 June 1934

northern Italy to set up a new Fascist regime under Hitler's supervision. It was a thoroughly brutal government. On 28 April 1945, while trying to escape to Switzerland with his mistress, he was captured by a group of Italian Communist partisans. They were put up against a wall and shot. The following day 'Il Duce' made his last public appearance, hanging by his feet from a Milan garage.

Exercise 8

Study the cartoon on page 78

a What did these two men have in common as political leaders?

b Why was Mussolini concerned to make sure that Germany kept 'on the other side of Austria'?

c In what way did Hitler fail to take notice of Mussolini's warning in the weeks after this cartoon (20 June, 1934)?

d What action did Mussolini take against Hitler over Austria?

e Which of the two men is shown by the cartoonist to be the dominant one? How does the cartoonist show this?

f In what way did the relationship between these two men change in the years after 1934?

Assignment unit

The Matteotti crisis

The date is 13 June 1924. The body of Giacomo Matteotti, the Socialist Deputy, has been found in a shallow grave. The car in which the struggling Matteotti was stabbed to death has been traced to two local Fascist *squadristi* or henchmen, Dumini and Volpi. Mussolini's regime is in crisis. You are asked to draw up two possible courses of action by '*Il Duce*'. For each of them state the likely results of the action for Mussolini and the Fascist movement. Entitle your options 'Velvet Glove' and 'Iron Fist'.

Velvet glove Possible steps:

a order the arrest of Volpi and Dumini and deny all knowledge and involvement: refer to the murder as an 'outrage', etc.;

b such a step is likely to get a good response from abroad and among liberals and from the Pope;

c this new, respectable image is not likely to go down well with the 'squadristi' – there is a possibility of a movement from within the party to overthrow '*Il Duce*' (see Exercise 4 for help here).

Iron fist Possible steps:

a pretend to punish those responsible so as not to provoke a serious crisis for the government and that way weaken the case of the opposition against the government;

b inform the 'squadristi' of your intention to release Dumini and Volpi from gaol after a 'few months';

c then declare to Parliament your responsibility for the murder and announce the abolition of opposition parties and press; Fascism means dictatorship;

d the response from liberals, the Pope, and foreign opinion is likely to be hostile but does this matter?

Finally be brave and make your own recommendation as to whether Mussolini should follow the 'Velvet Glove' or 'Iron Fist' approach and why.

Chapter 6

The Weimar Republic: from crisis to collapse

Germany's problems in 1919

Germany was a beaten nation by November 1918. Her armies were in full retreat. Her navy was in mutiny and her population, starved by the British blockade, was rioting in the streets. The **Kaiser**, William II, abdicated the throne on 9 November. A civilian government was allowed to take over on the advice of General Hindenburg and Ludendorff. They knew the war was lost. Perhaps, they calculated, a republican government would get better terms from the Allies. More to the point, the army would not be humiliated by having to sue for peace. That task was left to Philipp Scheidemann, the leader of the **Socialists**. Germany's new civilian government was getting off to a bad start. They had been 'set up'. The **armistice** was signed on 11 November. The First World War was over but Germany's problems were just beginning.

In January 1919 the German people elected an Assembly whose job was to draw up a **constitution** for the new republic. Germany's Parliament, the *Reichstag*, was to be elected by **proportional representation**. (See Chapter 5, page 68 for the problems caused by proportional representation.) A President was also to be elected who would have the power to appoint and dismiss the Chancellor or Prime Minister. He could also govern by decree in an emergency. This meant he could pass laws without Parliament's approval. Friedrich Ebert, a Socialist, became the first President of the Republic.

Although he was a Socialist, Ebert was not a revolutionary. He believed in the parliamentary system. But there were those in Germany who did not and their leaders were Karl Liebnecht and Rosa Luxemburg. These Spartacists – named after the leader of a slave rebellion against Rome, Spartacus – wanted a **Communist**-style revolution like the one in Russia. In January 1919 the Spartacists staged a rebellion in Berlin against the new government. After two weeks it was over. The rising was put down with great ferocity by the *Frei Korps* – an organisation of ex-servicemen violently opposed to Communism. On 15 January Luxemburg and Liebnecht were hunted down and murdered. Rosa Luxemburg's badly beaten body was thrown into a canal.

The Weimar Republic's first steps

The new republic was unable to set itself up in Berlin because of the fighting and instead it began its life in the town of Weimar. As a result, the period of German history between 1919 and 1933 is known as Weimar Germany – even though the government was soon able to return to Berlin. If seeking an armistice in November 1918 had been a bad enough blow to German prestige, worse was to follow. In June 1919

Ebert's republic was forced to sign the Treaty of Versailles. To many Germans this was an unforgivable crime – a shameful blot on Germany's proud tradition. The terms were considered to be harsh and humiliating. The Weimar Republic was to be always associated with the defeat and humiliation of the treaty for the rest of its short life. The army, though, could claim it was all the fault of civilian traitors: 'November criminals' as Hitler was to call them.

The parties that supported the Republic, the Socialists, the Catholic Centre Party and the Democratic Party were repeatedly abused by the Nationalists and later the Nazis. The Nationalists were a party of the rich landowners and industrialists. They wanted the Kaiser back on the throne, trade unions crushed and Communists dead. To help achieve this they set up the Frei Korps of ex-soldiers with no jobs and hungry for violence.

Kapp Putsch

In 1920 the Frei Korps, led by a Dr Kapp, attempted to take power by force in Berlin. The Kapp *Putsch* would have succeeded if the workers had not staged a general strike and paralysed the city. The professional army, the *Reichswehr*, had refused to fire on the rebels and the government had already fled the city. Most of the rebels went unpunished as most judges detested the government as well and longed to see the Kaiser back in power. The Weimar Republic might have survived the severe political threats of attempted revolutions by Spartacists and the Frei Korps but its economy was also beginning to disintegrate. The Republic might have lasted a lot longer if it had only had political *or* economic crises to deal with. The combination of the two was to prove fatal to **democracy** in Germany.

Exercise 1

a Why was Germany a beaten nation in November 1918?

b Why did the Treaty of Versailles weaken the Republic's chances of survival?

c What do you think the author means by the phrase that the civilian government had been 'set up'?

d What does the Kapp Putsch tell us about the stability of the government in 1920?

e Is your answer to question **d** confirmed by Source One and Two on the next page? Explain your answer.

Exercise 2

a The figures shown in the Spartacist poster on page 82 are elected representatives in the Weimar Republic's National Assembly. What do you think the attitude of the Spartacists was to such assemblies?

b Can you suggest with what the Spartacists would have replaced the Republic's parliament?

c The poster was used in one of the election campaigns for the National Assembly general election. Can you think of anything odd about the Spartacists' appealing for votes for the Assembly?

d Source Two is a photograph taken in May 1919 of some Frei Korps members in an armoured car in *Munchen* (Munich). How can you tell from the picture that the Frei Korps was composed mainly of ex-servicemen?

e What do you think the insignia of the Frei Korps was?

f The armoured car – unlike many used in the Spanish Civil war – is not 'home made'. What does it suggest about the Frei Korps' relations with the regular army? What have you read in the text so far that might confirm this opinion?

Source One
Spartacist Poster

g Generally speaking, what do both the pictures tell us about the nature of Weimar Republic politics?

h Of the two political groups referred to in these sources (Spartacists and Frei Korps) which had proved the biggest threat and why to the Weimar Republic up to 1923?

Source Two   *May 1919, Frei Korps in Munich*

The inflation of 1923

The First World War had been a crippling expense for Germany. The loss of much of her **industrial output** and reserves of iron and coal as a result of the Treaty of Versailles were going to make her chances of recovery that much harder. The German governments found it convenient to print more and more money to pay off debts. From 1921 onwards the value of the mark began to fall rapidly. Soon Germany fell behind with her **reparations** payments to France and Belgium. Poincaré, the French Prime Minister, and the Belgians sent in troops in January 1923 to the Ruhr – the industrial heartland of Germany. They were determined to take the coal for themselves. The German workers went on strike in protest and the already weak economy now ground to a halt. **Inflation** took off. A loaf of bread in 1918 had cost 0.6 of a mark. By January 1923 it cost 250 marks. By September the price was 1.5 million marks. In November of that year you would have paid 201 million marks! Workers collected their wages in laundry baskets or wheel-barrows. In a restaurant people paid for the meal before they ate it – it would cost twice as much at the end! German money was literally not worth the paper it was printed on. The savings of middle and working class people were wiped out overnight and could not even buy them a coffee.

Only the very wealthy escaped the terrible effects of the inflation because the value of their land and factories kept pace with the increase in prices. For the vast majority of Germans, though, it was a bitter experience. Many were never to trust the Weimar Republic and its politicians again. The middle-classes, who had suffered the most, soon began to give a hearing to the views of a little-known southern German politician, Adolf Hitler.

The Munich Putsch 1923: enter the Nazis

Adolf Hitler, an Austrian, served in the German army during the First World War. He had been a good soldier, winning Germany's highest award for courage, the Iron Cross. Like many other soldiers he was bitter about the armistice of November 1918 and felt humiliated and betrayed by the Treaty of Versailles. He was determined to avenge that dishonour and create a Germany which would once again be proud of itself and worthy of international respect. There would be no room for Jews in this Germany or Communists or, indeed, for democracy. The French occupation of the Ruhr and the terrible economic conditions convinced Hitler that the time had come for an armed seizure of power, or Putsch, in Munich in Bavaria. Once the Nazis (the National Socialist German Workers Party) had taken control there they would march on Berlin itself. Hitler and the First World War General Ludendorff formed the first rank of marchers who set off from a beer hall towards the Bavarian Parliament on 9 November 1923. The 3000 armed and brown-shirted Nazi Stormtroopers or SA (*Sturmabteilung*) looked a formidable sight. To Hitler's astonishment and horror the Bavarian police fired on the marchers. Sixteen were killed. Hitler was arrested and given a very light sentence of five years. He was released after just nine months of comfortable imprisonment. At his trial Hitler had declared to the court:

You may pronounce us guilty a thousand times over, but the goddess of the eternal court of history will smile and tear to tatters . . . the sentence of this court. For she acquits us.

The Hitler 'Battle Group' (Stosstrupp) in Munich, 1923. A Stosstrupp numbered from 20–60 men

The trial made Hitler into not just a national figure but an international one as well. But he had learnt a vital lesson. He would never again try to seize power by force alone.

Exercise 3

a Why was Germany's economy in such a poor state after the war?
b Do you think the action of the French and Belgian governments was
   i justified and
   ii worthwhile?
c Why do you think Hitler was surprised by the actions of the police towards the Nazi Putsch?
d The sentences quoted above were the end of Hitler's final statement to the court. Write another 20 lines for the rest of the speech you think Hitler might have made.

Germany 1924–29: the lull before the storm

Stresemann's achievement

This period is known as the 'Golden Years' of the Republic. During this time Germany was accepted back into the international community. Her currency was made stable and the economy began to prosper. The man given the credit for this achievement is Gustav Stresemann. He was the leader of the small People's Party and was Chancellor for three months from August 1923 and then Foreign Minister until his death in October 1929.

Stresemann's priority was to halt the inflation and establish a currency which Germans would feel confident enough to trust. In 1923 Germans virtually stopped using paper currency – they preferred to barter by exchanging goods rather than cash. Stresemann's new *Reichsmark* was backed by land and was soon accepted. He ordered the German workers back to work in the Ruhr and agreed to start paying reparations instalments again to the French. As a result the Franco-Belgian forces withdrew from the Ruhr in 1925. To help the Germans with these payments a huge loan of 800 million marks was negotiated from the USA – the Dawes Plan of 1924. Five years later the reparations sum itself was reduced from £6 600 million to £2 000 million in an agreement called the Young Plan. The repayments were scheduled to last until 1988. After 10 years the Allies were at least willing to take a more sympathetic view of Germany's problems. These loans did a great deal to stabilise Germany and provided a boost for the economy. However, such prosperity depended dangerously on economic conditions in the USA.

Germany's restored international status

Germany also ended her period of isolation from the international community. Up to 1925 Germany had friendly relations only with Soviet Russia. In 1922 the two countries had signed the Treaty of Rapallo. The treaty brought Russia and Germany into close co-operation. This co-operation was not only commercial but military as well. Secret tank and flying schools were set up in Russia in defiance of the Treaty of Versailles. In 1925 Germany signed a series of Locarno Treaties. The most important was signed with France. Germany recognised as permanent her borders with France and so gave up any claim to Alsace-Lorraine, ceded to France in 1919. Britain and Italy promised to make sure both sides kept to their agreements. Stresemann also signed an agreement with Czechoslovakia and Poland in which all three pledged to try and settle any future disputes over territory with international help. However, only France and not Britain guaranteed this treaty. In 1926 the Stresemann 'honeymoon' period continued as Germany was at last allowed to join the League of Nations.

As the economy prospered so the appeal of the Communists and Nazis lessened – though the Communists in 1928 still held 10% of the vote. However, there were signs – even before the Wall Street Crash of 1929 – that the German boom was beginning to falter. Unemployment had risen to 2 million and agriculture was in a state of depression already – a fact which had not escaped Hitler's attention. The Nazis first established real popular support among the small farmers and peasants of Bavaria and Lower Saxony.

The storm: 1929–33

One historian has written of Stresemann: '... if he had lived to guide Germany through the approaching world depression, Hitler might never have become Chancellor.' It is always dangerous to exaggerate the power of an individual in history. It is unlikely that even if Stresemann had lived on he would have been able to stop Hitler taking control of Germany. Stresemann could not have stopped the world economic crisis. Neither could he have prevented the United States calling back its loans from Germany. It is the effects of these two events that sealed the fate of the Weimar Republic. The reaction of Bruning, the Chancellor and leader of the Catholic Centre Party, to the crisis in 1930 was to cut unemployment and welfare benefits. The Centre Party's coalition partners, the Socialists, withdrew from the government in protest. This meant that Bruning's government did not have majority support in the Reichstag – Germany's Parliament.

Elections were called by the President, the First World War General Hindenburg, in September 1930, but this did nothing to solve the country's political crisis. In fact the situation got worse as the Nazis and Communists increased their share of the vote. Bruning, still without a majority of seats in the Reichstag, had to govern by decree, which meant that laws no longer had to be approved by the Reichstag. Long before Hitler took power in Germany the Reichstag had ceased to be the centre of political control. The increasing strength of the Nazis was reflected in the presidential elections of March 1932. Hitler won 13 million votes to Hindenburg's 19 million. The Communist candidate got 4 million. Bruning – the last Chancellor committed to the Republic – resigned in May 1932. He was replaced by Franz von Papen who was probably committed only to furthering his own interests. The elections that followed in July of that year saw a doubling of the Nazi vote to 38%. They were now the biggest party in the Reichstag. Von Papen lifted the ban on Hitler's private army – the SA, or storm troopers. Soon violent clashes between Nazis and Communists added to the chaos and sense of hopelessness. Unemployment reached 6 million in 1932. Only the Communists or the Nazis seemed to have solutions to Germany's problems.

Hitler: Chancellor, January 1933

New elections in November 1932 did nothing to break the deadlock – no party could win enough seats to govern on its own. In December a new Chancellor took over – von Schleicher – but he resigned on 28 January when Hindenburg refused to allow him to govern by decree. Finally the President played his last card, confident he could use the Nazi leader's popularity and then get rid of him when the crisis was over. On 30 January 1933 Hitler became Chancellor of Germany. The Weimar Republic had six months to live.

Nazi Propaganda vehicle 1932

Exercise 4

a Why do you think the appeal of the Nazis and Communists lessened during the period 1924–29?

b How did things begin to go wrong for the Weimar Republic in 1929?

c Why was the country in a state of 'political crisis' from 1930 onwards?

d The sub-heading to the previous section was 'Germany 1924–29: lull before the storm'. What does this phrase mean in general and why is it appropriate as a description of Germany at this time?

e What do the November 1932 election results suggest about the popularity of the Nazis?

Exercise 5

a According to the graphs below, which party during the period 1924–30 won the most votes in the elections?

b The DNVP, or Nationalists, was a right-wing party with ideas similar – though not as extreme – to the Nazis. What can you say about its share of the vote from 1924–32? Which party do you think benefited most from this?

c In which year did the KPD (Communist Party) reach the peak of its popularity? Can you give any reason for this?

d Stresemann was a member of the People's Party. What can you say about its share of the vote between 1924 and 1930? Why might this seem strange?

e The Z or Centre Party was a Catholic party which appealed to all classes of Germany. In general terms what can you say about its share of the vote during this period? Can you give any reason why this happened?

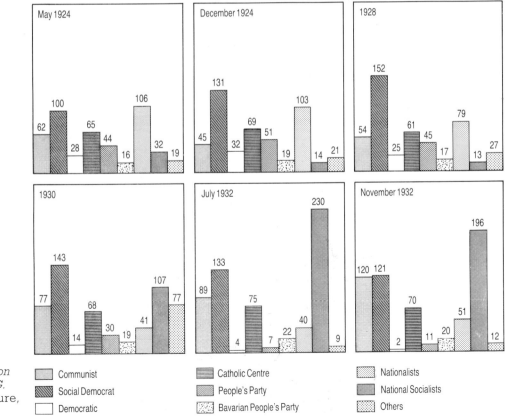

Source Three

Reichstag election results. (From: G. Mosse Nazi Culture, *1966)*

Legend:
- Communist
- Social Democrat
- Democratic
- Catholic Centre
- People's Party
- Bavarian People's Party
- Nationalists
- National Socialists
- Others

f In 1919 there were four major parties who believed in trying to make the Weimar Republic succeed. These were the Peoples' Party (Stresemann's party), the Democratic Party, the Centre Party and the Socialists. Find the total number of seats of these four parties in December 1924 and compare it with the same figure for November 1932. What does it show about the popularity of the Republic? Can you find any other supporting evidence for this view from the election results during the period? (Clue: compare this with the seats won by the Nazis and Communists over the same period.)

Exercise 6

a The number 48 on the coffin lid of the photo-montage in Source Four is a reference to Article 48 of the Weimar Constitution which allowed the President to make laws without Parliament. The building shown is the Reichstag. What is the point that the artist, John Heartfield, is trying to make in this poster from 1932?

b John Heartfield was actually a German who gave himself an English name. Looking at this poster, do you think he was likely to be a supporter or an opponent of Hitler?

Source Five
Nazi poster

Source Four

John Heartfield photo-montage

c Source Five is a Nazi election poster of 1933. The German means 'Our Last Hope'. To what class of people is the poster making its appeal? Why would these people have been likely to support Hitler in 1933?

d Source Six is another German Nazi propaganda poster. The words on the banner read: 'Loyalty, Honour and Order'. What do you think the woman next to Hitler represents? What impression is the poster attempting to get across about Hitler? Which of the three virtues on the banner do you think Hitler *least* represented and why?

e Of the two posters (Sources Five and Six) which do you think had the more general appeal to Germans and why?

Source Six *Nazi poster*

Germany: January to July 1933 – the beginning of the Nazi dictatorship

Hitler became Chancellor in January 1933 but he was far from being sole master of Germany. He soon called for new elections in the hope that he would receive more than 50% of the votes. In February the Reichstag was burnt down and a Communist was arrested for the crime. It provided Hitler with an ideal excuse to arrest and persecute leading Communists and break their organis-ation. Despite this terror the Nazis polled only 44% of the vote. So Hitler had to form a **coalition** with the Nationalists whose 8% gave him 52% of the vote. Before the end of the month Hitler put a new bill to the Reichstag called the Enabling Bill. This would give Hitler the power to make laws without parliament's approval for four years. In other words it would make him virtual **dictator** of Germany. The bill acquired its two-thirds majority with only the Socialists voting against. (The Communists had already been outlawed.) Hitler did not need four years to make himself dictator. Four months proved to be enough. In May the Socialists were banned and so were trade unions. In

(a) SA Brownshirt
(b) SS Standard Bearer

July the Centre Party was declared illegal. By 14 July the National German Socialist Workers' Party was the only legal political party left.

Why was Hitler able to come to power?

The Weimar Republic had the odds stacked against it from the very start. It was a government born out of defeat which many Germans believed the Allies had forced on them. The humiliation of the Treaty of Versailles and the 'War Guilt' clause which the new Republic had had to accept did not make it any more popular. Many of Germany's judges, top civil servants and army officers disapproved of democracy and conspired with right-wing forces like the Nationalists and then the Nazis to overthrow the Republic. The system of proportional representation encouraged small parties and made it impossible for any one party to get a majority of the votes. (For fuller discussion of the difficulties involved in proportional representation systems see Chapter 5 on Mussolini, page 68.) It meant that parties like the Socialists always had to govern in coalitions which were often unstable and broke up, as in 1930. The country could not be strongly governed from where it should have been – the Reichstag. It was left to an ageing President Hindenburg and politicians like him to try to control Germany's political affairs after 1930. Men like von Papen and von Schleicher were dangerous and stupid. They thought they could control Hitler.

Hitler's promises: all things to all men

But of course, one of the most important reasons why Hitler was able to become dictator of Germany was Hitler himself. He had a true politician's ability to understand what the people wanted and then promise it to them. He knew that the middle-classes in Germany wanted stability and no repetition of the disaster of 1923. The lower middle-class people like shopkeepers, small farmers and office workers, turned in large numbers to Hitler. Their memories of the disaster of 1923 and now the **Depression** strengthened their determination to do away with the Republic once and for all. Hitler knew that the workers wanted jobs and welfare benefits. He knew that the big industrialists and landowners like Krupp (armaments), Stinnes (coal), and Thyssen (steel) wanted the trade union movement made powerless and the Communists crushed. They were prepared to pay well for these 'improvements'. To all of these he told them exactly what they wanted to hear. To the army he offered massive expansion and new weapons, and the officer corps was only too happy to throw in its lot with him. In the meantime Hitler provided the Germans with someone to blame for the crisis they were in. Germany's 500 000 Jews were responsible for the humiliating defeat and peace terms. They had stabbed her in the back. The **Bolshevik** menace – Jewish inspired – threatened to destroy Germany's Aryan culture and society.

There were signs, however, that the situation may have begun to turn against Hitler. In the elections of November 1932 the Nazi vote actually dropped by 2 million. Perhaps Hitler's support was beginning to slide. The Socialists and Communists together could well have stopped the Nazi bully boys in the street with their own paramilitary forces. The Socialists and Communists had for a while co-operated against the Nazis but Stalin then ordered the German Communists to break with the Socialists. Divided they were easily crushed by the SA which, by 1932, was 400 000 strong. The SA and the more elite SS (*Schutzstaffel* or Protection Squad) provided tremendous appeal to many Germans – particularly former soldiers and unem-

Number unemployed

Jan. 6 000 000

Sept. 5 102 000

4 350 000

3 000 000

1 320 000

1929   1930   1931   1932   1933

A Nazi rally at Nuremberg: the smart uniforms, order and discipline of these rallies impressed many Germans

ployed. Their impressive uniforms and discipline inspired confidence. Nazi Party rallies at Nuremberg and elsewhere moved huge crowds into acts of hero-worship for the *Fuhrer* or leader. They hung on his every word and Hitler had full control of them.

Source Seven (top right) *Graph of unemployment in Nazi Germany*

1928		800 000
1930		6 400 000
1932	July	13 700 000
	Nov.	11 700 000

Source Eight (table) *Nazi votes in the Reichstag elections.*

	% Nazi Party members	% total population
manual workers	28.1	45.9
'white-collar' workers	25.6	12.0
'self-employed' (shop-keepers etc.)	20.7	9.0
officials and civil servants	14.9	9.3
teachers	1.7	0.9
farmers	14.0	10.6
others	3.3	

Source Nine (far right) *Occupation of Nazi Party members, 1930*

Assignment unit

Study the three sources above and answer the following questions

  a When did unemployment reach its peak in Germany?
  b When did the Nazis win the biggest number of votes in the elections?
  c Explain the link between these two statements.
  d What other evidence is there in the sources which confirms your answer to question c?
  e By studying Source Nine state in which types of occupation the Nazis were over-represented in terms of the total population.
  f In which type of occupation were the Nazis most over-represented?
  g In which occupation were the Nazis under-represented? What reasons can you suggest for this?
  h What evidence is there in Source Nine that the Nazi Party was much more a middle class than a workers' party?
  i From what you have read so far in the text and from sources such as the one above, put together a picture of a typical Nazi of 1933. Explain the kind of views he or she would hold over issues such as the Versailles Treaty, the Inflation of 1923, the Stresemann era, the Depression, Communism and why Nazism was the best solution for Germany's difficulties. (Exercise 7 will help you here.)

Exercise  7

Extract

Read this account of one Englishman's experience of life in Weimar Germany:

There were many, however, among one's friends and acquaintances . . .
who for the moment were ready to give their support to the new
government. It must be remembered that in the course of the fifteen years
which separated that day from the Armistice of 1918, Germany had
5   experienced governments of every kind of political combination and
complexion, had suffered terrifying national bankruptcy, had failed to
obtain any measure of treaty revision . . . and who genuinely believed that
economic breakdown, a paralysing inflation and a Communist 'Putsch'
were both possible, probable and imminent. On these fears and memories
10   Hitler had based his popular appeal. He had something for everyone in his
bag of promises, and above all he offered an attractive – almost a romantic
– prospect for youth. Where Bruning had called for sacrifices and had
gained no concessions in return, Hitler offered pledges and made no
concessions.
15   I offer these facts not in any way as an excuse for my friends' action but
as an explanation. 'He's our last chance', I heard all over and over again
. . . 'We've got to let him have this opportunity. After all the Nazis are a
minority in the government; the Old Man and 'Franzchen' are sound at
heart, and, if the worse comes to the worst, the Army can always turn the
20   Nazis out'.

(J. Wheeler-Bennet, *Knaves, Fools and Heroes in Europe between the
Wars*, 1974)

a Name the day on which the new government mentioned in lines 2–3 was
formed.
b Name the treaty referred to in line 7.
c To what year did the 'paralysing inflation' of line 8 refer?
d On what other fears, quoted in the text, did Hitler base his appeal?
e Give an example of the sacrifices called for by Bruning in line 12. Of what
party was he a member?
f Who were the Old Man and 'Franzchen' referred to in line 18? What had
been their role in bringing about this new government? Do you think the
author's faith in them was well placed?
g Why do you think the Army was unlikely to 'turn the Nazis out'?
h This account is a primary source, i.e. written by somebody who witnessed
the events he describes. A secondary source is one written from other
peoples' accounts – like this text book for example. What do you think the
advantages and disadvantages are of this primary source compared to
secondary ones for students of German history?

Exercise 8

Turn to the photograph of the Nazi propaganda vehicle on page 86. The middle
poster bears the words 'Work, Freedom and Bread' above a farmer sowing
seed. Now design your own Nazi poster for the elections of 1932.

Chapter 7

The National Socialist State

Totalitarianism

As you will remember from the chapter on the Weimar Republic Hitler wasted no time in establishing himself in a position of supreme authority in Germany. Trade unions were abolished in May of 1933. The **Communist** Party had been outlawed in March, the **Socialists** in June and the rest in July. In April a law was passed dismissing 'non-Aryans' or non-Germans from the civil service and anyone else whose loyalty to National Socialism was suspect. Joseph Goebbels was appointed Minister for Propaganda and set up sections which controlled and censored art, literature, music, the theatre, films, radio and the press. This kind of government control of all sources of news and ideas is one characteristic of a **totalitarian** state.

Militarism and **nationalism** are typical of totalitarianism also. Hitler wanted Germany to prosper as a nation which would be able to dominate other weaker nations. To achieve this nationalistic ambition Germany would require not only powerful armed forces but also an aggressive or militaristic spirit. The idea of racial superiority went hand in hand with this militarism. The Germans were entitled to enslave supposedly inferior nations, Hitler believed, because they were a master race, or *Herrenvolk*.

Hitler: 'The Fuhrer'

The creation of this new spirit of mastery would require new laws. It was vital that a totalitarian regime could rely on the law courts to deal with political opponents. Hitler ensured, therefore, that the system of justice took its orders from the government and that these 'Peoples' Courts' convicted those that Hitler wanted convicted.

Perhaps the most essential feature of totalitarian government is rule by a single individual in place of an elected parliament. Sometimes, as in the case of Hitler and Stalin, this all-powerful individual will have the backing of a party organisation. The organisation of the Nazi Party became the effective civil service of Germany and the Nazi Party was the personal instrument of Hitler. The final step to this supreme authority was taken by Hitler in 1934 when, on the death of President Hindenburg, Hitler abolished the titles of both Chancellor and President and made himself *Fuhrer*, or leader, of Germany.

The Nazi Party organisations

One of Hitler's first tasks was to clear out of public office all those who could not be trusted to carry out Nazi policy. Germany was divided into districts and each district was controlled by a '*Gauleiter*' appointed by Hitler. All important offices, such as judges and chiefs of police were held by Nazis. The Secret State Police or *Gestapo*, under the control of Heydrich, was given the task of identifying and bringing to 'justice' opponents of the Nazis. Some were opponents such as Communists and Socialists. Others were simply innocent of the 'crime' of opposition – they were merely Jews, homosexuals or gypsies. Heydrich controlled the Gestapo but

Three Nazi leaders: Rudolf Hess, deputy leader of the Nazi Party (second from left), *Hermann Goering, Air Force Chief* (third from right), *Joseph Goebbels, Minister of Propaganda* (far right)

Himmler controlled the regular police and the SS and was therefore his superior. But Hitler encouraged rivalry between the two just as he did with the other leaders of the party like Goebbels and Goering, the chief of the *Luftwaffe* (Air Force). These rivalries made sure that none was able to ever challenge Hitler's position of supremacy.

Anyone could be arrested by the Gestapo on suspicion and taken into 'protective custody' (imprisonment without trial). By April 1939 there were, according to the Gestapo's own report, precisely 162 734 people in protective custody. By this time there were a further 21 000 in the labour camps which were run by the SS. The numbers that met their deaths in these from SS beatings is not known though some 534 death sentences were officially carried out between 1934 and 1939 for political offences.

Night of the Long Knives, June 1934

The official title of the Nazi Party was the National Socialist German Workers' Party. Hitler had used the word socialist only to appeal to working class people. Two of the 25 Points of National Social-

ism drawn up in 1920 demanded 'profit-sharing in the great industries' and 'abolition of all incomes unearned by work'. This, in Hitler's view, was just for show as he hated socialism. However, many Nazis were attracted by these socialist ideas and their leader was Ernst Roehm. He was also commander of the SA whose Brownshirts numbered some 2 million in 1933. Roehm wanted to see these left-wing policies put into effect, including the **nationalisation** of the major firms. Furthermore, Roehm wanted Hitler to scrap the professional army, the *Reichswehr*, which numbered only 200 000 in 1933. He wanted it replaced by the SA with himself as commander-in-chief. Taking the major firms under state ownership would not please Hitler's big business supporters as they owned the firms. Roehm's ambition to see the Reichswehr replaced by the SA concerned the aristocratic army officers of the Reichswehr. They made it clear to Hitler that the regular army would give Hitler its full support once the SA was brought under control. Hitler knew what had to be done.

During the night of 30 June 1934 Himmler's SS moved against its old rival, the SA. At least one hundred (probably several hundred) SA leaders were shot out of hand by the SS. Roehm, a comrade of Hitler from the early days of the Nazi movement, was given the option of suicide rather than a firing squad:

> 'You have forfeited your life', said Eicke. 'The Fuhrer gives you one more chance to draw the right conclusions. He placed a pistol loaded with a single bullet on a table, then left the cell. Eicke waited in the passage for almost 15 minutes, then he and his deputies drew their own revolvers and rushed back into the cell. 'Chief of Staff, prepare yourself!' shouted Eicke. And, when he saw his

deputy's gun quivering, said 'Aim slowly and calmly'. Two shots reverberated deafeningly in the little cell. Roehm collapsed. 'My Fuhrer!' he gasped. 'My Fuhrer!'

(J. Toland, *Adolf Hitler*, 1976)

It was not only SA leaders that perished. Other old scores were settled as well. Von Papen, narrowly escaped death and Schleicher, the man who was Chancellor before Hitler also perished. Goebbels and Goering also took their opportunity to eliminate personal rivals within the party such as Gregor Strasser. The ruthless killings impressed the army and Hitler got his reward a month later when he became Fuhrer. The army swore an oath of personal loyalty to the leader of the Third Reich.

Exercise 1

a What was Goebbels' job as Minister for Propaganda?
b What task was carried out by the Gestapo?
c What reason did the Reichswehr have to fear the SA?
d What does the 'Night of the Long Knives' tell you about Hitler's political methods?
e When he was arrested Roehm commented that 'All revolutions devour their own children'. What do you think he meant by that phrase? Can you think of any other revolution that you have studied where the same could be said?
f What do Roehm's last words, ''My Fuhrer'', suggest about his attitude to Hitler?

Exercise 2

Extract: Roehm on Hitler

Adolf is a swine. He will give us all away. He only associates with reactionaries (extreme conservatives) now. His old friends aren't good enough for him. Getting matey with the Prussian generals. They're his cronies now ... Adolf knows exactly what I want. I've told him often
5   enough. NOT a second edition of the old imperial army. Are we revolutionaries or aren't we? ... The generals are a lot of old fogeys. They never have a new idea ... I'm the nucleus of the new army, don't you see ... The basis must be revolutionary.

(H. Rauschning, *Hitler Speaks*, 1939)

a Why was Roehm so angry about Hitler 'Getting matey with the Prussian generals'?
b How can you tell that Roehm had a personal relationship with Hitler?
c What do you suppose Roehm meant by the sentence 'He [Hitler] will give us all away'?
d How would you describe the tone of Roehm's comments concerning Hitler and Roehm's own ambitions?
e To what extent and why does Source One overleaf confirm the fears expressed by Roehm in lines 1–3?

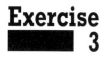

Exercise 3

Study Source One on page 96

a Identify the character standing next to Hitler and the one crawling on the ground.

THEY SALUTE WITH BOTH HANDS NOW.

Source One   *David Low cartoon: "They salute with both hands now", 3 July, 1934*

b What organisation is represented by the men standing with their hands in the air?

c How does Low, the cartoonist, get across the violence of the events of 30 June, 1934?

d Suggest the kind of promises Roehm might have had in mind by the crumpled paper 'Hitler's unkept promises'.

e What point is Low making by the ironic title 'They salute with both hands now'?

f Explain the significance of the words 'the double cross' on Hitler's arm band.

g Which people and groups of people benefited the most from the events this cartoon relates to and why?

Youth in Nazi Germany

Children were a special target for Nazi propaganda. Hitler believed that if the youth of Germany could be fed a diet of Nazi ideas from the earliest age then they would stay fanatically loyal to the new '*Reich*' or state. Young boys started at the age of six in the *Pimpfen* (Little Fellows) and at the age of 10 took a test. If they passed they graduated on to the *Jungvolk* (Young Folk) until the age of 14 when they could join the Hitler Youth. Between the ages of 18 and 25 a year of Labour Service had to be done and after 1935 there were two years of military service. Girls did not begin youth activities until the age of 10 with the Young Maidens, followed at 14 by the League of German Maidens. Hitler's view of the tasks of German womanhood was simple – they were to stay at home, marry and give birth to Aryan children: '*Kinder, Kirche, Kuche*' (Children, Church and Cooking). By 1938 these youth organisations had nearly $7\frac{3}{4}$ million members.

Source One
(right) *Weapon training for members of the Hitler Youth*

Education was also closely controlled. Biology and history were of special concern to the Nazis. All teachers had to join the National Socialist Teachers' League or be sacked. Biological 'evidence' was regularly produced in

lessons to show how non-Aryan races like the Jews and Slavs were supposedly inferior. Jewish children were constantly humiliated in front of their classmates. All lessons had to begin and end with the Nazi salute and '*Heil Hitler*'. The most able children were removed from ordinary schools and sent to Adolf Hitler Schools where they were trained to be the future leaders of the Reich. Much of this was tremendously exciting to young people. The work camps where they marched and hiked, sang Nazi songs and had military parades created the kind of enthusiasm for Nazism and for Hitler in particular which was to serve Hitler well in the early years of the war.

The churches

One source of possible opposition to Hitler came from the Christian churches. At first it seemed possible that Hitler might avoid a confrontation with the Catholic Church when he signed an agreement, or Concordat, with the Church in 1933. In this agreement Hitler promised not to interfere with the Church and its faith. The Church agreed not to interfere in political matters. The truce did not last long. The Catholic Youth League competed with the Nazi youth organisations so he banned it and then shut down Church schools. In 1937 Pope Pius XI condemned Nazism as anti-Christian. Priests and nuns were arrested and sent to labour camps. The Protestant Churches, led by Pastor Niemoller, also resisted and he and 800 pastors were imprisoned.

Treatment of the Jews

None but members of the nation may be citizens of the State.

None but those of German blood may be members of the nation. No Jew, therefore, may be a member of the nation.

This was one of the 25 Points of National Socialism, drawn up in 1920. Some of the 25 Points, as we have seen, were discarded by Hitler when it suited him. **Anti-Semitism**, the hatred of Jews, was one point which Hitler clung to throughout his life. Right from the beginning Hitler began a relentless campaign against the 500 000 Jews in Germany. However, Hitler began cautiously with his anti-Semitic policies, gradually stepping up the level of persecution. In April 1933 the SA organised a boycott of Jewish shops, goods, doctors and lawyers. Jewish civil servants were dismissed. The names of any Germans who continued to use Jewish services were published on posters for all to see. By 1935 Jews were forbidden to enter swimming baths, sports fields and public parks in some parts of Germany. In September 1935 Hitler took a bigger step against Jews with the Nuremberg laws. They were deprived of their citizenship, the right to vote and the right to marry Aryans and non-Jews. Many Jewish businesses were taken over and sold off cheaply to Germans. They were encouraged to leave the country. Some headed for Palestine (see Chapter 19 on the Arab–Israeli conflict). Others headed for Britain and the USA. Many were turned away and forced back to Germany. A fine of $1\frac{1}{4}$ billion marks was also levied on Germany's Jewish communities.

In 1938 a German diplomat was shot dead in Paris by a French Jew. The SS organised an attack on Jewish property in Germany as a reprisal. 'Crystal Night', as the event was called because of the shattering of countless thousands of panes of glass, led to the looting of 814 Jewish shops, the burning of 191 synagogues and the beating to death of

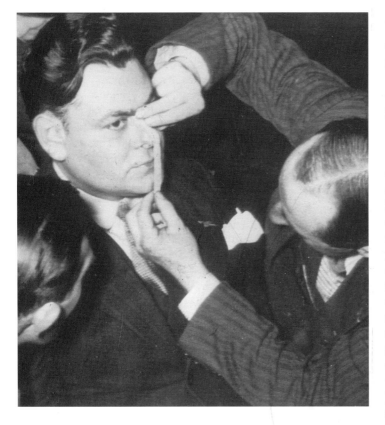

Hitler believed that Jews had large noses very different from those of his supposed 'master race'. Here a man is having his nose measured to check whether it is a 'Jewish' nose or not

Jewish composers were probably accepted by the majority of Germans without too much concern. Anti-Semitism was already established in Germany before 1914. All Hitler had done was to make a major political policy of it.

The 1936 Olympics

Only for a brief period leading up to and during the 1936 Olympic Games in Berlin did Hitler ease up on his attacks on the Jews. Anti-Semitic posters were removed and anti-Jewish papers disappeared from the news stands. A couple of token Jews were allowed to compete for Germany in the Games. All this was done to boost Germany's image abroad and Hitler succeeded. The Games were a triumph for Germany on and off the field: the Germans won the most medals and the many thousands of foreign visitors saw no evidence of ill-treatment of Jews. Hitler did fail to shake the hands of several black American winners – the idea of 'inferior' Negroes beating Aryans was hard for Hitler to swallow. He was told by the President of the Olympic Committee that, as guest of honour, he should shake the hands of all the winners or none. Hitler chose to shake the hands of none and so was never put in the position of actually refusing to shake the hand of the black American, Jesse Owens, who won four gold medals. Just before the Olympics began, the organiser of the Olympic Village, a German Jew, was replaced on the orders of Hitler. He shot himself. When the visitors returned to their countries, full of praise for the new Germany, the Jews once again faced their persecutors.

at least 36 Jews (though Heydrich admitted these official figures must have been 'considerably exceeded').

By 12 November – just a week after the killing in Paris – some 20 000 Jews had been sent to labour camps. It should be pointed out here that the deliberate policy of mass-murder of Jews in the concentration camps did not begin until 1942. Germany's Jewish population today numbers some 30 000 compared to the pre-war figure of 500 000. It is also worth pointing out that anti-Semitism in Germany was not the invention of Hitler. The policies against Jews, the burning of books by Jewish authors and the banning of music by

---

Exercise 4

a The title of the poster on page 99 is 'The eternal Jew'. Which particular physical feature, according to Nazi theory, is supposed to represent Jews?

b The caricature shows Jews as money-lenders, Bolsheviks and slave-drivers. Indicate how the poster gets these points across.

Der ewige Jude

Source Two   *Anti-Semitic poster*

c What country is represented in the figure's arm? What is the poster implying will be the fate of this country if the Jews are not stopped?

d The Jews are shown as both Communists and businessmen, lending money for profit. In what way does this poster reflect one of the contradictions of Nazi theories about the Jews?

e Why do you suppose so many Germans believed propaganda like this?

f Can you suggest any reasons why the Jews did not fight back against the Nazis?

g Why do you think countries like Britain and France did little to help the Jews in Germany?

Exercise 5

a Why were biology lessons of special interest to the Nazis?

b What was the appeal of Nazism for Germany's youth?

c Can you suggest any reason why, as it says in the text, Hitler 'began

b cautiously with his anti-Semitic policies'?

d What evidence is there in the text that anti-Semitism in Germany was not the invention of Hitler?

e Draw up a report of 25 lines from Himmler to Hitler on the events of 'Crystal Night', suggesting what the response should be to international criticism of the SS actions.

The armed forces and rearmament

Life in Nazi Germany was pleasant for those who were not Jews, Communists, Socialists, homosexual, priests or gypsies. Most Germans were none of these. All they saw was that Hitler had brought stability and increasing prosperity to the country. Hitler repaid his debt to big business for its financial sup-

A motorised military parade in 1935

port in the years before 1933 by abolishing trade unions and the right to strike. Wages were kept low and profits high. One of the reasons for this prosperity was rearmament. In 1934 Hitler began his rearmament policy and in 1935 announced conscription. Both of these helped to reduce unemployment considerably. In defiance of the Versailles Treaty the German leader openly developed an airforce, the Luftwaffe, which by 1939 numbered 260 000 men and 3 600 aircraft. The navy began work on powerful new battleships like the *Graf Spee*, launched in 1936, with still bigger ones like the *Bismarck* and the *Tirpitz* to follow. There were, however, high-ranking opponents of Hitler's plans for war in the renamed *Wehrmacht* or Armed Forces. In 1938 the commander-in-chief of the army, Fritsch, and the War Minister were forced to resign. Hitler himself became Minister of War. The traditional officer corps of the Armed Forces was being forced out and replaced by men prepared to do the Fuhrer's bidding. The more junior officer ranks of the forces were already occupied by committed Nazis, grateful to Hitler for their rapid promotion.

The Nazi economy

Hitler's economic ideas were straightforward. He wanted Germany to increase her exports, reduce her imports and end unemployment. He wanted Germany to be as self-sufficient as possible so that she would not have to rely on any other country for raw materials like oil, iron ore and rubber. To some extent this was a reaction against the interference by foreign countries in the German economy – the **reparations** bill, the Dawes and then the Young Plans. This policy of economic independence is known as autarky. The problem was that Germany could not hope to produce enough raw materials from within Germany herself. Countries rich in these materials would have to come under Nazi control or influence. This was why Hitler's ambitions were likely to lead to war sooner or later as Germany seized for herself the vital requirements for her economy from other nations.

'Guns before butter'

In order to carry out these economic targets Hitler's Minister of Economics, Dr Schacht, controlled the imports of raw materials. This meant that firms could only produce what the government wanted as the raw materials they needed came only from the government. For example, in 1934 Schacht cut down on the amount of raw cotton and wool imported. Instead he increased the level of iron-ore imports so that heavy industry could increase production. This industry, of course, was vital to armaments firms like Krupps. The increase in arms production was one of Hitler's central aims. By 1939 the Germans were spending 16 times more on military expenditure than they were in 1933.

This vast increase in money spent on the military also brought an end to unemployment – the number of unemployed in 1938 was just 200 000 compared to 5.6 million in 1932. Hundreds of thousands of workers were drafted into the factories to turn out the guns and tanks needed. As Reichsmarshall Goering commented: 'In the decisive hour it would not be a question of how much butter Germany has but how many guns'. More employment was created in huge public works schemes such as cheap housing for workers and motor (*autobahn*) construction. Even here there was a military purpose behind the road building. The steel, iron and concrete for these schemes came from private firms. Their profits rose steadily and there were no strikes for the employers to worry about. Trade unions had been abolished and with them the right to strike. Instead the workers got cheap theatre tickets, controlled rents and subsidised holidays.

Experiments were begun to produce synthetic raw materials to replace natural ones such as oil, rubber and wool. They were not very successful.

In 1939 Germany still imported some two-thirds of her oil and ore requirements. In fact, Germany's imports between 1933 and 1938 rose by 28% while exports rose by only 8% and she was actually selling less abroad than in 1932. From 1937 onwards Germany was spending more than the country earned in revenue from taxes and sales of goods. This did not concern Hitler. By 1939 he had an army of 730 000 men with another 1 million in reserve, and Germany's aircraft outnumbered Britain's airforce by two to one.

Exercise 6

a What does 'autarky' mean?
b Why was this policy likely to lead to conflict with other nations sooner or later?
c How did Schacht control the economy?
d What do you think Goering meant by the sentence quoted in the text?
e What do you think the military purpose was behind the motorway construction referred to in the text?

Exercise 7

a Draw two graphs, one from each of the tables below and on page 102.
b In percentage terms by roughly how much did military expenditure increase between 1937 and 1939? (Table One)
c What evidence is there in Table Two that Schacht's claim that Germany could not afford such military expenditure was correct?
d What percentage (approximately) of total government expenditure in 1939 was accounted for by military spending?
e Schacht was forced to resign in 1937 because he disagreed with Hitler's policy of concentrating on armaments production. Do you think that Goering was pleased to see the resignation of Schacht and if so why?

Table One: military expenditure 1933–39

Figures in millions of marks

1933	1 900
1934	1 900
1935	4 000
1936	5 800
1937	8 200
1938	18 400
1939	32 300

Table Two: Government receipts and expenditure 1933–39

(Figures in millions of marks)	Receipts	Expenditure
1933	7 700	6 300
1934	10 000	8 200
1935	10 700	10 200
1936	13 800	13 200
1937	17 000	17 300
1938	21 300	29 200
1939	27 400	49 500

(From: *Purnell's History of the 20th Century*)

Exercise 8

a This is a photo-montage by John Heartfield. He was a German Communist in the 1930s. The writing at the bottom of the poster reads: 'Hooray! The butter is finished!' To what statement is the poster referring?

b Why is the family eating bullets and bits of bicycle?

c Which of the following adjectives best describes Heartfield's poster and why:
  i bitter;
  ii heartless;
  iii ironic;
  iv humorous?

d How accurate a comment would you say the poster was on Germany's economy by the end of the 1930s? (Refer to the graphs on the next page in your answer.)

Source Three
John Heartfield photo-montage

Hurrah, die Butter ist alle!

Assignment unit

The Nazi economy

Write a confidential report in 1939 to Hitler from the Ministry of Economics discussing the strengths and weaknesses of the German economy. (The graphs on page 103 will provide you with additional information). Conclude your honest report with a recommendation as to whether Germany's economy is strong enough to support a war. You will need to make some reference to the condition of the Wehrmacht (the Armed Forces) for this. Comment not only on the level of armaments production but on the attitude of the generals to a war and their likely loyalty to the Fuhrer. (The section on the Armed Forces and rearmament will help here.)

Index of industrial production (1928 = 100)			Value in billions of marks of	
	total	production goods	consumer goods	imports	exports
1932				4.7	5.7
1933	66	56	80	4.2	4.9
1934	83	81	91	4.5	4.2
1936	107	114	100	4.2	4.8
1938	125	144	116	5.4	5.3

number employed (millions)

1928	1932	1933.	1934	1935	1936	1937	1938
18.0	12.6	13.1	15.1	16.0	17.1	18.4	18.8

number unemployed (millions)

1928	1932	1933	1934	1935	1936	1937	1938
1.4	5.6	3.7	2.3	2.1	1.6	0.9	0.2

Graphs showing the effects of National Socialism on the economy

	Wages (1936 = 100)	wholesale prices (1913 = 100)
1928	124.5	140
1932		
1933	87.7	93.3
1934	94.1	
1936	100	104.1
1938	108.5	105.8

size of the German army (in battalions)

	infantry	artillery	Panzer
1933	84	24	
1934	166	95	6
1935	287	116	12
1936	334	148	16
1937	352	187	24
1938	476	228	34

Chapter 8

The League of Nations: 1920–39

In 1918 President Wilson of the United States put forward his 14 Points as a basis for ending the First World War. The last of these points called for the setting up of an international organisation that would bring the nations of the world together to ensure peace. The League of Nations came into existence in January 1920. Despite Wilson's great hopes for it, the League soon ran into several difficulties. First of all, Congress, the law-making body of the United States, refused to give its approval to US membership of the League. America was to enter a period of **isolationism** that would keep it out of Europe's affairs until 1941. This was a devastating blow to the League. It soon became clear that Europe's two major Allied powers, Britain and France, also had little faith in the idea. They had paid lip service to it only to please Wilson. The truth of the matter was they had no intention of allowing the League to influence any of their policies. Finally, none of the defeated powers was allowed to join the organisation and this did little to create an atmosphere of peaceful co-operation in Europe. Nonetheless, the League was set up in 1920 with Geneva as its headquarters.

Aims and structure of the League

The League had two broad aims. Firstly, it was to maintain peace through **collective security**. This meant that all member states (42 in 1920) would act together or collectively to punish any nation that threatened or committed an act of war (called the aggressor) against another nation. This punishment could take two forms: economic or military **sanctions** or measures. Economic sanctions would involve refusing to trade with the aggressor. As a last resort military means could be used – in theory. In practice, the League never actually raised an army for such purposes and so the only sanctions which were ever applied were economic ones. The second of the League's aims was to encourage international co-operation in order to solve the world's economic and social problems. A variety of special commissions and committees was set up, such as the Health Organisation and the Disarmament Conference. All member states were required to sign the Covenant which was the **constitution** of the League, containing all its rules and the duties of the members. The League may have been lacking in some qualities but it certainly had good intentions.

The main bodies of the League were:

(a) the General Assembly;
(b) the Council;
(c) the Permanent Court of Justice;
(d) the Secretariat;
(e) the special commissions and committees.

The General Assembly This met once a year and all members attended. Each member had a single vote, no matter how big or small the country. All decisions taken by the Assembly had to be agreed by every member. In theory this could have meant that one vote against would be enough to stop any decision being made. In practice, a member state would abstain rather than vote against; so decisions were made. The Assembly had some real power in that it controlled the League's budget but the real running of the League was carried out by the Council.

The Council This was a much smaller body and met at least every three months. It had four permanent members – Britain, France, Italy and Japan. The USA, the fifth of the victorious powers, never joined the League. Four other members were to be elected by the Assembly for a three year period. By 1926 the number of non-permanent members had increased to nine. This prevented the major powers from dominating the League. The Council had to deal with crises that arose and settle political disputes unanimously.

The Permanent Court of Justice This was set up in the Hague and consisted of 15 judges. It dealt with legal, as opposed to political, disputes between members. Before any case could be submitted to the Court both sides had to agree to accept the verdict in advance.

The Secretariat This was the civil service of the League and drew up the resolutions and reports for the League.

The commissions and committees There were a variety of these to deal with specific issues and problems. The **Mandates** Commission made sure the mandated territories were being properly governed. Other commissions looked after the rights of racial minorities or discussed proposals for disarmament. Of the committees, the most noteworthy was the International Labour Organisation (ILO) which sought to spread trade union rights and improve wages and working conditions. It was led by a Frenchman, Albert Thomas, and because membership was not restricted to League members only, the United States also joined.

The ILO and the committee which tried to eliminate drug trafficking had a fair measure of success.

Teething troubles

One of the first countries to challenge the League was Poland. The Poles quickly displayed the kind of aggressive behaviour the League was intended to stop. The Poles first quarrelled over Teschen with Czechoslovakia (see map, page 34). Then in 1920 their troops seized another disputed area – Vilna – this time at the expense of Lithuania. The Lithuanians appealed to the League and the League decided that Lithuania was entitled to the area. However, the Conference of Ambassadors decided that Vilna should be Polish and not Lithuanian. The League gave way.

The Conference of Ambassadors had been set up as a temporary measure until the League had established itself. But major powers like Britain and France kept the Conference going until 1931. On some occasions the Conference actually worked against the League, considerably undermining the image and prestige of the League of Nations.

In 1923 five Italian soldiers were killed on Greek territory while mapping out the Albanian–Greek border for the Conference of Ambassadors. Mussolini, the Italian **dictator**, held the Greek government responsible and demanded huge compensation. The island of Corfu was first shelled and then occupied by the Italians. Greece appealed to the League against this obvious act of aggression. The League handed the matter over to the Conference of Ambassadors. Greece was forced to pay up.

The League's successes

After this rather poor start the League did begin to achieve some minor success. In 1920 it solved a dispute between Sweden and Finland over the Åland Islands. Similar success was achieved in quarrels between Chile and Peru (1925) and Colombia and Venezuela (1922). It successfully partitioned Upper Silesia between Poland and Germany (1921) and stopped a major war between Greece and Bulgaria. The problem was that these were all minor nations. Italy had already proved that the big powers could ignore the League and get away with it. Japan was to prove the point again in the 1930s. In 1924 Britain's first Labour Prime Minister, Ramsey MacDonald, drew up the Geneva Protocol by which all members were to accept as binding all decisions of the Court of Justice and agree to more vigorous action being taken against aggressors. However, MacDonald's government fell before it could be signed. The new Conservative Government considered that the Protocol went too far and it was shelved. Britain preferred to secure peace in its own way and with as little regard for the League as possible.

The League had a fair measure of success with its less well-known committees and commissions. The ILO has already been mentioned but the Mandates Commission deserves favourable comment as well. Its purpose was to ensure that the mandated territories (the former colonies of Germany and Turkey) were well governed and prepared for independence. Iraq, a British mandate, moved smoothly to independence in 1932. Most of the others became independent after the Second World War when the United Nations took over the work of the Commission. Much creditable work was done by various committees for child welfare, refugees and women's rights and by the committee against the drug traffic. The Disarmament Commission achieved some progress in 1922 with the Washington Conference in which the United States, Britain, France, Italy and Japan agreed to limit the size of their navies according to a specified ratio. Further progress towards the goal laid down by Article 8 – 'the reduction of national armaments to the lowest point consistent with national safety' – proved impossible. The Disarmament Conference of 1932 was attended by 60 nations. Hitler, once in power in Germany, angrily withdrew in October 1933 and then left the League altogether.

It can be said in defence of the League that it was something of an achievement for it to exist at all. It was the first truly international body designed to develop co-operation and understanding. The 19th century had produced only the international Red Cross as an example of co-operation between nations. The League also proved an important base from which to create another body whose aim has been to foster the international brotherhood of nations – the United Nations. It is still in existence.

Exercise 1

a What crucial weakness did the League suffer from the very start?
b Why were military 'sanctions' likely to prove ineffective?
c What failing of the League did the Corfu incident reveal?
d How did Britain undermine the position of the League?

Exercise 2

Study Source One on page 107.

a Name the President mentioned in the notice board on the left of the cartoon.
b What did the powers named on the bridge have in common in 1918?
c Which of these powers was not a permanent member of the Council of the League?

THE GAP IN THE BRIDGE.

d What is the significance of the missing keystone of the bridge, seen on the right?

e What institution might the figure on the right be said to represent?

f What is the point the cartoon is making about the prospects of the League? Was the cartoonist justified in his opinion?

Source One Punch *cartoon*

Exercise 3

OVERWEIGHTED.

PRESIDENT WILSON. "HERE'S YOUR OLIVE BRANCH. NOW GET BUSY."
DOVE OF PEACE. "OF COURSE I WANT TO PLEASE EVERYBODY; BUT ISN'T THIS A BIT THICK?"

a The man offering the branch is Woodrow Wilson, President of the USA. Given later developments concerning the United States and the League, before which year do you think this cartoon was drawn?

b What is the point the cartoonist is making by drawing such a thick olive branch? What does the branch represent?

c What do both these cartoons have in common as regards the League?

d Which of the cartoons do you consider to be more a statement of opinion rather than fact? Explain your answer.

Source Two Punch *cartoon*

The failure of the League

Manchurian crisis, 1931–39

The first 11 years of the League's life had been mixed ones with some successes and failures. However, once it came up against large and aggressive powers, its basic weaknesses were ruthlessly exposed. From 1931 onwards it went into a period of sharp decline, eventually ending in the disaster of the Second World War. The first of its major crises occurred in 1931 when Japan invaded the Chinese territory of Manchuria. China naturally appealed to the League to take action against the aggressor. The League condemned the invasion and ordered Japan to withdraw its troops. When the Japanese refused to do this, the League sent a commission under Lord Lytton to invest-

(Right) Japanese invasion of Manchuria

igate the affair (1932). It suggested that the League govern Manchuria. Japan was unimpressed and left the League in 1933. To make its point even clearer, Japan invaded the rest of China in 1937. There was no discussion of sanctions during the crisis. Britain and France were reluctant to risk a war with Japan.

Japanese troops pause behind a barricade in Shanghai, 1937. Note how well equipped these troops are

Exercise 4

THE DOORMAT.

Source Three

David Low cartoon

a Name the country represented by the figure in military uniform.

b Why is Geneva written on the pillar on the right?

c What is the significance of the word 'League' written on the woman on the ground?

d What international incident is the cartoon describing?

e The title to this cartoon is 'The Doormat'. Do you think it is an appropriate title and why?

f The figure on the right is the British Foreign Secretary, Sir John Simon. What point is the cartoonist making by positioning the box labelled 'Face-Saving Outfit' by the Secretary?

g What other technique does the cartoonist use to show that the League was not able to stand up to the aggressor nation?

The invasion of Abyssinia 1935

Mussolini had watched Japan flout the authority of the League and get away with it. He now felt that it was time for Italy to claim its rights as a great power. In this case this meant invading the East African state of Abyssinia. The fact that Abyssinia was an independent African nation with a poorly equipped army added to its attractions in Mussolini's eyes. The League was once again faced with an unprovoked act of aggression by the Italians as their troops poured across the border from Italian Somaliland.

On this occasion the League responded swiftly. Within a week economic sanctions had been imposed on Italy but the sanctions did not extend to oil, steel and coal. These were the very materials Italy needed for a successful conquest. The Soviet Union and Rumania both called for an oil embargo

Italian invasion of Abyssinia

or blockade on Italy but Britain and France would not agree. A glance at the map above will show you how well placed Britain was to take effective measures against the Italians but she even allowed Italy to use the Suez Canal to transport war materials. Britain and France actually tried to work out a solution behind the back of the League. The British Foreign Minister, Hoare, and the French Prime Minister, Laval, worked out a pact by which Italy would control two-thirds of Abyssinia. This would leave the Emperor of Abyssinia, Haile Selassie, a thin strip of land. The world denounced this shameful plan. Hoare and Laval were forced out of office and Mussolini rejected the proposal anyway. He wanted all of Abyssinia. In 1936 Haile Selassie appealed to the League of Nations for assistance with words which were to prove so justified three years later (see page 112). Britain and France were desperately keen not to lose Italy's support against Germany but the unity of the Stresa Front (see Chapter 5, page 77) had already crumbled. Nonetheless, the sanctions, feeble as they were, were enough to anger Mussolini. The fact that Germany had refused to impose any sanctions at all brought the two dictators, Hitler and Mussolini, together in the Rome–Berlin Axis of 1936 (see Chapter 5, page 77).

Italian troops amid burning native huts during the Abyssinian campaign

Haile Selassie appealing to the League of Nations in 1936 over the invasion of his country by Italy. 'International morality is at stake', he warned

Why did the League fail?

From the very start the absence of the United States was a crippling blow to the League. It was from then onwards deprived of the leadership and authority of the world's greatest power. It is probable that Britain and France could have filled the gap left by the USA – if they had made a real effort to make the League succeed. But as we have seen, these two major powers were more interested in making deals which bypassed the League altogether. They were reluctant to use their power to make the organisation stronger, afraid that they would be faced with a decision with which they did not agree. Other great powers also played little part in the League. Germany was not allowed to join until 1926 and she left in 1933 when the World Disarmament Conference, set up by the League, collapsed. Without an army to enforce its 'military sanctions' the League was powerless against the aggressive dictatorships of Germany, Italy and Japan. The one European nation that was willing to make a stand against Hitler, the Soviet Union, did join the League in 1934. But it saw the weakness of Britain and France as Hitler repeatedly broke the Treaty of Versailles which the League was supposed to safeguard. The feebleness of the response of Britain and France to the occupation of the Rhineland (1936) and the Anschluss with Austria (1938) convinced Stalin that the West would never oppose Nazism. In 1939 Stalin and Hitler signed the Nazi–Soviet Pact. The League of Nations ended its short life without a whimper. Unfortunately for the history of the world, it also went out with a bang.

Exercise 5

MORAL SUASION.

The Rabbit. "MY OFFENSIVE EQUIPMENT BEING PRACTICALLY *NIL*, IT REMAINS FOR ME TO FASCINATE HIM WITH THE POWER OF MY EYE."

Source Four

Punch *cartoon: 'Moral Suasion' (meaning persuasion)*

a Why is the League depicted as a rabbit?

b Explain the reference to 'offensive equipment'. Why was it 'practically nil'?

c Name two international incidents of the 1930s which the snake could be said to represent.

d Other than offensive sanctions, what other methods could the 'rabbit' resort to against an aggressor?

e Looking at the sources used so far, what can you say in general about the opinion of many cartoonists of that time on the League of Nations? Can you think why the United Nations has not been treated in a similar manner?

f Which of the sources do you think is most critical of the League? Explain your answer.

Exercise 6

Extract

Study this extract from a speech to an international assembly in 1936, and then answer questions a to f which follow:

> I, Haile Selassie, Emperor of Ethiopia, am here today to claim that justice which is due to my people, and the assistance promised eight months ago, when fifty nations asserted that aggression had been committed.
>
> 5 It is my duty to inform the governments of the deadly peril which threatens them. It is a question of trust in international treaties and of the value of promises to small states that their integrity shall be respected. In a word, international morality is at stake.
>
> Apart from the Kingdom of God, there is not on this earth any nation that is higher than any other. God and History will remember your judgment.

a By what other name was Ethiopia usually known at this time? To what international organisation would Haile Selassie have made this speech?

b Against the aggression of which country and ruler was Haile Selassie appealing?

c What promises (line 2) had been made to small nations by this organisation?

d What did the speaker mean by the use of:
  i 'integrity' (line 6)?
  ii 'judgment' (line 9)?

e What action did the international organisation take against the aggressor?

f What decision by the international community, not mentioned in this speech, indicates that not all sense of 'international morality' had been abandoned?

g Which of the previous sources on the League most supports Haile Selassie's view? Give reasons.

Chapter 9

The USA 1919–41: prosperity, poverty and recovery

Decade of prosperity

The First World War had been good for American business. Production had risen sharply to meet the massive requirements of the war. After the war was over European countries continued to buy American goods. The Republican governments of Presidents Harding (1921–23), Coolidge (1923–29) and Hoover (1929–33) encouraged this 'boom' (a sharp increase in business and profits) in the United States by increasing import duties on foreign goods coming into the United States. The Fordney–McCumber tariff (1922) therefore encouraged Americans to buy American-produced goods rather than the more expensive foreign ones. These presidents also cut taxes so people had more money to spend and generally believed in what is called '*laissez-faire*'. This means that when possible they let businessmen run their affairs without any government control. Between 1923 and 1929 wages rose by 8%. Although this was not a great deal it did mean workers had that bit more to spend on the new consumer goods like radios, washing-machines, vacuum cleaners and cars. Many bought these items through another invention of the 1920s: hire purchase. It all helped to keep the economy in top gear. Prospects seemed excellent – as long as the goods kept on being sold.

Why did the boom collapse?

Even before the famous Wall Street Crash of October 1929 there were signs that things were going wrong. Farmers had found life increasingly difficult since the end of the war. The widespread use of machinery had led to the production of more food than was needed – in other words, '**overproduction**'. Little of this could be exported as European countries were beginning to produce plenty of their own food. As a result, prices fell steadily during the 1920s. Many farmers could not meet the mortgage payments on their farms and the banks took their farms from them. Much the same began to happen in industry. Too many goods

Girl in a short skirt powdering her knees. Such fashions led to unemployment in the textile industries

were being produced for the home market. Unsold goods began to pile up and so the manufacturers produced less. As a result workers were laid off and because there was no unemployment benefit they could not afford to buy much. Less was sold and so more workers were laid off. The vicious cycle went on repeating itself. Had wages kept pace with profits between 1923 and 1929 the situation might never have arisen. Profits had increased by 72% whereas wages rose only by 8%. But American business was much more powerful than the unions and it had been able to keep wages down.

In some cases it was not just a matter of industries producing too much. Some industries were in decline anyway. The coal industry could not compete with newer forms of energy like petrol, electricity and gas. These now supplied over half of America's energy needs. Needless to say, many miners were sacked or were forced to accept wage cuts. The textile industry was in similar trouble. Cotton was in much less demand. This was partly because women's fashion now required shorter clothes and less material and also because artificial fibres like rayon were beginning to replace cotton.

The Wall Street Crash, October 1929

Firms might have been able to export what they could not sell at home but many countries had imposed tariffs on American goods in retaliation for the Fordney–McCumber tariff. World trade was grinding to a halt. Another problem was speculation on the Wall Street stock market. The idea behind speculation is to buy shares at a low price and sell them at a higher one. For example, shares of the Radio Corporation of America in early 1928 cost $85 each. By September 1929 each share was valued at a staggering $505! The skill was knowing when the value of the shares had reached its peak. That was the time to sell. It seemed a fool-proof way to make money. Around a million people spent their savings or borrowed money in order to buy shares. As long as the value rose everybody was happy. But some investors knew the boom could not last. Towards the end of 1929 a few began to sell while prices were high. Other investors got nervous and sold their shares. Soon the stock market was gripped by a panic to sell off its shares as quickly as possible. On Black Thursday, 24 October 1929, 13 million shares were 'dumped'. Prices collapsed. The president of Union Cigar, stunned when his company's shares plummeted from $113.50 to $4 in a day, fell or jumped to his death from the ledge of a New York hotel. Hundreds of thousands of people had lost all their savings or were in debt for thousands of dollars because of the shares they had bought on credit. 'Buddy, can you spare a dime?' was the haunting melody that could be heard across America.

Exercise 1

a What two methods did the Republican governments of the 1920s use to encourage Americans to buy home-made goods?

b In what ways was the depression that affected agriculture similar to the industrial depression of the late 1920s?

c Explain the point of the sentence: 'Had wages kept pace with profits between 1923 and 1929 the situation [the depression] might never have arisen.'

d Why could it be said that the Fordney–McCumber tariff eventually back-fired on the United States?

e Write an article as a financial journalist in early 1929 expressing your concern about the current boom and explain why you think investors should sell now. (Can you think of any reason why you might do better to keep the advice for yourself and throw the article in the bin?)

Other problems in the 1920s

These economic problems made worse the problem of poverty which existed in the United States even during the 'boom' years of the 1920s. In 1929 16 million families, 60% of all American families, had an income of less than $2500. This placed them below the poverty line. Between them they owned less than a quarter of the nation's income.

Another difficulty which the United States faced in this period was self-made. In 1919 the US Congress passed the 18th Amendment, forbidding the manufacture and sale of alcohol. It was thought that this would put a stop to drunkenness and absenteeism from factories. It is worth pointing out, though, that this was not really as drastic a step as it seems. By 1918 two-thirds of the United States was already 'dry' –

Ku Klux Klan Parade 1925

in other words, alcohol was already illegal. What 'Prohibition' in fact achieved was the creation of another social evil. Gangsters soon stepped in to supply illegal 'liquor' – 'bootlegging' was the name given to this trade. The illegal drinks were sold in bars called 'speakeasies'. Al Capone controlled the bootlegging industry in Chicago and may have made as much as $100 million a year from his criminal activities. Many judges, politicians and policemen were on his payroll – bribed to turn a blind eye to his 'business activities'. He was eventually arrested by the Federal Bureau of Investigation for not paying his income tax.

Ku Klux Klan

Even more disturbing than the activities of these gangsters were those of the Ku Klux Klan. The Ku Klux Klan was confined mainly to the southern states where 75% of America's 12 million negroes lived. By 1925 the Klan had 5 million members. Its 'activities' (lynchings, burnings, beatings) were not confined to blacks, either. Hitler would have admired the enthusiasm with which they set about Jews, Communists and Catholics.

However, the United States Congress must take some of the blame for the new climate of racial intolerance which the Klan exploited. In 1917, 1921 and 1924 Congress passed a series of laws designed to cut down immigration from southern and eastern European countries. People from these areas were considered to be of 'inferior stock'. Congress did nothing to prevent the continued discrimination against blacks in the South where the 'Jim Crow' laws stopped them using the same buses, hotels and schools as whites. Many were barred from voting and no black could serve on a jury. All the same, there was some good news for minorities in America. In 1924 Indians were granted full citizenship and then forgotten about on their reservations.

Exercise 2

Source One
German cartoon

a This is a German cartoon of 1927 on the 'World Economic Conference'. What sort of people are
　i　the group at the bottom intended to represent?
　ii　the group at the top intended to represent?
b What do you think the people at the bottom are appealing for? What is the response of the group at the top?
c Why do you think the cartoonist depicted the men at the top on the edge of the cliff face?
d In what ways do you think the cartoon is an accurate prediction of future economic developments?

Roosevelt and the New Deal

Unemployed queuing for bread in New York, 1930. Millions had to rely on charity for basic needs

The depression, after the collapse of the Wall Street stock market, continued to cripple the American economy. As each firm was bankrupted more workers were sacked and forced on to the breadline. They queued at soup kitchens and lived in shanty towns called 'Hoovervilles' because they could no longer afford to pay the rent. As there was no unemployment benefit for them to claim these cardboard and canvas slums became their homes. By 1932 unemployment had reached 12 million – three times what it was in 1930. At least 25% of the workforce had no job. The presidential election of 1932 proved an easy victory for the Democratic candidate, Franklin Delano Roosevelt, over the Republican, Hoover. Hoover's slogans of 'a chicken in every pot', 'a car in every garage' rang hollow to most Americans who believed that Hoover's ideas of self-reliance or 'rugged individualism' would do nothing to improve the economy. Roosevelt, on the other hand, promised vast government expenditure to stimulate demand and create jobs. He vowed that his administration would 'interfere' as much as possible in the economy and provide relief for the poor and out-of-work.

The first 100 days

Roosevelt had promised Americans a 'new deal' and he quickly set about honouring his promise. His programme was to be in three stages. The first was to be 100 days of vigorous activity to tackle immediate problems. Then the First New Deal from 1933 to 1935 would create jobs and set the USA on the road to recovery. The Second New Deal from 1935 to 1939 would be concerned with improving welfare services. Of America's 25 000 banks 10 000 had shut down by 1933. Roosevelt's first aim was to convince Americans that their savings would be safe in the bank. The Emergency Banking Act shut down the weak banks and only allowed the sound ones to reopen. Roosevelt explained the banking system to the people in one of his radio 'fireside chats'. Once again Americans began to invest their savings in the banks. Confidence in the financial system had been restored. The Federal Emergency Relief Act provided $500 million of aid for the unemployed and hungry. It did not provide charity but work. To show that everybody was tightening his belt during the crisis the salaries of state employees were cut by the Economy Act. To encourage a little gaiety Prohibition was abolished.

Exercise 3

Source Two
American cartoon

a Name the man carrying the dustbin and the one walking away.
b What event has just taken place and why is the man on the right shown reading a timetable?
c Explain the reference to three of the items in the dustbin.
d To what extent do you think the optimism shown in the cartoon was proved to be justified?
e What methods does the cartoonist use to show his disapproval of the policies of the man reading the timetable?

The first New Deal

The first New Deal set about creating the hundreds of thousands of jobs that were going to be needed if the economy was to begin working again. The Civilian Conservation Corps (CCC) provided work for young people in the countryside, planting trees and reforesting. By 1940 about 2.5 million young people had spent a six month period with the CCC. The Works Progress Administration (WPA) financed road, school and hospital building as well as dams and bridges. The WPA came under the National Industry Recovery Act which also created the National Recovery Administration. This abolished child labour and set up a minimum wage and an eight-hour day. This legislation was not compulsory for employers but those firms which did not accept the new laws faced government-encouraged boycotts. The Tennessee Valley Authority was one of the biggest schemes. It set up a series of dams along the Tennessee river through seven states to generate hydro-electric power and irrigate the Tennessee valley. Farmers also came in for government assistance in the Agricultural Adjustment Administration (AAA). The AAA subsidised farmers to produce less food. As food became scarcer prices rose and by 1937 the income of farmers had almost doubled. However, the AAA was one of Roosevelt's most controversial measures because it encouraged farmers to produce less food at a time when millions of Americans were still hungry.

The second New Deal

The second New Deal from 1935 helped the poor and unemployed who, in 1935, still numbered 10.6 million. The Social Security Act provided pensions for the old, widowed and maimed. Workers could also contribute, along with the government and employers, to an insurance scheme against unemployment. But there was still no provision for sickness benefit. The Wagner Act gave trade unions the legal right to negotiate wages for their members and their

hours of work and wages were fixed by the Fair Labour Standards Act (1938). The National Housing Act reduced rents and built new homes. The American people were grateful to FDR. He was re-elected in 1936, in 1940 and again in 1944. Even so it must be remembered that he did not end the depression in the USA. In 1940 there were still 8 million unemployed. It did not fall to 1 million until 1943 because of the increase in war-time production.

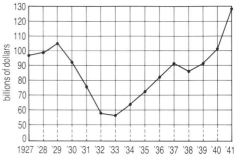

Source Three
(above) *US National Income 1927–41*

Source Four
(below) *US unemployed 1930–40*

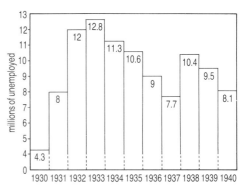

a What was the US national income in the year of the stock-market crash?
b What was the US national income when the depression was in its worst year?
c What can you say about the national income in the years after 1933?
d What year is responsible for disrupting this general pattern?
e Can you give any reason for the dramatic rise in income for 1941?
f Now look at the unemployment graph. Which two years represent the worst period for the increase in the rate of unemployment?
g In what year did unemployment reach its worst level?
h Which year represents a sharp change in the general pattern for unemployment in the years after 1933?

Exercise 5

a Plot both sets of statistics on page 118 on the same graph for 1930–40.
b What can you say, in general, about the relationship between national income and the number of unemployed?
c What evidence can you find in the graph that:
  i 1933 was the worst year for the depression?
  ii the years 1934–37 marked a general improvement in America's economic situation?
  iii 1938 represented the beginning of another depression?
  iv the approach of war pulled the US out of the depression?
d What reasons can you give for the general improvement in the US economy in the years after 1933?

Roosevelt's opponents

Roosevelt remained tremendously popular with ordinary Americans right until his death in 1945. But he got little support from the wealthy businessmen of the United States. They objected to his interference in the way businesses were run; they objected to those of his policies which strengthened trade unions. They also believed that it was the individual's responsibility to ensure that he had enough money for his old age. Government 'hand-outs' in the form of pensions or sickness benefit would lead Americans to lose their rugged, independent spirit. Roosevelt was accused of being a socialist, and many of his supporters, 'New Dealers' as they were called, were treated very badly during the 1950s in the United States and lost their jobs because of 'anti-Communist' witch-hunts. The most serious opposition came from the Supreme Court. The job of the Supreme Court is to make sure that governments do not break the laws of the **Consti-**

tution of the United States. The Supreme Court generally disapproved of Roosevelt's policies and often declared them illegal. This angered Roosevelt so much that he threatened to replace some of the judges with his own supporters. He, after all, had been elected while the judges had not been elected by anyone, so he argued. Fortunately for Roosevelt, the Supreme Court, from 1937, began to take a more favourable view of the New Deal and raised no more opposition. This was just as well as the President did not have the power to sack the judges anyway.

Roosevelt's period of office (1933–45) is a very important one for the United States. He restored the faith of ordinary Americans in their country and its system. As he himself pointed out: 'People who are hungry and are out of a job are the stuff of which dictatorships are made'. His New Deal, far from costing the Americans their freedom, had probably made sure that the USA would remain a **democracy**. Fifteen years after Roosevelt's death, another president, John F. Kennedy, would try to rediscover that same spirit with his 'New Frontier' policy.

Exercise 6

a How did Roosevelt restore faith in the banking system?
b Why was the Agricultural Adjustment Act so controversial?
c What evidence does the text give that Roosevelt's policies were popular with most Americans?
d Which of Roosevelt's policies do you think most angered businessmen?

e What do you think Roosevelt meant by the quotation 'People who are hungry and are out of a job are the stuff of which dictatorships are made.?

f What events in Europe at that time prove the truth of Roosevelt's opinion?

g Would Roosevelt have agreed or disagreed with the view expressed in the cartoon (Source One) about the dangers of wide differences of wealth? Explain your answer.

Source Five (left) ***and Source Six*** (right) *Two contemporary views of the New Deal*

a What sort of people does the cartoon in Source Five claim to benefit?

b Show how Roosevelt's policies tried to ensure that each of the three slogans at the top of the cartoon were carried out.

c Who do you think the figure on the left helping the old man is intended to be?

d How does the cartoonist in Source Six show his opinion that
   i   Roosevelt's efforts to pump life into the economy are failing?
   ii the New Deal is a waste of public money?

e How much money, according to the cartoonist, has already been poured away or is about to be poured away?

f Who, does the cartoon claim, is paying for all this wasted money?

g Which type of people would have agreed with
   i   Source Five?
   ii Source Six?

h Which of the two cartoons, in your opinion, is more effective in putting across its view and why?

Chapter 10

The Thirties: the road to war

The 1920s in Europe were a decade in which the leading powers made reasonable efforts to maintain the peace. The Locarno Pacts of 1925 typify the period. Germany, France, Italy, Belgium, Poland, Czechoslovakia and Britain signed a number of different agreements. The most important was the one signed by Germany, Belgium and France. In this agreement they promised to respect the frontiers that had been laid down at the Treaty of Versailles. Britain and Italy promised to go to the aid of any country attacked by whichever power broke the agreement. However, in the 1930s there was a major change of attitude by three big powers: Italy, Germany and Japan. Each of these nations began a policy of aggressive action which weakened and then finally shattered the peace of Europe and then the world.

In 1931 Japan invaded Manchuria, the northern industrialised province of China. The invasion was a success but its most important result was the feeble response of the League of Nations to this act of aggression. Hitler, not yet in power, took note – as did Mussolini. Once in power, Hitler at first moved cautiously before beginning to put into effect the policies he had openly outlined in *Mein Kampf* in 1924.

Hitler's foreign policy: 1933–39

Hitler's most basic aim was to make Germany a great power. He intended to achieve this by destroying the hated Treaty of Versailles which, along with most Germans, Hitler considered both a humiliation and an insult to Germany's honour. The dismantling of the treaty would allow Germany to regain lost territories such as the Polish Corridor and the full use of the demilitarised Rhineland. But Hitler's ambitions went beyond the Versailles settlement and its destruction. He also wished to bring under German rule all German speakers. The Paris Peace treaties had led to several million Germans finding themselves as minorities in other nations. Hitler intended to bring into his Third Reich the 1 million Germans living in Poland, the 3 million Germans in the Sudetenland area of Czechoslovakia and the 7 million Germans that made up Austria. His long-term plans were more ambitious. Because the Germans were a master Aryan race Hitler believed that they were entitled to conquer extra 'living space' or *Lebensraum*. So called 'inferior races' like the Poles and Russians would be cleared from their fertile lands and 're-

Japanese troops enter Manchuria, 1931

settled' or simply used as slave labour. Fertile areas like the Ukrainian wheat fields could be put to use to feed Germany's armies, and Russia's oilfields in the Caucasus would help to transport them. No less importantly, the conquest of the Soviet Union would also bring about the destruction of 'Jewish **Bolshevism**'.

1933–36: cautious advance

Germany in 1933 was still a weak power in military terms and Hitler had to make slow, cautious progress towards fulfilling his ambitions. He began by withdrawing from the World Disarmament Conference and the League of Nations within his first year in power. At the same time he declared that Germany was more than happy to disarm as long as everyone else did as well. This policy of acting agressively and then making peaceful statements to soothe the fear of Britain and France is one which Hitler followed time and time again. Time and time again Britain and, to a lesser extent, France allowed themselves to believe Hitler's promises of good intentions. They did so because they were desperate for peace. Hitler knew this and ruthlessly exploited their willingness to reach a peaceful settlement with Germany. Another aspect of Hitler's foreign policy was his ability to do the unexpected. This unpredictablity showed itself in January 1934 with a ten year non-aggression pact with Poland. Hitler's anger over the loss of the Polish Corridor in 1919 was seemingly forgotten. This pact prised away from France her most important ally in Eastern Europe and threatened the stability of the Little **Entente** (a series of agreements between the small East European states of Czechoslovakia, Yugoslavia and Rumania with each other and with France against Germany).

The murder of Dollfuss

1934 also saw a more ambitious move by Hitler. It was his only real set-back in the years before the outbreak of war. The *Anschluss*, or union, with Austria's 7 million Germans was a project dear to Hitler's heart – the more so because Hitler was also an Austrian. Austrian Nazis, encouraged by Hitler, staged a revolt and murdered the Austrian Chancellor, Dollfuss. Whatever Hitler's plans were, Mussolini put a stop to them by sending troops to the border with Austria with orders to move against German troops if they crossed over the border into Austria. Mussolini was furious because only a month earlier Hitler had promised to respect Austria's independence. Mussolini raged at the 'savage barbarism' of Nazism and then had to break the news of Dollfuss' murder to the Austrian's family who were Mussolini's guests at the time.

Collapse of the Stresa Front

In January 1935 the Saar was returned to Germany after a **plebiscite** resulted in 90% of the Saar's inhabitants voting in favour of union with Germany. This was a step in accordance with the Treaty of Versailles but his next, in March 1935, was not. Hitler announced that Germany would rearm and set a target of 600 000 troops – six times the limit laid down by the treaty. This led to the setting up of the Stresa Front in April 1935 in which Italy, Britain and France agreed to oppose any further violations of Versailles.

However the spirit of Stresa was short-lived. It was snuffed out by Britain two months later with the signing of the Anglo–German Naval Agreement, and its early death was confirmed by Mussolini's invasion of Abyssinia in October 1935 (see Chapter 5, page 77, for further details.) In the Anglo-German agreement Britain agreed that Germany should be allowed a navy 35% the size of the British fleet. Not only was this a breach of the Versailles

Italian Blackshirts in Abyssinia in 1936

Treaty, which Britain had promised to safeguard at Stresa, but it was also signed without consulting France or Italy. It was, by chance, the 120th anniversary of the Battle of Waterloo. Hitler had skilfully driven a wedge between Europe's two major democracies and France was already seeking security elsewhere. In May 1935 France and Russia had signed a treaty, promising to assist one another in case of attack. It was followed by another in which both promised to assist Czechoslovakia – though Russia would only do so if France did so first.

Exercise 1

a Apart from 70 million Germans in Germany, where else were Germans to be found in Europe?

b Why did Britain allow herself to be taken in by Hitler's promises of good intentions?

c Why was Hitler's non-aggression pact with Poland such a surprise?

d What does the effectiveness of Mussolini's action over Austria in 1934 indicate might have been one way of dealing with Hitler?

e Describe Hitler's techniques of foreign policy in the years up to 1936.

1936–39: full speed ahead

Mussolini's invasion of Abyssinia in October 1935 and the feeble response to it of the League of Nations and Britain and France convinced Hitler that his next step would not meet with any serious opposition. He ordered a token force of German troops to march into the Rhineland – an area demilitarised at Versailles – in March 1936. Should the French oppose the move, the troops were under orders to beat a retreat. In other words, the whole exercise was a gigantic bluff. This reflects another of Hitler's methods of foreign policy – the ability to bluff and intimidate his opponents into defeat. He was convinced that Britain would not respond. The coming to the throne of Edward VIII further encouraged him since the King was known to support many of Germany's ambitions. To most Britons Germany was merely 'going into their own back garden'. France saw it differently and appealed to Britain for support in defence of the Treaty of Versailles. Baldwin, the British Prime Minister, made it clear that there would be no British military assistance. The French tanks, sent to the border with Germany, stayed put. The French could probably have driven the Germans out of the Rhineland. The truth of the matter was that they were no more willing to make a stand over the Rhineland than the British. Hitler's instincts had been proved right. The remilitarisation of the Rhineland was a turning point for Hitler's foreign policy. He was now convinced of Britain's weakness and knew that the French were powerless without British backing. His new friendship with Italy as a result of Germany's support for

Mussolini's invasion of Abyssinia further strengthened Hitler's hand – now there would be no opposition from Italy over the Anschluss with Austria.

Exercise 2

A *Punch* cartoon, February 1936

TROUBLE AMONG THE LOCARNO "QUINS."

Source One

a Identify, from left to right, four of the five nations which made up the 'Locarno quins'.

b What do the letters 'F.R.' on the figure in the middle represent? Why is she shown clutching a 'Russian' teddy bear?

c Explain the significance of the figure in the foreground attempting to strangle the doll, 'Abyssinia'.

d Over what issue is the sitting figure threatening the little girl in the middle? (Remember the date of the cartoon.)

e What action did the little boy take to settle the dispute the month following this cartoon?

f How would you describe the attitude to the quarrel of the figure wearing a hat in the background? Did this prove an accurate prediction of this nation's attitude to events in the following month?

Anschluss: 1938

For the time being Hitler was content with the success of the remilitarisation of the Rhineland and the tremendous popularity it brought him in Germany. A firm alliance was signed with Italy in October 1936, the 'Rome–Berlin Axis'. Both agreed to send assistance to General Franco's rebel forces in the Spanish Civil War. This conflict had broken out in July of that year when Franco led a rebellion against Spain's elected Republican Government, a government backed by **socialists** and **Communists**. A prolonged war in Spain would help distract attention from Hitler's plans elsewhere in Europe and neither Hitler nor Mussolini wished to see a Communist-backed government triumph in Spain. While Italy and Germany were soon sending substantial aid to Franco, Britain and France agreed on 'non-intervention' which meant allowing Spain's elected government to fall to another right-wing dictator. Hitler also struck up an agreement with another militaristic power in late 1936 – Japan. Both these nations signed the Anti-Comintern Pact in which they pledged to stop the spread of Communism and the activities of the Communist International (the Comintern).

The year 1937 saw further developments in Hitler's favour. Japan launched a full-scale invasion of China – an event which should have been of grave concern to Britain. It certainly worried the Americans, and President Roosevelt suggested to Chamberlain, the new British Prime Minister, that Britain and the United States set up a naval blockade of Japan. Chamberlain refused to co-operate and, instead, stepped up his policy of '**appeasement**'. Chamberlain believed that Hitler should be treated favourably and his demands, where reasonable, agreed to. In this way, Hitler would learn that sensible negotiation and not confrontation was the way to settle disputes. With Britain firmly committed to appeasement under the leadership of Neville Chamberlain, described by Hitler as a 'little human worm', the German dictator directed his thoughts to the Anschluss.

Schuschnigg abandoned

In February 1938 the Austrian Chancellor, Schuschnigg, was summoned to Hitler's mountain retreat at Berchtesgaden. Hitler demanded the release of Austrian Nazis gaoled by the Chancellor. Furthermore, Seyss-Inquart, an Austrian Nazi, was to be made Minister of Interior. Schuschnigg, bullied and threatened, meekly agreed. This only served to encourage the Austrian Nazis who continued to clash with anti-Nazi Austrian patriots. Schuschnigg decided to hold a plebiscite in March on whether Austrians wished to remain an independent state or unite with Germany. Hitler could not allow this to take place since defeat for the Anschluss would deprive him of his propaganda claim that the Austrians wanted to join with the Third Reich. Hitler decided that the time had come to strike. He demanded the resignation of Schuschnigg and his replacement by Seyss-Inquart and the cancellation of the plebiscite. Schuschnigg appealed for help to Italy and Britain. Mussolini, firmly tied to Hitler, offered no assistance. Chamberlain replied that His Majesty's Government 'are unable to guarantee protection' to Austria. Schuschnigg resigned. On 12 March German troops rolled across the border in answer to an appeal from Seyss-Inquart to help restore order. Hitler had returned to his native Austria as triumphant ruler.

Hitler driving through Vienna after the Anschluss. Hitler's plebiscite after the Anschluss claimed 99.75% in favour of union with Germany

---

Exercise ▬ 3

a Why was the occupation of the Rhineland a 'gigantic bluff'?
b How did the remilitarisation reveal the division between Britain and France?
c Why did Hitler intervene on the side of Franco in the Spanish Civil War?
d What was the idea behind appeasement?
e Why, in your opinion, was Hitler's Anschluss with Austria achieved so easily?

Czechoslovakia recedes into the darkness

'It is my unshakable will to wipe Czechoslovakia off the map ...' Hitler declared to a top level Nazi meeting at the end of May, 1938. The international situation favoured such a move. He was convinced that Britain and France would not act forcefully against him, and Italy had indicated her approval. That left only Russia, and between Russia and Czechoslovakia stood Rumania and Poland. Both these states had made it clear they would not allow Russian troops across their territory. Besides, Russia was only committed to defend the Czechs if France did so as well.

Konrad Henlein, the leader of the Sudeten German Nazis in the Sudetenland area of Czechoslovakia, was told to step up his campaign of anti-government activities, claiming that the Sudeten Germans were being ill-treated by the Czech leader, Benes.

Chamberlain arrives at Munich airport for the Peace Conference, accompanied here by Hitler (left) and Ribbentrop (right)

Chamberlain decided to fly to Hitler's mountain retreat at Berchtesgaden to discuss the Sudeten question on 15 September. Hitler demanded that a plebiscite be held in the Sudetenland and that those areas voting for union with Germany should be transferred. Chamberlain returned to London to seek the approval of his Cabinet and the French Prime Minister, Daladier. Benes also, reluctantly, agreed to the plebiscite.

When Chamberlain met Hitler again at Godesberg on 22 September he was astounded to hear that the plebiscite was no longer enough. Hitler demanded the immediate transfer of the whole of the Sudetenland. Hitler had once again shown that when given an inch he would take a mile. Chamberlain was angry and refused to agree. War seemed likely. The Czechs had already mobilised their large and well equipped army which numbered some 2 million men and was only just smaller than Germany's at this time. Britain's fleet was also mobilised for war. Hitler seemed shaken by this show of strength and when Mussolini suggested a meeting at Munich for 29 September with Chamberlain, Daladier and the two **dictators**, Hitler quickly agreed. The meeting rapidly decided that the evacuation of the Sudetenland should begin on 1 October and that the area would be occupied by Germany. It was just as Hitler had demanded. Benes, when informed of the decision, resigned. The new Czech leader put the situation in a nutshell: 'It was a choice between a reduction of our territory and the death of the nation'. Chamberlain returned to Britain a hero for having guaranteed 'peace for our time'. The fate of the 'vile race of dwarfs', as Goering described the Czechs, was quietly forgotten. Hitler announced that the Sudetenland was his last territorial demand in Europe. Six months later in March 1939 German troops occupied the rest of Czechoslovakia.

Exercise 4

Munich – a comparison of views

Extract One: **Churchill's speech in the house of Commons, September 1938**

All is over. Czechoslovakia recedes into the darkness. She has suffered in every respect from her association with the Western democracies. She has suffered in particular from her association with France. I think you will find that in a period of time which may be measured by years, but may be
5 measured only by months, Czechoslovakia will be engulfed in the Nazi regime. When I think of the fair hopes of a long peace which still lay before Europe at the beginning of 1933, when Herr Hitler obtained power, and all the opportunities of arresting the growth of Nazi power, I cannot believe that a parallel exists in the whole of history. We are in the
10 presence of a disaster of the first magnitude which has befallen Great Britain and France.

Extract Two: **Historian A.J.P. Taylor**

President Benes believed that Hitler was bluffing and would give way if faced with a firm, united opposition. When Hitler did not give way, even Benes in the last resort preferred surrender to war. The Czechs, Benes held, were a small people, who must preserve their lives for a better
5 future. Their country had been occupied before and they had survived. They would survive again. In a sense, his arguments were justified by events. The Czechs were abandoned by the Western powers. Their country fell under German tyranny for six years. But only one or perhaps two hundred thousand of them lost their lives. Prague, their capital was the
10 only great city of Central Europe to remain undamaged in the Second World War, and Czechoslovakia emerged with unbroken spirit, at the end. In contrast, Poland was guaranteed by the Western powers, who went to war for her sake. As a result six million Poles were killed. Warsaw was reduced to a heap of ruins, and Poland, though restored, lost much of her
15 territory and of her independence.
(*Purnell's History of the 20th Century*, Vol. 12)

Source Two
Swiss cartoon, 1938

a Which country does Churchill single out for blame for the result of the Munich conference?

b Suggest one occasion which Churchill might have considered an opportunity of 'arresting the growth of Nazi power' before 1938.

c How good a prophet did Churchill prove to be on Czechoslovakia's fate?

d Which of these two extracts would you describe as being in favour of Chamberlain's policy of appeasement at Munich? Explain your answer.

e Source Two features the word '*Pax*' meaning peace in Latin. What point is the cartoon making on the events at Munich?

g With which of the two written extracts is the cartoon in agreement? Give reasons for your answer.

Exercise 5

Munich – your view

Most public opinion in Britain welcomed Chamberlain's action at Munich. The opinion of Winston Churchill, quoted in Extract One, was in the minority – though today it is easy to claim that he was right to denounce the Munich Agreement. Write an article or a radio or film commentary of Chamberlain's return to Heston airport, making clear your support or opposition to the agreement just reached at Munich. Be careful to include only details and facts known at that time.

Stalin's earlobes ... and cigarette: the Nazi–Soviet pact

The occupation of the rest of Czechoslovakia had only been a matter of time. The loss of the Sudetenland not only stripped the Czechs of 70% of their industry but also of the most modern defensive fortifications in Europe. With the Sudetenland also went the largest arms factory in Europe, the Skoda Works. When German troops marched into the rest of the country, supposedly 'by invitation' of the Czech President Hacha, Chamberlain at last realised that Hitler was not a man of his word and could not be trusted. In April both Britain and France promised to assist Poland if attacked by Germany. Hitler now demanded that Poland hand over the German-speaking port of Danzig and access to it by road and rail. The Poles refused.

Hitler was merely biding his time before invading the country. He stepped up claims of Polish ill-treatment of Germans in the Corridor and began negotiations with Russia on a non-aggression pact. The Russians had lost patience with the West. Negotiations with Britain had been dragging on since May before the Germans arrived in Moscow. The Russians were willing to have a military alliance with Britain and France against Germany but the British were making only half-hearted efforts to reach agreement. To the astonishment of the world, on 24 August 1939, the Russian Foreign Minister, Molotov, and his Nazi opposite number, Ribbentrop, announced the signing of the Nazi–Soviet Non-Agression Pact in which both countries promised not to fight each other for 10 years. A secret clause, not made public, also revealed that both Germany and Russia were to invade and divide

Tearful Czechs forced to salute the Nazi take-over of the rest of Czechoslovakia in March 1939

SOMEONE IS TAKING SOMEONE FOR A WALK

The Nazi–Soviet Pact. David Low, the cartoonist, was quick to spot the real mistrust behind the pact

Poland between them. Hitler was over-joyed as he now had a free hand in Poland. He carefully scrutinised the press photographs of the signing ceremony before release. He examined Stalin's earlobes to check whether they were 'ingrown and Jewish or separate and Aryan'. According to the earlobe test Stalin was not a Jew. However, Stalin did have a cigarette dangling from his lips in every photograph and Hitler had them all painted out because it did not add dignity to such an import-ant occasion.

With Russia out of the picture as far as opposition was concerned, that left only 'the worm' Chamberlain and the French. Hitler never believed that Britain and France would honour their promise to defend Poland. After all, they had backed down over **rearma-ment**, over the Rhineland in 1936, over the Anschluss and the Sudetenland in 1938 and over Czechoslovakia in 1939. Why would Poland be any different?

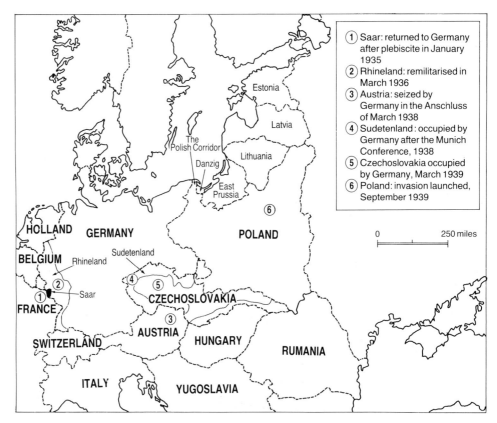

① Saar: returned to Germany after plebiscite in January 1935
② Rhineland: remilitarised in March 1936
③ Austria: seized by Germany in the Anschluss of March 1938
④ Sudetenland: occupied by Germany after the Munich Conference, 1938
⑤ Czechoslovakia occupied by Germany, March 1939
⑥ Poland: invasion launched, September 1939

The expansion of Nazi Germany 1935–39

Exercise
▆▆▆▆ 6

a Why was it difficult for the Russians to come to the aid of Czechoslovakia by military means in 1938?

b How did Hitler step up his demands over the Sudetenland to Chamberlain?

c Why do you think Hitler readily agreed to Mussolini's suggestion of a conference at Munich?

d Why do you think the Russians decided to go for an agreement with the Nazis in August 1939?

e What evidence is there that Hitler miscalculated over the reaction to his attack on Poland?

Why did war break out?

Once again there are as many views about the real causes of this war as there are historians. Most put the blame squarely on Hitler and his plans of conquest. They argue that Hitler had always planned a major war against Russia and that the conquest of Poland was just a preliminary. If Hitler's other aims, such as the inclusion of German speakers inside the Third Reich, had been his real objective then he should have settled for just the Polish Corridor and Danzig in September 1939 – areas where there were indeed Germans. But his invasion plans were for the whole of Poland.

Other historians argue that Hitler would never have launched an invasion of Poland if he had been convinced that Britain and France would have stood up to him. For this reason they claim some of the blame must be placed on the appeasers, like Chamberlain, for continually giving way to Hitler. Some defenders of Chamberlain have written that he was merely playing for time at Munich in order to build up Britain's armed forces. If this is true then Czechoslovakia would have made a much better ally than Poland did 12 months later. Czechoslovakia was militarily strong and had a very sound defensive position in the Sudetenland. Poland had none of these advantages and in this sense was the wrong country over which to go to war with Germany. Furthermore, Czechoslovakia was a democracy whereas Poland was a military dictatorship. To go to war on behalf of one military dictatorship (Poland) against another (Germany) never had the same appeal to moral values that a defence of Czechoslovakia would have had.

The most forceful defence of Chamberlain and Munich has come from A. J. P. Taylor. In his book *The Origins of the Second World War*, Taylor wrote:

> The settlement at Munich was a triumph for British policy . . . not a triumph for Hitler . . . It was a triumph for all that was best and enlightened in British life; a triumph for those that preached equal justice between peoples; a triumph for those who had courageously denounced the harshness and short-sightedness of Versailles, Brailsford . . . wrote in 1920 of the peace settlement: 'The worst offence was the subjection of three million Germans to Czech rule'. This was the offence redressed at Munich.

German forces poured across the border into Poland at 4.15 am on 1 September. Hitler was confident that this too would be an easy campaign. Britain and France would make loud noises of protest, he claimed, and then would let the matter drop. Two days later, on

Sunday, 3 September, Britain and France stood by their promise to Poland and declared war on Germany. Clearly, Poland was going to be 'different'.

THE DAILY MIRROR — Page 10 — Monday, September 4, 1939

WANTED!

FOR MURDER . . . FOR KIDNAPPING . . . FOR THEFT AND FOR ARSON

ADOLF HITLER
ALIAS
Adolf Schicklegruber, Adol, Hittler or Hidler

Last heard of in Berlin, September 3, 1939. Aged fifty, height 5ft. 8½in., dark hair, frequently brushes one lock over left forehead. Blue eyes. Sallow complexion, stout build, weighs about 11st. 3lb. Suffering from acute monomania, with periodic fits of melancholia. Frequently bursts into tears when crossed. Harsh, guttural voice, and has a habit of raising right hand to shoulder level. DANGEROUS!

Can be recognised full face by habitual scowl. Rarely smiles. Talks rapidly, and when angered screams like a child.

Profile from a recent photograph. Black moustache. Jowl inclines to fatness. Wide nostrils. Deep-set, menacing eyes.

FOR MURDER Wanted for the murder of over a thousand of his fellow countrymen on the night of the Blood Bath, June 30, 1934. Wanted for the murder of countless political opponents in concentration camps.

He is indicted for the murder of Jews, Germans, Austrians, Czechs, Spaniards and Poles. He is now urgently wanted for homicide against citizens of the British Empire.

Hitler is a gunman who shoots to kill. He acts first and talks afterwards.

No appeals to sentiment can move him. This gangster, surrounded by armed hoodlums, is a natural killer. The reward for his apprehension, dead or alive, is the peace of mankind.

FOR KIDNAPPING Wanted for the kidnapping of Dr. Kurt Schuschnigg, late Chancellor of Austria. Wanted for the kidnapping of Pastor Niemoller, a heroic martyr who was not afraid to put God before Hitler. Wanted for the attempted kidnapping of Dr. Benes, late President of Czechoslovakia. The kidnapping tendencies of this established criminal are marked and violent. The symptoms before an attempt are threats, blackmail and ultimatums. He offers his victims the alternatives of complete surrender or timeless incarceration in the horrors of concentration camps.

FOR THEFT Wanted for the larceny of eighty millions of Czech gold in March, 1939. Wanted for the armed robbery of material resources of the Czech State. Wanted for the stealing of Memelland. Wanted for robbing mankind of peace, of humanity, and for the attempted assault on civilisation itself. This dangerous lunatic masks his raids by spurious appeals to honour, to patriotism and to duty. At the moment when his protestations of peace and friendship are at their most vehement, he is most likely to commit his smash and grab.

His tactics are known and easily recognised. But Europe has already been wrecked and plundered by the depredations of this armed thug who smashes in without scruple.

FOR ARSON Wanted as the incendiary who started the Reichstag fire on the night of February 27, 1933. This crime was the key point, and the starting signal for a series of outrages and brutalities that are unsurpassed in the records of criminal degenerates. As a direct and immediate result of this calculated act of arson, an innocent dupe, Van der Lubbe, was murdered in cold blood. But as an indirect outcome of this carefully-planned offence, Europe itself is ablaze. The fires that this man has kindled cannot be extinguished until he himself is apprehended—dead or alive!

THIS RECKLESS CRIMINAL IS WANTED—DEAD OR ALIVE!

A 'Wanted' poster from the Daily Mirror, *4 September 1939*

Exercise 7

A Russian view

Study Source Three on page 132. The signpost arm pointing to the left reads 'Western Europe' and the other arm reads 'USSR'.

a Identify the two countries represented by the policemen.

b Which country is represented by the car? Name two of the occupants.

c In which direction are the policemen pointing the car? What is their purpose, according to the cartoonist, in doing this?

d Given that the policeman with the moustache is intended to be Chamberlain, explain why the year of the cartoon's publication cannot have been
   i   before 1937;
   ii after 24 August, 1939.

e In general what view of the Western powers' attitude to Russia is the cartoon trying to get across? Is there, in your opinion, any justification for the Soviet view about the attitude of the countries represented by the policemen?

Source Three
Russian cartoon

Chapter 11

Aspects of the Second World War: 1 From Poland to the Blitz

On 1 September 1939 the German invasion of Poland began. It came as a surprise to few people. The British and French had made a commitment to defend Poland after Hitler had seized all of Czechoslovakia in March of that year. For once this guarantee was honoured and Britain and France declared war on Germany on 3 September. The Poles were jubilant, confident that the Germans could now be defeated. Within four weeks the Polish army had been crushed at the cost of just 8000 German dead. The British and French had barely fired a shot in anger. What had happened?

Blitzkrieg

The short answer is '**blitzkrieg**'. This new type of warfare means 'lightning war'. It was based on the speed of the tank and motorised infantry. The stages of a blitzkrieg attack were as follows. First, the enemy headquarters and communications centres would be bombed and shelled by long range artillery and dive-bombers. Parachutists would be dropped behind enemy lines to cause further chaos and panic. Second, the armoured spearhead of tanks and infantry in vehicles would punch a hole in the weakest part of the enemy frontline. The strong-points of the enemy position would be encircled in the third stage by troops following up the attack, cutting the enemy off from any reinforcements and forcing them to surrender. In the meantime the motorised columns would drive their way at rapid speed through the surprised and demoralised enemy troops. The Germans had understood that the tank should be treated as a vital and independent weapon and not a weapon to be used to support slow moving infantry – as the French believed. The diagrams below and on page 134 show the major differences between French and German thinking at this time.

The German blitzkrieg was not the only problem the Poles had to deal with. In the middle of September the Russians, as agreed in the Nazi–Soviet Pact, struck at Poland too. Stalin wanted his

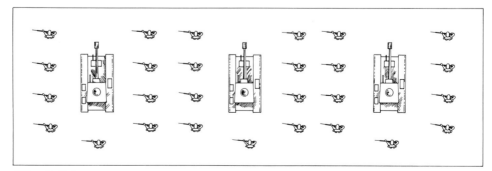

Source One

French tactics in the Second World War: tanks dispersed among infantry

(After P. F. Speed 'A Coursebook in Modern World History')

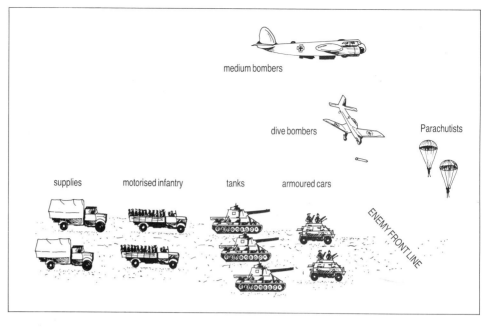

Source Two

German tactics
(Blitzkrieg) in the
Second World War
(After P.F. Speed)

share of the spoils. Faced with such a task the Polish army soon collapsed. The RAF did drop 18 million leaflets over Germany but the actual bombing of Germany was ruled out because it would have meant the destruction of 'private property'! (By July 1940 the mood of the British had changed drastically as Churchill ordered the Royal Navy to sink the French fleet, after France's surrender, to stop her ships falling into German hands. At least 1300 French sailors died.) By the time France's large conscript army had fully mobilised, the Polish campaign was over anyway and the Germans had a good defensive position along the 90 mile stretch along the border where the French would have been able to attack.

Exercise 1

a What was the basic idea behind the strategy of the blitzkrieg?
b How did the second stage of the blitzkrieg strategy make sure that the attack would maintain its speed?
c What two points can be made to explain France's inactivity during the Polish campaign?
d Look at Sources One and Two and explain the major differences between French and German tactics at the start of the war.

The 'phoney war': October 1939 – April 1940

The British Expeditionary Force (BEF) did not suffer a single casualty until December 1939. This period from the fall of Poland until the invasion of Norway is known as the 'phoney war' because there was no fighting on land at all – though there were several bitter naval engagements. The tension in Britain began to ease. Children, evacuated from London in the early days of September, began to return. People stopped walking about carrying their gas masks.

Churchill, the First Lord of the Admiralty and in charge of the Royal Navy, was determined to strike at Germany somehow. He drew up a plan to seize the port of Narvik in neutral Norway. Through this port 80% of Germany's iron ore arrived from Sweden by rail. During the winter months the Gulf of Bothnia freezes up and the ore had to be taken to Narvik for eventual shipment to Germany. Chamberlain hesitated. He was afraid Britain might lose world sympathy by attacking a neutral state. Hitler was aware of the threat and on 9 April 1940 he launched an invasion of Norway and neutral Denmark. British and French troops were rushed over to help the Norwegians but in May they were forced to withdraw. The Germans had secured their iron ore supplies and now controlled the Norwegian fjords which would provide excellent bases for attacks on British shipping. Although some serious damage had been inflicted on the German navy the campaign was a blow to morale. Chamberlain, who months earlier had boasted that Hitler 'had missed the bus', was forced to resign as Prime Minister on 10 May. He was succeeded by Churchill. On the same day Germany launched an invasion of Holland, Belgium and France.

The evacuation at Dunkirk, Operation Dynamo

The fall of France

The British and French generals were convinced that they were about to fight a repetition of the First World War. They expected the main German attack through Belgium and that is where the bulk of the BEF and France's few mobile armoured units were sent. It was going to be the Schlieffen Plan Mark Two. That was exactly what Hitler wanted the Allies to think. Holland surrendered after four days and Belgium, backed by the finest Allied troops, fought on. The French were confident that their Maginot Line of underground forts and gun emplacements would hold off any German attacks further south. The only possible gap was the Ardennes forest region – but that was impassable to tanks. General Rundstedt, with 45 divisions massed on the other side of the Ardennes, had different ideas. Against this overwhelming force stood two poor French divisions. Supported by hundreds of Stuka dive bombers, Guderian's XIX *Panzer* Corps (Tank army) crashed through the French line at Sedan on 12 May. The French tanks, spread thinly and grouped in small numbers, were swept aside as Guderian raced for the Channel coast. In eight days he covered 151 miles, trapping one-third of the French army and the BEF's 10 divisions. Nearly 340 000 Allied troops were penned in around the port of Dunkirk. Hitler decided not to use his tanks in a costly assault in unsuitable built-up terrain. The *Luftwaffe* (the German Air Force) pounded the beaches for nine days. Many bombs failed to explode in the soft sand. Almost the entire BEF of 200 000 men and 140 000 French troops were evacuated in 'Operation Dynamo' between 27 May and 4 June.

Once the best of the Allied troops were out of the fighting it was only a matter of time before the rest of General Weygand's army collapsed. Paris fell on 14 June and finally on 22

June the French signed an armistice in the same railway carriage in which the Germans had surrendered in 1918. Marshall Petain, the hero of Verdun in 1916, became Prime Minister of a new government prepared to work with the Nazis from the town of Vichy.

Why did France fall?

The evacuation of 340 000 troops from under the noses of the Germans was the only bright point in what was really a military disaster. Of the British troops 68 000 had been killed, wounded or captured. Over 90 000 rifles, 475 tanks, 1000 heavy guns, 400 anti-tank guns and 7000 tons of ammunition were left behind. The losses would take between three and six months to make up. Why had the French collapsed so quickly? General Gamelin had tried to blame 'inferiority of numbers, inferiority of equipment, inferiority of method'. Only the last point has any truth to it. French numbers matched those of the Germans, and their equipment, especially the excellent French tanks, also equalled the Germans. But they had the wrong strategy and the wrong mentality, convinced they were safe behind their Maginot Line.

Some Frenchmen, like Petain and Laval, who led the Vichy Regime, also believed that a defeat by Germany was a fair price to pay for the end of Reynaud's hated government. Reynaud, made Prime Minister in March 1940, had been a bitter opponent of Petain's policies as Minister of War during the 1930s. With northern France under Nazi occupation and the south in the hands of Petain's Vichy Government Britain stood alone and prepared for the expected invasion.

Exercise 2

a Why was Narvik so important to the Allies and Germany?
b What error of judgement did the Allied generals make when the Germans began their invasion of France, Belgium and Holland?
c How did Hitler take the Allies totally by surprise?
d In what sense was 'Operation Dynamo' a 'miracle' as well as a disaster?
e Write a 20-line confidential report for Churchill on the military lessons to be learnt from the fall of France and what changes ought to be made inside the British High Command's thinking. Comment on the effectiveness of the *blitzkrieg* tactics and the inappropriate tactics of the French concerning the use of tanks. (You might find it helpful to study Exercise 3 first.)

Exercise 3

Map work

Copy the map of the Invasion of the West (Source Three) into your book. The 29 divisions under General Bock (Army Group B) were to be the decoy attack which was to draw the Allied troops into Belgium. In the meantime, the major offensive was to come further south from Rundstedt's Army Group A (45 divisions).

a Using bold arrows mark in the following routes taken by Group B on your map:
i one attack on Amsterdam along the northern Dutch coast;
ii one attack on The Hague;
iii one attack on Rotterdam from the south;
iv one attack on Brussels across the Albert Canal.

Source Three
*Invasion of the West
10–20 May 1940*

b Using the same method now mark
   in the routes of Army Group A's
   assault:
   i   one attack between Namur and
       Sedan through the Ardennes
       forest towards Cambrai;
   ii one attack by Guderian's XIX
       Panzer Corps through Sedan,
       then Amiens, Abbeville and on to
       Boulogne.
c Using a small semi-circle mark in
   the Allied perimeter defence ring
   around Dunkirk which held off the
   Germans while the evacuation took
   place.
d How does the map illustrate the
   failure of the Maginot Line?

The Battle of Britain: July–October 1940

Hitler now turned his attention to
Britain. A plan, 'Operation Sealion', was
drawn up for the invasion of Britain. For
a seaborne invasion to take place the
Germans had first to eliminate the RAF
as air power was the only real threat to a
German invasion. (The Royal Navy
could not operate in the narrow waters
of the Channel at the mercy of the
Luftwaffe's planes and the deadly U-
boats and torpedo boats.) The Battle of
Britain was a battle for control of the
skies and the fate of Britain and Europe.

The Fighter Battle

Numerically the odds seemed in favour
of the Luftwaffe. The Germans had
nearly 2500 aircraft available: 969 bombers; 336 Stuka dive bombers; 869

ME 109 fighters and 268 twin engined
ME 110 fighter bombers. Against this
the RAF pitched 820 fighters – the bombers played no role in the battle.
However, these statistics only tell a part
of the story. There were several factors
which helped to shift the balance towards the British. First of all, the
Luftwaffe's bombers were not a threat
to the RAF's fighters, neither were the
Stukas or really the ME 110 fighter-
bombers – the last two types were far
too slow and cumbersome to take on a
Spitfire or a Hurricane. As far as fighters were concerned the two sides
were evenly matched. The Spitfire was
probably the best fighter of its time. It
was faster than the ME 109 and had a
more effective fire power. But the
German fighter was rather faster and
more manœuvrable than the Hurricane
– which made up about two-thirds of the
RAF's fighter strength. Most of the
German pilots were very experienced,

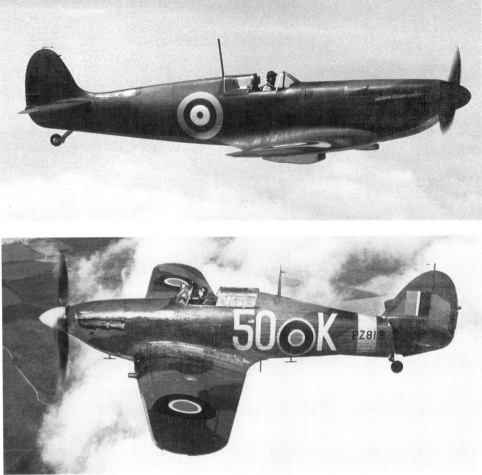

Spitfire (above) and Hurricane (below) fighters of the Battle of Britain: the Hurricanes took on the role of attacking German bombers while the Spitfires tackled the ME 109s. Of the 48 fighter squadrons in August 1940, 29 were Hurricane squadrons

having fought in the defeats of Poland and France; some had served in the Spanish Civil War as well. One serious handicap for the German fighter pilots was that they only had about 20 minutes flying time over south-east England because of fuel limits. This limited their manœuvrability. However, the use of radar greatly aided the RAF because it meant they could concentrate their fighters to intercept the German raiders in large numbers at the right spot without wasting time looking for the enemy.

Exercise 4

Assessing the odds

In order to get a clearer picture of the strengths of the Luftwaffe and the RAF divide your page into columns like this:

	RAF	Luftwaffe
Aircraft numbers:	—	—
Fighter quality:	—	—
Pilot quality:	—	—
Fuel restrictions:	—	—
Value of Radar:	—	—
TOTAL:	—	—

Give each of the two sides a mark out of ten for each of the five scoring areas. Then add up the respective totals to see which of the two, on paper, should have won. Which one of the five areas, in your opinion, was the most important in deciding the outcome of the battle?

The five stages of the Battle of Britain

At first, Goering, the commander of the Luftwaffe, concentrated his attacks on Channel shipping and the ports (10 July – 7 August). During this stage the RAF concentrated on building up its fighter strength – production reached 500 a month in July. From 8 until 23 August the Germans wisely concentrated on bombing radar stations and forward fighter bases. This was a severe test as the fighters were often unable to use their damaged bases. The radar masts proved very difficult to destroy and Goering, fortunately, soon gave up trying to knock them out. During the third phase (24 August – 6 September) the Luftwaffe struck at inland fighter bases and, very crucially, aircraft factories. Had Goering persisted with this tactic there is little doubt that the RAF would soon have been unable to get enough fighters in the air. However, Goering once again grew impatient and from 7 to 30 September he attempted to bomb London into submission. This was partly in revenge for a British raid on Berlin on 25 August. It gave the RAF time to repair their bases and get fighter numbers up again. The climax of the whole battle took place on 15 September when Goering launched one final massive air assault in which 60 German planes were shot down. The 'Blitz' on London went on for 57 nights in a row but Hitler knew the battle was over and on 17 September 'Operation Sealion' was postponed indefinitely. The 'Blitz' continued right through the last stage of the battle until 31 October.

Radar beacons – difficult targets for the Luftwaffe

Exercise 5

a Why was the Battle of Britain really an air and not a sea battle?
b Why did the Luftwaffe have less of an advantage – despite their numerical superiority of planes?
c What three errors of judgement did Goering make during the battle?
d Why could 7 September be seen as the real turning point of the battle?

Exercise 6

Counting the cost

Aircraft losses: the RAF figures are fighters only; the Luftwaffe totals include fighters and bombers:

	RAF	Luftwaffe
10 July – 7 Aug.	169	192
8 – 23 Aug.	303	403
23 Aug. – 6 Sept.	262	378
7 – 30 Sept.	380	435
1 – 30 Oct.	265	325

a Total up the losses for each side. (Of the RAF pilots shot down 414 were killed.)

b Why are the figures for German aircraft losses slightly misleading?

c In which period did the battle reach its peak for aircraft losses?

d Was this period, in your opinion, also the most decisive one? If so, why, and if not, which stage of the battle was the most important in eventually deciding who won the battle?

e Why do you think the figures for the numbers of RAF pilots killed are more important than the numbers of planes shot down?

f Explain why the Luftwaffe pilots shot down, even if uninjured, were unlikely to play any further part in the battle.

Exercise 7

The Propaganda War

Study the cartoon – Source Four – and answer these questions.

a Identify the character seated on the left. What was his job in Nazi Germany?

Source Four
David Low cartoon

b Name three ways in which the cartoonist, Low, shows how ineffective British war propaganda was.

c How does Low indicate his opinion that German propaganda was much more effective?

d Apart from the fact that the cartoon is in English (and Low is British) how can we tell that the cartoon backs Britain?

e What further point is Low trying to make by his reference to British propaganda leaflets – 'Leaflets dropped from the air (and remaining well above the enemy's head)'.

Exercise 8

Source Five
Vichy poster

The action of the Royal Navy under Admiral Somerville, to attack the French fleet at Mers-El-Kebir on 3 July 1940, caused great bitterness in France. It made the decision of some Frenchmen to work with the Nazis much easier. This Vichy poster of Churchill after the attack shows how use was made of the 'treachery' of the British. Admiral Darlan had promised that no French ship would fall into German or Italian hands but he rejected Somerville's call to sail the fleet into neutral waters. Design your own poster in the style of this one from the point of view of the Vichy Government about the 'vicious betrayal' by the Royal Navy.

Chapter 12

Aspects of the Second World War: 2 North Africa, Barbarossa, Normandy and the war in the Pacific

The war in North Africa: 1940–43

When the Second World War broke out in September 1939 Mussolini decided, wisely, that Italy was not in a position to wage a modern war. However, the speed of Germany's victories in the west in May and June convinced him that the war was almost over. He needed a 'few thousand' Italian dead so that Italy could justify her share of the winnings before the war was finished. On 10 June 1940 Italy declared war on Britain and France. Churchill commented that 'People who go to Italy to look at ruins won't have to go so far as Naples and Pompeii again'. Churchill was to be proved right. Italy was no more ready for war in June than she had been in September 1939. She had practically no anti-aircraft guns and only enough fuel for seven months. Italy was desperately short of rubber, coal and steel. Her sizeable army of 800 000 men was badly equipped and poorly led. Mussolini knew all this, of course, but chose to ignore it. He was determined to carve out a huge North African Empire at the expense of Britain before it was too late.

In August the Italians cleared the British out of British Somaliland – the British forces were far too small to offer any serious resistance. The same should have been the case in Egypt where Marshall Graziani had 240 000 troops in neighbouring Libya poised to attack General Wavell's 36 000. The Italians made slow progress into Egypt as Wavell retreated until 9 December when he was ready to launch a counter-attack against Graziani's badly supplied troops. (Supplies and weapons had been diverted to the Italians' faltering campaign in Greece invaded in October 1940). Within two days 38 000 Italian prisoners were taken for the loss of 624 British casualties. Mussolini's navy had fared no better. It was a modern navy with fine ships but

The War in Africa

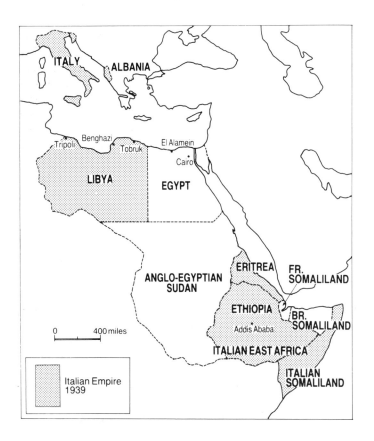

Italian Empire 1939

timidly led, and during 11–12 November it was crippled at its base in Taranto by torpedo bombers and three battleships were put out of action.

The arrival of Rommel

Early in 1941 Hitler stepped in to assist his weak Axis partner (Italy). By the time Lieutenant-General Rommel arrived in Libya in April a further 100 000 Italians had been taken prisoner by Major-General O'Connor's 13th Corps. The Axis forces under Rommel soon drove the British back out of Libya, leaving only Tobruk in British hands. Churchill became desperate for a morale boosting victory against the Afrika Korps (German and Italian troops stationed in Africa) and urged Wavell to launch an offensive in June before he was really ready. It was heavily defeated. Churchill sacked Wavell and replaced him with General Auchinleck. He resisted Churchill's demands for an offensive until he was fully prepared. On 18 November 1941 'Operation Crusader' was launched. 'Crusader' was the first British victory over the Germans of the war. The Afrika Korps fell back and Tobruk was relieved on 7 December. Both sides quickly set about preparing for new offensives but Rommel struck first in May 1942 and virtually destroyed the British tank force under Ritchie. The 8th Army was chased back to Tobruk which fell in a single day – along with 80 000 British prisoners by the end of June. Churchill

An official government photograph showing an Italian anti-tank gun emplacement on the Egyptian border 'near Sollum'. The 47 mm anti-tank gun was a weapon of which the Italians had very few. Details like this, though, were conveniently forgotten for official government purposes

was determined to have a decisive victory in the Western Desert – though to Hitler the campaign was never more than a side-show. British resources were poured into North Africa. Montgomery took over the 8th Army in August and steadily the British forces grew.

Montgomery was to prove two things in the battle of El Alamein (23 October – 4 November 1942): the power of the British artillery and the effectiveness of British tanks when deployed in large numbers. The Axis tanks were outnumbered two to one and so were its 100 000 troops. It was a shattering British victory against a heavily outnumbered enemy – only 36 German tanks out of 249 survived the battle. More importantly it prevented Egypt and the Suez Canal – and beyond that the Middle East oil fields – from falling into German hands.

The end of the war in North Africa

From El Alamein onwards Rommel was in retreat. On 8 November 1942 Anglo–American landings took place in Algeria and Morocco and Rommel's forces were squeezed into Tunisia where the remnants of the Afrika Korps (275 000 German and Italian troops) surrendered. The war in North Africa was over. Hitler later blamed Italy for contributing to Germany's eventual defeat in the Second World War because troops had to be diverted away from the invasion of Russia to assist Mussolini first in Greece and then in North Africa. But Hitler only sent four divisions to North Africa and seven to Greece. It is unlikely that these would have made a great deal of difference to the 153 divisions committed to the invasion of Russia. Indeed, it was a mistake on Hitler's part not to take the war in the Mediterranean much more seriously – as his naval advisers had urged – as the Middle East was of great importance strategically to Britain's **empire**.

Exercise 1

a In what ways was Italy unprepared for war in 1940?

b What defeat did the Italian navy suffer in November 1940?

c What do you think Churchill meant by the sentence: 'People who go to Italy to look at ruins won't have to go so far as Naples and Pompeii again'?

d What evidence is there in the text that Churchill sometimes let his impatience for a victory get the better of good military judgement?

e Why was El Alamein such an important victory for Britain?

Exercise 2

This is a Bulgarian cartoon drawn at the time of France's surrender in 1940.

a Identify the three characters in the cartoon.

b State the exact date the event in the cartoon took place. (Remember that Italy's armistice with France was signed two days after Germany's armistice).

c What relationship is the cartoonist suggesting existed between Italy and Germany?

d Based on what you have read about the North African Campaign, give evidence to support the cartoonist's view of the nature of the Axis partnership.

e Suggest a title for this cartoon and explain why you think it is a good one.

Source One

Exercise 3

Extract One

This is part of the text of a telegram Churchill sent to the United States' President in May 1941:

> We must not be too sure that the consequences of the loss of Egypt and the Middle East would not be grave ... We shall fight on whatever happens but please remember that the attitude of Spain, Vichy, Turkey and Japan may be finally determined by the outcome of the struggle in this theatre of
>
> 5   war.
>
> If all Europe, the greater part of Asia and Africa, became a part of the Axis system, a war maintained by the British Isles, United States, Canada, and Australasia against this mighty agglomeration would be a hard, long, and bleak proposition ...
>
> 10   Mr. President, I am sure that you will not misunderstand me if I speak to you exactly what is in my mind. The one decisive counterweight I can see to balance the growing pessimism ... would be if the United States were immediately to range itself with us as a belligerent Power ...
>
> We are determined to fight to the last inch and ounce for Egypt,
>
> 15   including its outposts of Tobruk and Crete ... In this war every post is a winning post, and how many more are we going to lose?

(Churchill Papers 20/38)

a Who was the president to whom the telegram was sent?

b Who were the leaders of Spain and Vichy (France) at this time?

c What did Spain, Vichy, Turkey and Japan all have in common at this time?

d What 'theatre of war' was Churchill referring to in lines 4–5?

e What fate befell Tobruk in December 1941 and June 1942?

f What, essentially, was Churchill appealing to the President to do? (see lines 10–13).

g What event had taken place the month before this telegram was sent which made it look as though Britain would lose several more 'winning posts'?

h What reason of overall strategy does Churchill give to persuade the Americans to enter the war 'immediately'. (See lines 6–9.)

The Normandy Landings, 6 June 1944

As we shall see later, in June 1941 the Germans launched their invasion of the Soviet Union. Britain and the USSR automatically became allies. The United States joined them when Japan, Germany and Italy declared war on the USA in December 1941. Soon Stalin began urging the Western Allies to launch an invasion of France – to open up a 'Second Front' – so the Germans would be forced to withdraw troops from the Russian front and ease the pressure on the Soviet forces. In November 1943 at the Teheran Conference Roosevelt promised Stalin that Anglo–US forces would open up a second front provided the Soviet Union agreed to declare war on Japan after Germany's defeat. But Churchill's objections to the plan delayed the invasion

from 1943 to 1944. He insisted that a successful invasion of Italy would help draw German troops from France into Italy and so the invasion would meet less resistance when it took place. The invasion of Italy – first Sicily in July 1943 and then the Italian mainland at Salerno in September – proved to be a much more difficult task than Churchill had thought. Rome did not fall until June 1944. 'Operation Overlord' – the code for the invasion of France – was fixed for June 1944, after another postponement in May.

The American General Eisenhower was placed in charge of 'Overlord'. The obvious target for an invasion was the Calais area and Eisenhower encouraged Hitler to expect an attack there. The Calais area was heavily bombed and dummy camps were set up in England facing Calais. In fact, the 'D-Day' landings were to be in Normandy, taking the Germans totally by surprise. On 6 June 1944 six Allied divisions (three American, two British and one Canadian) landed on the Normandy beaches. Only on 'Omaha' beach was fierce resistance encountered. Hitler was convinced that this was only a decoy attack and held back his heavy armour for the expected attack at Calais. By the end of 6 June 130 000 Allied troops had been landed. By the end of the first month 1 million troops had been landed. Floating harbours called 'Mulberries' were towed across to unload vital supplies, and fuel was provided by PLUTO (Pipeline Under The Ocean). The land forces under the overall command of General

From left to right, Stalin, Roosevelt and Churchill at Teheran in December 1943. It was agreed to open a 'Second Front' in Europe. Anthony Eden (right, rear) was himself to become a British Prime Minister in 1955

A Sherman tank undergoing inspection. US industrial power was a decisive factor in the war. The Americans manufactured 296 000 aircraft and 102 000 tanks during the war. Germany's war-time aircraft production was less than a third of that of the United States

August with De Gaulle's Free French forces (the French Army serving with the Allies) leading the way. Belgium and Antwerp followed in September. By then the Germans had suffered 500 000 casualties – twice as many as the Allies, and most of France had been freed from Nazi occupation. Germany made one final attempt to prevent the invasion of the 'Fatherland'. In December 1944, 30 German divisions, using the last of the fuel, were pitched into the Ardennes Offensive (the 'Battle of the Bulge'). By the middle of January it was all over. Hitler lost 120 000 more casualties and 600 tanks and guns. The invasion of Germany could begin.

Montgomery soon broke out from their bridgehead. Paris was liberated on 25

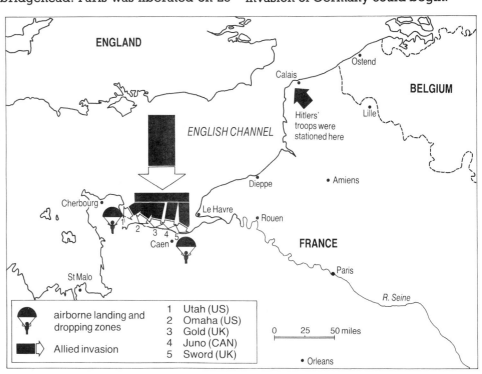

Normandy landings

Exercise 4

a Why did Stalin urge the British and Americans to open up a 'Second Front'?

b Why did Churchill insist on the invasion of Italy first?

c How did Eisenhower trick the Germans into expecting the attack in the wrong place?

d Why do you think De Gaulle's Free French were given the honour of entering Paris first?

e What phrase in the text makes it clear that the Ardennes Offensive by the Germans was their final attack?

Exercise 5

Source Two

German cartoon, 1943 'Little Winston's fear of water'

Study the German cartoon above, published in 1943, and then answer the following questions.

a Identify the two characters shown above.

b In the direction of which country is the larger figure pointing?

c How does the cartoonist show little Winston's reluctance to:
  i get wet;
  ii make use of his navy for the 'invasion'?

d Describe Germany's relations with the country represented by the standing figure at the outbreak of the Second World War. How did this relationship suddenly change midway through 1941?

e What propaganda point do you think the cartoonist is trying to make concerning the relations between little Winston and the standing figure? What evidence can you find in the text to suggest that there is some truth in the German cartoonist's view?

f How, eventually, was the cartoonist proved wrong?

'Operation Barbarossa': the war in Russia

The strategy

The invasion of Russia and the destruction of **Communism** had always been Hitler's number one priority. In June 1941 he decided the time had come to fulfil his dream. It was to become an obsession which cost Germany the war. There were important strategic objectives too. In the south stood the huge wheat fields of the Ukraine which would feed Hitler's armies and in the Caucasus were the vital oil supplies for a mechanised army. Hitler thought he had learnt the lesson of Napoleon's defeat in 1812. He would not allow the Russian armies to retreat deep into Russia, drawing his troops after them and stretching his supply lines. Instead, he would encircle the enemy in a series of rapid **'blitzkrieg'** movements. Once encircled in these 'battles of encirclement' huge armies could be destroyed. To some extent this tactic worked, but Hitler's overconfidence proved to be Germany's undoing. Confident that the

Barbarossa:
June–December 1941

'Kicking in the door'

Stalin, despite warnings from Britain, was taken completely by surprise. Within a few hours 1200 Russian aircraft had been destroyed, allowing the Luftwaffe a superiority of 4 to 1. Everything went according to plan. Over 300 000 Russian prisoners fell with the capture of Smolensk in July. However, Guderian was diverted from Army Group Centre to assist Rundstedt's southern group. The rapid advance on Moscow slowed down. Kiev was taken in September along with 660 000 prisoners. In the north Leeb was laying siege to Leningrad by October – a siege which was to last three years and cost the lives of 800 000 Leningraders. By October Bock's 'final' offensive for Moscow was ready and in early December the Germans were within 60 kilometres of the capital. Then the Russians, led by General Zhukov, launched a counter-offensive which drove the Germans back. Moscow was saved. By the end of the year the 'battles of encirclement' had yielded a staggering 3 million prisoners. But here the first of Hitler's errors became obvious. He had estimated the Soviet forces at 140 divisions – in fact they were able to deploy more than 320. Secondly, the Russian winter began to take its toll with 100 000 cases of frost-bite around Moscow alone. Goebbels' 'emergency relief' drive proved hopelessly inadequate. One German later complained his battalion of 800 men received 16 greatcoats between them! Thirdly, Hitler had expected by now to have control of the bulk of Russia's industry but Stalin had managed to move over 1500 factories eastwards, far from the fighting. There they were already in production – often before roofs and walls were complete.

war would be over before the winter, no winter clothing was issued. As the Russians fell back they 'scorched the earth', destroying crops, livestock and buildings so that the Germans had no food or shelter from the terrible 'General Winter' – Russia's constant ally.

Hitler's 153 divisions – roughly 3 million men – were divided into three Army Groups. Army Group North under General Leeb was to head for Leningrad, the centre of Russia's armaments industry. Army Group Centre under Bock was given the task of capturing Moscow, and Army Group South, under Rundstedt, was to capture the Ukrainian wheat fields and then the oil of the Caucasus. On 22 June 1941, 3 million men, supported by 3500 tanks and 5000 aircraft moved into Russian-occupied Poland. 'Barbarossa' had begun. 'We have only to kick in the door and the whole rotten structure will come crashing down', Hitler had told his generals.

a How did Hitler plan to avoid repeating the mistakes of Napoleon?
b What benefits, other than the destruction of Communism, did Hitler expect to gain from his conquest of Russia?

c What tactical mistake did Hitler make as regards the attack on Moscow early on in the campaign?

d Of the three errors of judgement that Hitler made (referred to in the text) which do you think was the most serious and why? (As in most cases of historical opinion there is no 'right' answer – a well-argued answer will do.)

Exercise ■ 7

Extract Two

This is taken from an account by a German soldier home on leave to his wife:

'At first it was fine' Rudolf went on. 'We swept on, adding towns and villages by the score. Then the troops began to get stale. Do you know how we behaved to the civilians? . . . We behaved like devils out of hell.'

5 We sat in awful silence for a moment. Then Rudolf went on to tell us more details of the partisans behind the lines.

'We shoot the prisoners on the slightest excuse,' he said. 'Just stick them up against the wall and shoot the lot. We order the whole village to look while we do it, too . . . It's a vicious circle. We hate them and they hate us. Another of our mistakes was in the Ukraine. I was one of those who

10 marched in to be received, not as a conqueror but as a friend. The civilians were all ready to look upon us as saviours. They had had years of oppression from the Soviets . . . What did we do? We turned them into slaves under Hitler'.

(E. Wendel, *Hausfrau at War*)

a Explain the term 'partisans'. What kind of activities did they carry out during the war?

b How were captured partisan prisoners treated by the Germans, according to Rudolf?

c Why do you think the whole village was ordered to watch the event?

d What does Rudolf state was a serious mistake committed by the Germans in their treatment of civilians?

e What kind of historical source are both Extracts One and Two?

f In what ways are these two extracts different and in what different ways are they of use to historians?

Stalingrad: the turning point

The Russians launched counter-attacks early in 1942 but these were beaten back. Hitler decided that the main German war effort would be concentrated in the south of Russia with the Caucasus oil fields as the target. It was then that Hitler made a serious error. He decided that both oil fields and Stalingrad would be captured. This meant that his forces would have to be split. In order to capture both he risked gaining neither – and Stalingrad had no real military value. General von Paulus, in charge of the VI Panzer Army, was told to take the city. By September he was in the suburbs of Stalingrad where the Russians fought desperately for each street and each building. In November, Zhukov was ready to launch his offensive with two pincer attacks from north and south of the city. Paulus' army of 250 000 men were surrounded and cut off from any help. Hitler refused to allow any talk of retreat – which would

In December 1941, the Russians counter-attacked the Germans at Moscow. The Soviet troops were well-equipped, as the photograph shows, and prepared for the sub-zero temperatures – unlike their German enemies

have been nearly impossible anyway as the Germans had little fuel left – or of surrender. Eventually on 31 January Paulus did surrender along with the remaining 91 000 of his men. The Germans were forced to retreat from the south and the oil fields escaped capture.

This retreat was an important victory of morale for the Russians and a shattering blow to the Germans. From now on they were almost continually on the defensive. They launched only one further offensive in July 1943 at Kursk. It

was the biggest tank battle in history, in which 2700 German tanks faced 3600 Russian tanks. Not only were the Germans now continually out-numbered but the Russians also had the best tank of the war – the T.34 which was much better suited to the conditions with its wide tracks and excellent reliability. The attack at Kursk failed and the Russians rapidly recaptured their cities: Smolensk in September; Kiev in November and Leningrad, finally, in January 1944. By August the only German soldiers left on Russian soil were either dead or prisoners – and few of them survived the war.

The war in Russia was crucial to the Allied victory. At least 75% of Germany's troops and war material had been sent to the Russian front, which in June 1944 tied down 228 German and Axis divisions (some 4 million men) and 5250 tanks. German divisions in Western Europe at this time totalled just 61. However, the Russians paid dearly with some 20 million dead between civilians and troops. Britain and the United States' civilian and military dead totalled around 800 000.

Assignment unit

The Second Front

Write an exchange of letters between Stalin and Roosevelt in early 1943. In the first letter Stalin puts the Russian case for the opening of the Second Front in 1943. Tell Roosevelt of the tremendous victory at Stalingrad but point out information of a German counter-attack at Kursk and why immediate relief is needed by the hard-pressed Soviet forces.

In the second letter describe Roosevelt's sympathetic view of Stalin's needs. Mention Churchill's different strategy for an attack on Italy instead but promise to help Stalin at the earliest opportunity and suggest a meeting of the 'Big Three' (Stalin, Roosevelt and Churchill) at Teheran to discuss the issue.

Exercise 8

a Identify the two characters shown in Source Three.

b In which sea do you think the sinking figure is most likely drowning?

c What campaign do you think is represented by the weight around the drowning figure's neck?

d Which battle could the snare trapping the figure on land most likely represent?

Source Three
Russian cartoon

e Suggest a year in which the cartoon might have been published from the following possibilities: 1940; 1941; 1942; 1943; 1944. State why you have chosen that particular year as your answer and not the others.

f Compare Source Two (page 147) and this cartoon as political propaganda. For example, why might Source Two be considered more threatening to the Allies' alliance than Source Three to the Axis alliance?

The war in the Pacific: 1941–45

No country which wants to become a major world power can do so without the necessary raw materials – especially rubber and oil in the case of Japan. The Japanese had always considered that South East Asia should be under their control or **hegemony**. To establish that control they needed markets in which to sell their goods and raw materials. In 1931 they began their expansion with the invasion of China's industrial centre – Manchuria. Six years later they followed this up with an attack on the rest of China. This guaranteed the Japanese a huge market but it angered the Americans who were now unable to sell their products in the area. When France fell in 1940 Japan took over French Indo-China and the Dutch East Indies' oil supplies. But there were bigger supplies of oil and rubber in British-owned Burma and Malaya. With Britain heavily involved in war in Europe only the United States stood in the way of Japan's ambitions. Relations between Japan and the United States had been strained since the Japanese invasion of China in 1937. Japan's military commanders had in fact been unhappy ever since the 1922 Washington Treaty which permitted them to build only three ships for every five built by the United States and Britain. In July 1941 Roosevelt demanded the withdrawal of Japanese troops from China and Indo-China and blocked the sale of oil to Japan. Negotiations between the two countries achieved nothing and prospects for a peaceful solution faded rapidly in November. In that month General Tojo, a militarist determined to have war, became Prime Minister. He assured Emperor Hirohito that Japan could win a war.

Pearl Harbour

The Japanese decided to strike a devastating blow against the American fleet in its base at Pearl Harbour. Admiral Yamamoto launched over 200 aircraft early on Sunday morning, 7 December 1941. There had been no declaration of war and the US Pacific Fleet was taken completely by surprise as two waves of bombers pounded the stationary ships. As a result 2350 men were killed; 5 battleships were sunk and 3 put out of action and 200 aircraft were destroyed. Of the Japanese planes 29 were shot down. For six months the Americans were powerless to halt the Japanese advance across South East Asia. The only bright spot for the Americans was that their three aircraft carriers were not in Pearl Harbour that morning. It was an error that was to have serious consequences for Japan. Still, with 10 carriers of their own, Tojo was confident that he had done enough to win. By May 1942 Japan controlled Malaya, Singapore, Burma, Hong Kong, the Philippines and two US bases at Guam and Wake Island. The loss of Singapore in February was a bitter blow for British morale as 80 000 troops were taken prisoner.

Just as the war on the Eastern Front had its decisive battle at Stalingrad and North Africa its El Alamein, so the war in the Pacific had its turning point. This was the battle of Midway, fought in June 1942. The Japanese attack on Midway Island contained five aircraft carriers with nearly 400 planes and some 5000 troops. Though out-numbered, the Americans sank 4 Japanese carriers and 296 planes for the loss of one carrier and 132 aircraft. Midway put a decisive halt to the string of Japanese victories and turned the tide against Japan. Within nine months, the Americans were to have 19 carriers in the Pacific as against Japan's 10. Though the Japanese were to continue with a larger number of battleships, it was clear that the Pacific war was to be won by carriers and huge numbers of aircraft – especially dive-bombers.

While the British pushed forward with a drive against the Japanese in Burma, the Americans planned an assault by General MacArthur from the south-east and one by Admiral Nimitz from the east. Both of these attacks were to converge on the Philippines.

'Leap frogging'

The Americans decided to avoid trying to capture every one of the many islands occupied by the enemy. Instead, they 'leap-frogged' from one island to another, by-passing the more heavily defended islands and so cutting them off to 'wither on the vine', as

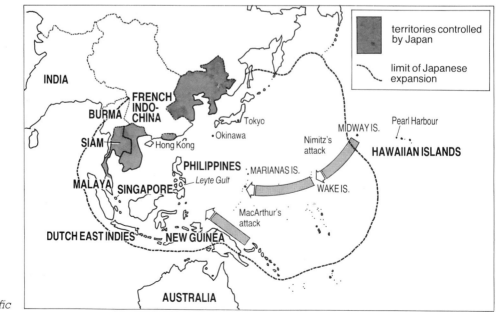

The war in the Pacific

MacArthur described it. The Battle of the Philippine Sea in June 1944 enabled Nimitz to take control of the Marianas Islands from which B29 bombers could now launch constant raids on Japan itself. This victory was followed by another in October for the Philippine Islands at the Battle of Leyte Gulf. The largest sea battle in history cost the Japanese 4 carriers and 3 battleships, 10 cruisers and 11 destroyers with a further 10 500 sailors and pilots killed. This battle also saw the first appearance of 'kamikaze' suicide pilots who flew their planes packed with explosive straight at the US ships. The Americans suffered casualties too. Three carriers were lost and over 200 aircraft were shot down – though the Japanese had lost 500. Over 2800 servicemen also perished. However, it was also an important strategic victory since the Japanese were now cut off from their oil supplies in the Dutch East Indies and most of the Japanese fleet had been sunk. After four months of very bitter fighting the island of Okinawa fell in June. From here an invasion of Japan itself could take place.

The Japanese at Okinawa had fought to the death and 130 000 had died. In Japan 2 million more troops faced the Americans. American bombing raids were reducing the islands of Japan to rubble – one raid on Tokyo in March killed 80 000 in a huge firestorm. Japan's largely wooden houses proved especially easy targets for incendiary bombs. President Truman, who had taken over after Roosevelt's death in April 1945, decided that an invasion of Japan would cost too many US casualties. He decided to drop two atomic bombs in August – one on Hiroshima on the 6th and one on Nagasaki three days later. In Hiroshima 80 000 perished at once and a further 80 000 died within a few weeks. The war was shortened – Japan surrendered on 14 August, unconditionally. Probably just as importantly from Truman's point of view, the United States had shown the Russians the terrible power of their new weapon.

Exercise 9

a Why were Burma and Malaya obvious targets for Japanese expansion?
b What serious error prevented the Japanese from claiming a total victory at Pearl Harbour?
c Why was Midway an important victory for the US?
d What was the strategic importance of the Battle of Leyte Gulf?
e What other reason than to shorten the war did Truman have for dropping the atomic bomb on Japan?

Exercise 10

Pacific time-line

Read through the text on the Pacific War. Divide your page like this:

Event	Date	Description	Result
Pearl Harbour	December 1941	Japanese attack on US fleet: 5 battleships sunk; 200 planes destroyed; 2350 killed.	Japanese able to control Pacific for next six months; US carriers escape.

Fill in the information for the following months as shown above:
February 1942; June 1942; June 1944; October 1944; March 1945; June 1945; August 1945.

Chapter 13

The Cold War in Europe: 1945–49

The origins of the Cold War

Relations between the Western Allies (Britain, the United States and France) and the Soviet Union were always likely to be strained once the war was over. Indeed, evidence of that strain was apparent before the war ended. Stalin had always suspected that Britain and the USA had deliberately delayed the opening of the 'Second Front' – the invasion of Normandy – so that Russia would suffer further casualties against Germany. There is no proof of this but in the situation of tension and distrust that existed between the former allies the truth did not and does not matter. What matters is what each side *believes* to be the truth. Besides, the Russians could always point to the efforts by Britain, France and America to overthrow the **Bolsheviks** in 1919–20 as evidence of their hostility to the Soviet Union. The Russians, on their part, had never made any secret of their eventual aim: the overthrow of the **capitalist** system.

The 'Big Three' at Yalta

As long as the Allies faced a common enemy in the shape of Nazi Germany these differences were put to one side. Once the defeat of Hitler was secured these differences emerged more strongly. In February 1945 Stalin, Roosevelt and Churchill met at Yalta in the Crimea in Russia to discuss what was to be done in Europe once Germany had surrendered. There was agreement on most issues. Germany was to be divided temporarily into three zones of Allied occupation, and a fourth, that of France was added later. Berlin was to be divided in the same way, as was Austria and Vienna. Free elections were to be held in the liberated states of Eastern Europe and Stalin agreed to declare war on Japan. On the whole the meeting was successful and friendly. The only cloud concerned Poland. The British and Americans eventually agreed to Stalin's demand that all territory east of the line formed by the rivers Oder and Neisse should be handed over by Germany to Poland. Poland had been occupied by the Red Army and already had a Communist government. Stalin was determined that the states of Eastern Europe would act as a buffer zone against any possible attack from the West. There would be no repetition of Germany's sudden attacks in 1914 and 1941 or, for that matter, Poland's in 1920. Stalin did agree to allow some members of the London-based Polish government to join the Communist government in Lublin and also to support the setting up of the United Nations Organisation.

When the next Allied meeting took place in July at Potsdam near Berlin the situation was very different. Roosevelt had died in April and had been replaced by his Vice-President, Harry Truman. Churchill was replaced during the conference as a result of his defeat in the General Election by Clement Attlee's Labour Party. The death of Roosevelt was bad news for Stalin. Roosevelt had always been prepared to go out of his way to see things from Russia's point of view. Roosevelt had shared Stalin's suspicion that Britain was determined to use the post-war

A different big three at Potsdam – Truman has replaced Roosevelt

occupation of Germany up to the Oder–Neisse on behalf of Poland and had driven out some 5 million Germans.

Once Germany had surrendered, the Yalta agreements could be put into effect at Potsdam: the division of Germany was begun and the Russians started collecting **reparations** from the eastern zone. 'De-Nazification' was the priority in all four zones and local Nazis were purged from any important posts. There were 21 top Nazis who were put on trial at Nuremberg and 11 who were hanged. Himmler, the SS chief, Goering, head of the Luftwaffe and Goebbels escaped the hangman's noose by suicide. Four days after the Potsdam conference closed Truman ordered the dropping of the atomic bomb on Japan on 6 August. The Russians had not known about this terrible weapon. Stalin was alarmed at its power and, no doubt, felt threatened too. The '**Cold War**' tension tightened still further.

settlement to strengthen her **empire** and force monarchies on post-war states like Italy and Greece. Truman, however, had no illusions about Russia's stand on **democracy** and anti-imperialism. Indeed, Roosevelt had come to much the same conclusion himself after Stalin had made his view clear about the future of Poland at Yalta. The Russians had continued with their

The trial of Nazi war criminals at Nuremberg: Goering, left, and Ribbentrop (the Nazi Foreign Minister) right, with Rudolf Hess (the Nazi Party deputy leader in 1941) in the centre. Ribbentrop was hanged and Hess sentenced to life imprisonment

Exercise 1

a Why did Stalin distrust the Western allies in 1945?

b What action was agreed over Germany at Yalta?

c What issue at Yalta caused friction between the Allies?

d Why was the death of Roosevelt a disappointment to Stalin?

e The idea of 'war criminal' was a new one. It was used to try, imprison or execute many Nazis. What sort of arguments do you think the Allies put forward to justify these trials?

The Cold War – further tension

Relations between Stalin and Churchill had never really been friendly and Churchill and the Russian leader viewed each other with great suspicion. Although no longer Prime Minister, Churchill continued to warn of the dangers of Soviet expansion into Eastern Europe and elsewhere. In March 1946 he made a speech at Fulton, Missouri, in which he spoke of this threat: 'From Stettin in the Baltic to Trieste in the Adriatic, an Iron Curtain has descended across the Continent. Behind that line are all the capitals of the ancient states of central and eastern Europe – Warsaw, Berlin, Prague, Budapest, Belgrade, Bucharest and Sofia. All these famous cities and the populations around them, lie in the Soviet sphere.'

Source One

(below)
Expansion of the Soviet Union and Communism after the Second World War

(Right)   Daily Mail cartoon
'Churchill takes a peep under the iron curtain'

The map below clearly shows the extent of that Soviet expansion into Europe at the expense of the Baltic States, Poland, Germany and Rumania. Churchill and Truman were both convinced that this expansion was the result of Stalin's aggressive plans for the future. Others were later to see this growth of **Communist** control as a defensive measure to ensure Russia's own security against attack from the West. Whatever the truth of the matter, Churchill's 'Iron Curtain' speech served only to add to the sense of fear and suspicion that was now dividing Russia and the Western powers.

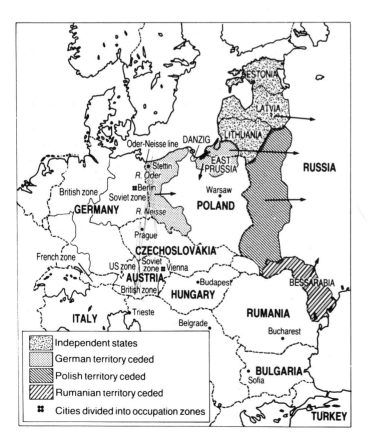

Independent states
German territory ceded
Polish territory ceded
Rumanian territory ceded
Cities divided into occupation zones

Stalin was encouraged to press ahead with the 'Sovietisation' of Eastern Europe. By the end of 1947 Bulgaria, Rumania, Poland, Hungary and Albania had Communist governments in power. Czechoslovakia followed in 1948.

Not everything went Stalin's way, though. Churchill had assumed that Tito's Yugoslavia was firmly part of the 'Soviet sphere' because it was a Communist state. But Tito's Yugoslavia did not owe its liberation from Nazism to the Red Army as did the other East European states. Tito's Communist partisans had driven the Germans out on their own and so there were no Red Army troops in Yugoslavia to ensure that Tito followed Moscow's policies. When Stalin tried to force Tito to adopt Russian-style Communism in 1948 Tito refused and was expelled from the Cominform – the Communist Information Bureau set up by Stalin in 1947 and which all East European and some West European Communist Parties had joined. Its purpose was to ensure that these parties co-operated with each other and followed the policies laid down by Moscow. Stalin decided not to send in troops to bring down Tito as he was unsure of the reaction of the British and Americans. He was not prepared to risk a war and was confident that Tito could be overthrown from within Yugoslavia.

Exercise 2

Map work: Source one

a Pair up the capitals listed in the extract from Churchill's 'Iron Curtain' speech with their respective countries.

b Which two countries and their capitals were divided into zones of occupation after the war?

c Churchill's error in naming Stettin as the northern end of the 'Iron Curtain' is dealt with in another chapter. Why was he later to be proven wrong in naming Trieste as the southern end of the 'Curtain'?

d Russian, British, French and American troops were all withdrawn from Austria in 1955. Austria became an independent state. The Russians withdrew, after certain guarantees had been made that Austria would always be a neutral nation, without any fuss. Look at Austria's geographical position on the map. What evidence is there that Austria was not vital to Russia's security? A year later in 1956 Hungary attempted to break free of Soviet control. The rising was fiercely put down by the Russians. Looking at the map, can you suggest why the Russians could not permit the loss of Hungary?

e Write half-a-dozen lines on why maps are useful aids to understanding history.

The Truman Doctrine and Marshall Aid

It was not only Stalin who was having difficulty hanging onto his 'spheres of influence'. Since the end of the war Britain had been involved militarily in a campaign to crush the popular Greek Communist movement, EAM. The Greek Civil War seemed a clear example of the fate that awaited the rest of the Mediterranean – especially Turkey – if something were not done. Greece, it was agreed by Stalin, Churchill and Roosevelt, was to be part of the Western spere of influence. As a result Stalin would not come to the aid of the Greek Communists and raised no objection to Britain's involvement. But Churchill had made it clear that Britain would have to cease all military and financial aid to the Greek royalist army at the end of 1947 because of the cost.

Defeat of EAM

In March 1947 Truman made an appeal to the US Congress for $400 million of military and financial assistance for Greece and Turkey to ensure their survival as 'free nations'. The speech, known as the Truman Doctrine, outlined the President's tough anti-Communist position and committed the United States to assist any nations having '**totalitarian**' regimes forced upon

Marshall Aid arrives in Europe. Marshall Aid put further strain on US–Soviet relations

Doctrine was also to lead to major American involvement in the wars in Korea (1950–53) and Vietnam (1965–73). (See Chapter 17.)

Truman was a shrewd man and knew full well that a more effective method of halting the spread of Communism was to ensure economic prosperity in Europe. Prosperous nations are stable nations and, what is more, they buy American goods. In the Europe of the late 1940s there was little prospect of a prosperous Europe without massive American help. In June 1947, the US Secretary of State, George Marshall, announced that the United States was willing to make funds available to all the states of Europe. To begin with the Americans sent food, and later fuel and raw materials. European output increased by 25% in two years. The $13 billion spent under the Marshall Plan between 1948 and 1952 proved to be well spent: Communism made no further inroads into Europe. As Truman said, the Truman Doctrine and Marshall Aid were 'two halves of the same walnut'.

them against their will'. It was a firm commitment to oppose the spread of Communism anywhere in the world, and by the use of military power if necessary. Its first significant success was the outright defeat of the Greek Communists by 1949. The Truman

Exercise 3

a What sort of countries lay to the east of Churchill's 'Iron Curtain'?
b How would Stalin have justified this expansion of Russian influence in eastern Europe?
c Why do you think that the Red Army in Europe in 1946 still stood at 5 million men while the Western powers had less than a million men under arms in the same year in Europe?
d Why do you think that ensuring economic prosperity in Europe was a more effective method of halting the spread of Communism?
e What reason of self-interest is hinted at in the text concerning the United States' offer of Marshall Aid?

Exercise 4

Extract: The Truman Doctrine (1947)

The peoples of a number of countries of the world have recently had totalitarian regimes forced upon them against their will. The Government of the United States has made frequent protests against coercion and intimidation, in violation of the Yalta agreement, in Poland, Rumania and
5   Bulgaria ...

At the present moment in world history nearly every nation must choose between alternative ways of life ...

One way of life is based upon the will of the majority, and is

10 distinguished by free institutions, representative government, free
elections ...
The second way of life is based upon the will of the minority forcibly
imposed upon the majority. It relies upon terror and oppression ... and
the suppression of personal freedoms ...

15 It is necessary only to glance at a map to realise that the survival and
integrity of the Greek nation are of grave importance ... If Greece should
fall under the control of an armed minority, the effect upon its neighbour
... would be immediate and serious.

(*Documents of American History*, Ed. H.S. Commager)

a Name two other states which Truman could have mentioned in addition to
those on lines 4–5.
b In what way had the Yalta agreement been violated to enable these
totalitarian regimes to come to power?
c What names are usually given to describe the ways of life described in lines
8–10 and in lines 11–13?
d Why was Truman so concerned about the 'survival and integrity of the Greek
nation'? What organisation was threatening this nation?
e Who was the neighbour referred to in line 16? Were Truman's fears about
the future of these nations later proved justified and why?
f Write a paragraph of 20 lines explaining the background to this statement by
Truman in March 1947.

The Berlin Airlift 1948–49

Stalin suspected that Marshall Aid was a ploy by the Americans to extend their influence into Eastern Europe and undermine Russia's control. He forbade the Communist states to take part in the scheme, preferring instead to set up his own version in the form of 'Comecon', the Council for Mutual Economic Assistance. Only Yugoslavia of the Communist states was willing to accept American money, though the $109 million received was very small compared to the $3000 million received by Britain, $2700 million by France and $1400 million by Italy.* Marshall Aid was administered by the Organisation of European Economic Co-operation (OEEC), consisting of the 16 nations receiving the assistance. The decision of the three Allied powers in the western sectors of Germany to go ahead with Marshall Aid without Stalin's consent focused attention once more on Germany as the heart of the East–West dispute. In June the Western allies also decided to introduce a new currency into the western sector and into West Berlin. It seemed to Stalin that the West was determined to create a separate West German state – a violation of the Yalta agreement which had decided that Germany would be reunited as soon as possible.

The blockade of Berlin

Stalin's response on 24 June 1948 was to cut off all rail and road links between Berlin and the West. It was probably his intention to force the Western powers to leave West Berlin and hand it over to Russia. The options open to the Western Allies seemed unpromising. Berlin was 100 miles inside the Russian sector of

*One other country which did show interest was Czechoslovakia but after a Communist take-over in February 1948 it was forbidden to take up the offer.

East Germany. Any attempt to drive through the blockade on land would probably result in war and the Russians had some 5 million men at hand. To evacuate West Berlin and hand over its $2\frac{1}{2}$ million inhabitants to Russia would make a mockery of the Truman Doctrine. It was decided that West Berlin would be supplied by an airlift. It was a remarkable undertaking as the West Berliners would need 4000 tons of supplies a day just to keep alive. The largest transport plane could take just 11 tons per flight. Over the next 11 months a flight left for Berlin from bases in West Germany every 30 seconds. The crisis point was reached in January 1949 when West Berlin was down to one week's supply of coal and three weeks' of food, but by March the American and British pilots were flying in 8000 tons a day.

Stalin realised he could not win. His efforts to tempt West Berliners in to the east of the city with promises of food and supplies failed. Only 2% of the population were desperate enough to go over to the east. In May 1949 Stalin called off the blockade. The blockade of Berlin was the closest that the Cold War

in Europe came to becoming a real war and it greatly increased the tension. The West, though, felt it had won a moral victory in standing up to and defeating Stalin. It also decided to set up an organisation to co-ordinate the defence policies of the major Western nations: the North Atlantic Treaty Organisation (NATO) set up in April 1949. Each of the 11 nations undertook to assist any member attacked by an aggressor. West Germany joined in 1955. It was clear that there was no hope at all of Germany being once again a single nation and so in August 1949 the German Federal Republic (West Germany) was established. It was followed in October by the creation of the German Democratic Republic (East Germany). Konrad Adenauer became West Germany's first Chancellor.

After 1949 the Cold War continued to exist as a state of tension between East and West but it was increasingly marked by real wars, such as the Korean War. In 1955 the Russians responded to NATO with their own military alliance of Communist states – the Warsaw Pact. Europe was now firmly divided into two hostile, armed camps.

Exercise 5

Punch **cartoon February 1948**

Source Two

The Missing Valentines 'Nothing yet from Greece or Turkey?'

a Identify the character standing by the fire.

b What do all the 'Valentine' cards on the mirror have in common?

c Which one of them would shortly be torn down and why?

d From which country was the Valentine in the hand of the figure with the moustache most likely to have come? (Clue: date of cartoon.) Explain your answer.

e Why was a card expected from Greece? Did it ever arrive? Give your reason for your answer.

Exercise

6

Punch cartoon July 1948

Source Three

The Bird Watcher

a Identify the figure in the chimney.

b What is the destination of the storks and from where have they come?

c Why are they carrying supplies of coal and food?

d What action is the figure in the chimney contemplating? Did he ever take such action? What would have been the likely consequence of such a step?

e Why did the figure in the chimney eventually give up his threatening attitude to Berlin?

f Describe in a paragraph of 20 lines the causes, course and results of the incident portrayed in this cartoon.

g What opinion of the Cold War and those responsible for it do both these cartoons (Sources Two and Three) show? In what sense are the cartoons themselves part of the Cold War?

Assignment unit

The Russian point of view

The views of historians on major (and minor) issues of history tend to be shaped by the society in which they live. Western historians tend to see the Cold War from the point of view of the West – if only because public record material and original documents giving the West's point of view are much more easily available. This book is no exception, despite efforts by its author to see events from more than one viewpoint.

Write an article for the Soviet newspaper *Pravda* at the end of 1949, reviewing the events in Europe from 1945 to 1949 from the Russian point of view. To do this you will need to go back to the Russian Civil War and comment on the help given by the West to the Whites (see Chapter 3). These points will also help you: lack of co-operation by the West with Russia against Hitler before the war; Russia's fears about the atomic bomb; Churchill's 'Iron Curtain' speech; the Truman Doctrine; Marshall Aid; the creation of the Federal Republic of Germany; NATO.

Chapter 14

The USSR from Stalin to Khrushchev and relations with the Soviet Bloc

The Second World War had been a tremendously costly one for the Soviet Union. Out of a population of 170 million, 25 million people were homeless and 31 000 factories had been destroyed or seriously damaged along with 98 000 collective farms. In 1946 a new Five Year Plan was begun to make good these losses and its remarkable success is clear from this table:

	1940	1945	1950
Industrial Output	100	92	173
Agricultural Output	100	60	99

(the index number 100 is the amount produced in 1940, the last full year of peace.)

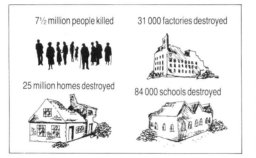

War damage in the Soviet Union

Those that hoped that the defeat of Germany would lead to a relaxation of life inside the Soviet Union were soon disappointed. This incident, told by Khrushchev in 1955, on the fate of a writer called Voznesensky is as good an example as any. Voznesensky had just written a book about the Soviet Union's war-time economy, full of praise for Stalin's leadership, but which suggested that there might be a case for some changes now the war was over:

The three of us, Malenkov, Molotov, and myself, immediately asked for an interview with Stalin, and we were received by him at noon. We stated that we had seen and approved the measures proposed by Voznesensky. Stalin listened to us, and then he said: 'Before you go on, you should know that Vosnesensky was shot this morning.

There you are. What could we do? A man is prepared to be a martyr, but what use is it to die like a dog in the gutter? There was nothing we could do while Stalin lived.

(Quoted in R. Payne, *The Rise and Fall of Stalin*, 1966)

De-Stalinisation

It seems that Stalin was planning yet another major purge when he died suddenly of a brain haemorrhage on 5 March 1953. Just as Lenin had died in 1924 without an obvious successor, so Stalin's death left the Soviet Union with no clear leader. Two men emerged as possible leaders. Malenkov became Chairman of the Council of Ministers, or Prime Minister, and Nikita Khrushchev became **Communist** Party Secretary. Power was also spread to other men like Bulganin and Molotov. It seemed that the Soviet Union was really to be ruled by group or 'collective' leadership. Malenkov, however, resigned in 1955 after a disagreement with Khrushchev over industrial policy and the latter had emerged by 1956 as the most powerful figure in the Soviet Union.

Nikita Khrushchev outside the Kremlin

was partly a secret speech, never made public inside Russia. A report of the speech was published in the West and the Russians have never denied its accuracy. For the first time, members of the Communist Party heard of the terrible crimes committed by Stalin during the purges of 1934–38 and the forced collectivisation. Stalin's 'personality cult', in which he raised himself to almost God-like status, never able to make a mistake, was also condemned. The Party must never again allow one man to acquire such terrible power. All this was secret but some, more mild, criticism was made public – such as Lenin's 'Testament' about Stalin. Some of Stalin's victims had their reputations restored – but not Trotsky. This speech was to have tremendous results for Russia and the world Communist movement. It also helped to firmly establish Khrushchev as the leader of the Soviet Union – but only as long as he kept the support of the Party's inner group of leaders, the Politburo. One other important aspect of the speech, also made public, was Khrushchev's call for the West and Communist world to live together in peace, for 'peaceful coexistence'. The 'Thaw' in the chilly East–West relations was beginning.

This was not the same country that Stalin had ruled. There were to be no more purges – people like Malenkov who disagreed with Party policy were not shot or suddenly made to disappear. Gradually Russia was undergoing 'de-Stalinisation'; that is, the methods of the old dictator were being changed for a more reasonable way of government.

'De-Stalinisation' was given a further boost in 1956 when Khrushchev made a very important speech to the Twentieth Congress of the Communist Party. It

Exercise 1

a How much damage had Russia suffered as a result of the war?

b What evidence is there in the text that the new Five Year Plan, started in 1946, was a success?

c What does the Vosnesensky incident tell you of Stalin's intentions on how to rule Russia after the war?

d Can you think of any reason why the whole of Khrushchev's speech was never made public to the Russian people?

e In the extract from Khrushchev's account of the Vosnesensky incident, he ends with the sentence: 'There was nothing we could do while Stalin lived'. Do you sympathise with Khrushchev's point of view? Explain why.

Khrushchev

Not all the Soviet Union's Communist leaders were very happy with Khrushchev's attack on Stalin. Malenkov and Molotov led the campaign against Khrushchev. But Khrushchev, like Stalin before him, had supporters in key positions and the Party backed him against his opponents. Malenkov and Molotov were 'retired' from office in June 1957 and Khrushchev was to remain firmly in control until his downfall in 1964.

Khrushchev was determined to make important changes in the Soviet economy. Industry was to concentrate on turning out consumer goods like television sets and refrigerators which would help to raise the standard of living of ordinary Russians. The number of refrigerators produced, for example, rose from 49 000 in 1953 to 360 000 in 1958. By 1966 there were five times more sewing machines than there were in 1955 and a staggering 77 times more washing machines. The standard of living certainly rose because not only did the average Russian have much more to buy now but he also had more money to spend as wages rose in real terms as well – 38% for non-agricultural workers between 1952 and 1958. Industry was also made more efficient. The old Stalinist system of centralised control was abolished. Now decisions could be made by new Regional Economic Councils and no longer had to be referred back to Moscow for approval. Factory managers were encouraged to make profits – the higher the profits, the bigger the wage packet for him and his workers. But there continued to be problems. Russia's terrible housing shortage was not solved by Khrushchev and remains one of the most serious difficulties today, and in 1958 the average Russian family had less room than it did 30 years earlier.

Another problem area which Khrushchev tackled, and which still remains a problem, was agriculture. In 1954 he began the Virgin Lands Project in which 75 million acres of new land in Siberia and Kazakhstan were to be turned into farm land. It was a bold scheme and soon produced impressive results. Output from these areas rose from 27 million tons of grain in 1953 to 58 million in 1958. But soon the figure dropped because the soil became exhausted and was blown away in dust storms and much of the land was of poor quality. Because of the failure of the Virgin Lands Project grain output fell from 140 million tons in 1962 to 110 million the next year.

The removal of Khrushchev

The failure of several harvests in the early 1960s led to an increase in food prices which caused some discontent in the cities. Khrushchev's fall from power in October 1964 happened quite suddenly. The lack of success in agriculture was certainly one reason, but there were others as well. Officially, he had resigned 'in view of his health and age'. In fact, his more conservative Politburo comrades had been embarrassed by his occasionally unconventional behaviour. During one United Nations meeting he had banged his desk with his shoe to make a point. He had a rough, hearty sense of humour, typical of the peasant stock from which he came. He was not a **Marxist** intellectual but similar to Stalin in this respect. Unlike Stalin, though, he liked to be seen out and about and would sometimes walk the streets of Moscow, shaking hands with surprised Muscovites. More seriously, he had been forced by Kennedy to back down over the Cuban Missile Crisis (see Chapter 17, pages 223–27) and his policies had led to a split with the world's most populated Communist power, China. He was also criticised later in *Pravda* for developing a personality cult like Stalin and giving important jobs to his relatives. Khrushchev was 70 when he was forced from power by the vote of the Politburo. He finished life in comfortable retirement and died in 1971. The fact that he could live the rest of his life without fear of sudden 'disappearance' or execution shows just how much the Soviet

Union had changed from Stalin's days. One English journalist paid this tribute to him, that he would be remembered because he had: 'left his country a better place than he found it, both in the eyes of the majority of his own people, and of the world.'

Exercise 2

a How did Khrushchev finally establish firm control of the Soviet Union in 1957?
b How did he intend to raise the standard of living of the people?
c How was economic decision-making improved?
d What caused the failure of the Virgin Lands Project?
e 'The fact that he could live the rest of his life without fear of sudden "disappearance" ...' Why is the word 'disappearance' in inverted commas? In what way was Khrushchev's retirement period different from Stalin's time?

The Soviet economy under Khrushchev

| | Goods per 1000 of the population | | |
	Russia 1955	Russia 1966	USA 1966
Cars	2	5	398
Radios	66	171	1300
TV sets	4	82	376
Refrigerators	4	40	293
Washing-machines	1	77	259
Sewing-machines	31	151	36

(From: J.N. Westwood in *Purnell's History of the 20th Century*)

a What word is usually given to describe the type of goods listed above?
b Which sector showed the biggest percentage increase over the period?
c Do these statistics confirm the view of Khrushchev's industrial policy given in the text? Quote the sentence in the text which backs up your answer.
d Although the *increases* in output are impressive, what factor should you bear in mind to assess Russia's standard of living in 1966? (Clue: output to start with.)
e Why are the statistics quoted in the last column about the USA also helpful in judging the Soviet Union's real progress during this period?

Exercise 3

Extract: **the Khrushchev memoirs, or getting a camel from Moscow to Vladivostok**

During his retirement from 1964 until his death in 1971 Khrushchev spent 180 hours dictating his memoirs into a tape recorder. Though Khrushchev remained a loyal Communist and Soviet citizen throughout his life, his memoirs could never have been published in the Soviet Union because they do reveal some criticisms of the system. The recordings were smuggled out to the West and first began appearing in printed form in 1970. Some Western historians thought they were forgeries and Khrushchev also claimed that he had never passed on the material to the West. However voice analysis of the tapes has proved that Khrushchev did dictate the memoirs and people agree that the memoirs fit in well with the type of man Khrushchev was. However, the memoirs are mainly of value because of what they tell us about Khrushchev and why he acted and made decisions the way he did:

> I met a man recently who asked me, 'Say, Comrade Khrushchev, do you think a camel could make it all the way from Moscow to Vladivostok?'
>
> I could tell from the way he was smiling that there was more to the question than met the eye. I answered cautiously, 'Well, the camel is a
> 5   strong animal with lots of stamina, so I think he could probably walk all the way to Vladivostok!
>
> 'No, comrade Khrushchev, you're wrong. The camel would be lucky to make it as far as Sverdlovsk.'
>
> 'Why?'
> 10   'Because, assuming he gets to Sverdlovsk, the people there would eat him.'
>
> There's a certain amount of truth in that story: it says something about the shortage of food in the towns and villages across our country. I look forward to the day when a camel would be able to walk from Moscow to
> 15   Vladivostok without being eaten by hungry peasants or villagers along the way.
>
> Food, of course, is the most essential need of our people, but we must also satisfy their aesthetic demands. Man loves flowers. Without flowers life would be terribly tedious. It's time for our leadership to realise that
> 20   those goods which add to the beauty of life are not superfluous – they are basic.

(N. Khrushchev, *Khrushchev Remembers, the Last Testament*)

a Why did the questioner think it unlikely that the camel would make it to Vladivostok?

b What do you think Khrushchev meant by the sentence quoted in lines 13–16?

c How much of a contribution do you think Khrushchev made to achieving that goal with his Virgin Lands Project?

d What sort of goods did Khrushchev have in mind in line 20 which 'add to the beauty of life'?

e What criticism is Khrushchev making of Russia's leadership at that time (i.e. late 1960s)?

f How much did he do to ensure while he was leader of Russia that the Soviet people acquired 'those goods which add to the beauty of life'?

g Why do you think Khrushchev denied that he had ever written these memoirs when they appeared in the West?

h What sort of impression do you get of the kind of man Khrushchev was from reading this extract from his autobiography?

i Why do you think historians were so interested in these memoirs once they were accepted as genuine? Why, nonetheless, do historians still have to treat the memoirs with caution when it comes to trying to piece together events in the past that Khrushchev was involved in?

After Khrushchev

Khrushchev was replaced once again by group leadership in which two men seemed to dominate. Leonid Brezhnev became Party Secretary in place of Khrushchev and Kosygin took over the post of Prime Minister. They largely continued Khrushchev's policies but in a less flamboyant style. There was, however, a tightening up of control over criticism and artistic freedom. Khrushchev had allowed the publication of material which showed the truth about the Stalin years. Solzhenitsyn's novel, *One Day in the Life of Ivan Denisovich*, which told of the author's years in one of Stalin's labour camps was published under Khrushchev, but the new leadership put a stop to any criticism of Stalin. Solzhenitsyn was expelled from Russia in 1974. Kosygin resigned from office in 1980 and Brezhnev died in 1982. The former chief of the KGB was elected to replace him. In his 15 months in office Andropov began a vigorous anti-corruption campaign but his death in February 1984 left the Russian leadership with a problem. They had a choice between the old generation in the shape of 73 year old Chernenko and Mikhail Gorbachev, 20 years his junior. The cautious, conservative nature of Russia's leaders won the day and Chernenko was chosen. Chernenko was a sick man and by early 1985 the Soviet Union had a new leader in the form of Gorbachev who represents a new and less traditional generation of Soviet leaders.

Gorbachev in power

Gorbachev, like other Soviet leaders before him, is committed to a major reform of the Soviet system of government. He wants to see more effective decision-making at a local level. Andropov had begun a system by which Soviet factories were to be given more power to make their own decisions without consulting Moscow. By 1985, however, only 6% of Soviet factories were operating in this way. Gorbachev plans to extend this scheme throughout Soviet industry by 1987. A bonus (and penalty) scheme will be introduced to ensure more prompt and better quality production. Unlike some leaders, though, Gorbachev has set modest targets for growth in the new Five Year Plans. Unfortunately for the people of the Soviet Union these modest targets also apply to growth in incomes. One area where the new leader has allowed his hopes to get the better of him is agriculture. Grain output is set to reach 250–255 million tonnes by 1990. This is likely to prove beyond the Soviet Union's still backward agricultural system. The 1981–85 Plan aimed at an output of 239 million tonnes and fell short.

'Star Wars'

Perhaps Gorbachev's most startling impression has been in the area of foreign affairs. He has made a favourable impact on the Western press and television networks as well as on Western leaders. During a visit to Britain in 1985 Mrs Thatcher, the British Prime Minister, described Gorbachev as a man she could 'do business with'. In November 1985 President Reagan met Gorbachev for the Geneva Summit to discuss super power 'business'. The key issue was the control of nuclear weapons. Both sides seemed willing to agree on substantial cuts in the nuclear arsenal but the Soviets were determined to get Reagan to abandon further development of his 'Strategic Defence Initiative (SDI, more commonly known as 'Star Wars'). This would lead the United States to setting up a space based anti-missile system which would destroy Soviet nuclear missiles in space before they could reach the United States. Gorbachev has argued that this would merely force the Soviet Union to de-

President Reagan and the Soviet leader, Gorbachev, at the Geneva summit in November, 1985. Relations between the two leaders seemed friendly enough but little in terms of concrete progress emerged

(Right) *Gorbachev's Geneva Summit 'bubble' could get a prickly response from the Soviet military's 'hedgehog'*

velop their own 'Star Wars' system and the arms race would simply go another step further. Reagan, however, was determined not to give way on the issue. No agreement was reached on 'Star Wars' but other improvements in East–West relations seem set to go ahead. More Jews may be allowed to leave the Soviet Union for Israel and Gorbachev hinted that he would like to see a solution to the problem of Afghanistan, under Soviet occupation since 1980.

However, all of Gorbachev's problems are not to be found in his relations with the United States. He, like Reagan, had powerful forces at home to satisfy – the Soviety military is as influential as the Pentagon (the US Defence Department). The Soviet leader knows that the military is keen to develop its own 'Star Wars' system and probably views Gorbachev's suspension of nuclear tests as a sign of weakness. The refusal of the United States to join the Soviet ban means that the Soviet Union will probably re-begin nuclear testing in the near future. As the cartoon above indicates the Soviet military is only too willing to bring Mikhail Gorbachev back to earth with a bang. The test of the Soviet leader's skill is whether he can keep his own military leaders happy and still continue with his search for successful arms limitations – especially in the 'Star Wars' field.

Relations with the Soviet Bloc

Within three years of the end of the Second World War, Poland, Hungary, Rumania, Czechoslovakia and Bulgaria all had pro-Russian Communist governments in control. In some of these countries, notably Czechoslovakia, Communists had already been well-established and popular – a popularity which grew as a result of the major role of Communist partisans in driving out the Nazis

(Right) *Marshall Tito: he stood up to Stalin to ensure that Yugoslavia developed its own independent form of Communism*

during the war in the Eastern European states. But it was the Soviet Union's Red Army which had been decisive and Stalin had no intention of allowing the countries of Eastern Europe to develop any system other than pro-Russian Communism. To begin with the Communists formed **coalition** governments with other parties that had opposed the Nazis – mainly Liberals and non-Marxist Socialists. In these coalition governments Communists usually held key posts, such as responsibility for the police and army. Gradually, the non-Communist parties were intimidated and finally banned, leaving only Communist parties in control. Only Czechoslovakia of these East European states had been a democracy before the war and so in most cases these countries simply passed from one form of dictatorship to another.

Czechoslovakia

In free elections in Czechoslovakia in 1946 the Communists won 38% of the vote and held a third of the ministerial posts in the coalition government. The Prime Minister, Klement Gottwald was a Communist though Benes remained President, and a liberal, Jan Masaryk was Foreign Minister. For a while the government functioned well enough until new elections were due in May 1948. The rejection by the Communists of US financial aid in the form of Marshall Aid in 1947 looked like costing them votes. An armed take-over or **coup** was staged in which Masaryk died in mysterious circumstances – officially he had committed suicide by throwing himself out of his office window. Unofficially he was pushed. In the May elections only Communist-backed candidates could stand. They 'won' 88% of the votes. In the other East European states the story was much the same. By the end of 1947 Communists were in sole control of Hungary (under Rakosi), Poland (under Gomulka), Rumania, Bulgaria (under Dimitrov) and Albania (under Hoxha).

Albania and Yugoslavia

The cases of Albania and Yugoslavia are somewhat different from the others. The Albanian Communists, led by Enver Hoxha, had successfully fought off the Italians and Germans without Soviet help in the shape of the Red Army. The Albanians were, for the time being, happy to ally themselves with Stalin.

The Yugoslavian Communists, led by Josip Tito, had also successfully freed their country without Stalin's Red Army. Unlike Hoxha, though, Tito had no intention of allowing Yugoslavia to become a Russian puppet state or satellite. Stalin's efforts to remove Tito from power failed and the Yugoslavs were able to develop their own distinctive brand of Communism which involved close links with the West.

Germany

The situation in Germany belongs to

another chapter as Germany was the centre of the **Cold War** in Europe. After the failure of the Berlin blockade in 1948–49 however, Stalin resigned himself to the presence of the Western Powers in Berlin; but in 1949 the division of Germany became permanent with the creation of the pro-Western German Federal Republic and the pro-Soviet German Democratic Republic (East Germany). Another country which had been divided between the Allies into French, British, American and Russian zones was Austria. Its capital, Vienna, was also split into four zones. Many feared that it would also become a source of conflict between East and West, but in fact the Russians withdrew their forces from the country in 1955.

Exercise 4

a List all the countries of Europe which had Communist governments by the end of 1949.

b In which one of these countries were the Communists a genuinely popular force at the end of the war?

c What evidence is there in the text that proves the popularity of the Communists in this country?

d In what way were the Communist governments of Albania and Yugoslavia different from the others?

e Can you think of any reason that might account for the Russian decision to withdraw from Austria in *1955*? (Clue: Russia's new leadership.)

Exercise 5

a Which two countries have boarded the bus of the US President Truman?

b Suggest two other countries which were to join Hungary in Stalin's bus by the end of *1947*.

c What evidence is there in the cartoon that Hungary was not a willing passenger in the bus?

d What evidence is there in the cartoon that the passengers in Truman's bus are more willing?

e Which country followed Bulgaria onto Stalin's bus in 1948?

f How appropriate a title do you think the name above Truman's bus is? Explain your answer.

g How justified were the fears of the cartoonist that Austria would soon be joining the others in the Russian bus?

h In what sense is this cartoon of 1947 itself a part of the Cold War?

Source One   Punch *cartoon*

The Soviet Bloc since Stalin

Stalin ruled the Communist states of Eastern Europe in the same way he controlled Russia. Those East European Communists that dared to follow a different line to the one laid by Stalin were lucky to escape with imprisonment. The Polish leader, Gomulka, was fortunate to get away with a prison sentence for supporting Tito in Yugoslavia in 1948. Stalin's death in 1953 seemed to have had the effect of bringing to the surface all the discontent of some of the peoples inside the Soviet Bloc. In May a demonstration by 100 000 workers for better pay in East Berlin was broken up by Russian tanks. In June 1956 Polish workers in Poznan went on strike in protest about high prices, wage restrictions and heavy taxes. Russian troops inside Poland once again put down the strikers but Khrushchev decided that some sort of compromise was needed. Gomulka was brought out of gaol and was once again allowed to become leader. Russian troops withdrew from Poland. Gomulka was allowed to develop the Communist system in his own way – provided Poland stayed loyal to Russia and her newly created military alliance, the Warsaw Pact. This had been set up the previous year (1955) and linked all the European Communist states in a military alliance with the Soviet Union. Relations with the powerful Polish Catholic Church were improved and the Church was allowed to function freely as long as it stayed out of politics.

The Hungarian Rising

Events in Poland, though, were nowhere near as bloody and tragic as those that took place in Hungary five months later. There had been serious disagreements inside the Hungarian Communist Party for a long time. Rakosi, the first leader, was a keen supporter of Stalin's methods but he had been consistently opposed by another Communist, Imre Nagy, who favoured a more liberal and less harsh method of rule. But little economic progress was made under Nagy and he was replaced as Prime Minister in 1955, two years after taking over. Rakosi was once again in control but in October 1956 the anger of the people of Budapest against the harshness of the Rakosi Stalinist regime exploded onto the streets. The victims of the Rakosi Secret Police probably numbered 2000 executed and a further 200 000 in prison. Khrushchev's speech to the Twentieth Congress earlier in the year and the return to power of Gomulka encouraged the Hungarians to think that there could be real changes in their country.

The secret policemen were hunted down in the streets and Russian troops were forced to withdraw from the capital, Budapest. Khrushchev made concessions, as he had in Poland earlier. Nagy was allowed to return as Prime Minister and the gaoled head of the Catholic Church in Hungary, Cardinal Mindszenty was released. But here the similarity with Poland ended because Nagy began a policy of encouraging political debate and freedoms. Government control of the press and radio was ended. People demanded that Hungary withdraw from the Warsaw Pact and that free elections take place. On 1 November 1956, Nagy announced that the government agreed to carry out these policies. The removal of Hungary from the Warsaw Pact was not something that Khrushchev would tolerate. On 4 November the Soviet tanks rolled back into Budapest. The people of the city and units of the Hungarian Army fought back but their resistance could never have succeeded. In the street battles 20 000 Hungarians and 7000 Russians were killed and wounded. Nagy was tempted out of his safe refuge in the Yugoslavian Embassy by a Russian promise of safe conduct. He was immediately arrested. Two years later the Russians announced that he had been shot. Over 200 000 Hungarians were luckier and managed to escape across the border to the West. Nagy was replaced by Janos Kadar, a reliable Communist still in control in 1986. Khrushchev had shown that he was not prepared to allow change to threaten Russia's own security. Kadar, however, was not a Communist in the Rakosi mould. Under his skilful leadership Hungary now provides considerable choice of consumer goods and economic independence from Russia.

Exercise 6

a Why was the Polish leader, Gomulka, imprisoned in 1948?

b What concessions did Khrushchev make to the Polish rebels in 1956?

c Why were the Hungarians encouraged to think that there would be major changes in their country by Khrushchev's speech to the Twentieth Congress and by the return to power of Gomulka in Poland?

d What were the two policies declared by Nagy that led the Russians to crush the Hungarians in 1956?

e To which country did the Hungarians that escaped in 1956 flee? Why would this country have been unlikely to welcome them over twelve months earlier? (See the map, Source Two, for help in answering this.)

Source Two
Changes in Eastern Europe after 1945

Exercise
7

a In which city did the events shown in Source Three occur?

b Whose statue has been pulled down? Why was it a likely target for such treatment?

c Other than the fallen statue, what evidence is there of violence in the photograph?

d In addition to the civilians shown in the photograph, what other body was active in the resistance to the invasion?

e What evidence is there in the photograph that the people shown were not in danger at that time?

f Would you date this photograph before the events of 4 November 1956 or after? Explain the reasons for your answer.

Source Three *Hungary, 1956*

Assignment unit

The Hungarian Rising

The Hungarians defended Budapest with fierce courage. Civilians used ingenious methods against tanks. Roads were covered with liquid soap to stop the tank tracks gripping. Upturned soup plates were left in the streets. The Soviet tank commanders, taking them for anti-tank mines, would not try to pass them. Agents of the hated Hungarian Secret Police (the AVH) often met the fate of the man in the photograph on page 174 when captured by the rebels. One *Daily Mail* reporter filed this report:

> As I moved deeper into the city, every street was smashed. Hardly a stretch of tramcar rails was left intact ... Hundreds of yards of paving stones had been torn up, the streets were littered with burnt-out cars. Even before I reached the Duna Hotel, I counted the carcasses of at least forty tanks ... at the corner of Stalin Avenue ... two monster Russian T.54 tanks lumbered past, dragging bodies behind them, a warning to all Hungarians of what happened to fighters ...
>
> (Quoted in D. Pryce-Jones, The *Hungarian Revolution*, 1969)

Your assignment is to continue with the report filed above. Like all good journalists you must remember the golden rule: 'Who, What, Where, When, Why?' Try to answer these questions in your report, giving the background to the Rising, its major events, who was involved etc. Some of these questions could be answered through an interview with a Hungarian fighter. Finish your report with likely future developments in Hungary and say why Western assistance for the rebels was very unlikely. (Turn to Chapter 19 for the Suez Crisis at this time and you will see that the West had serious problems of its own.)

The body of an AVH (Hungarian Secret Police) man, strapped to a tree. The AVH, under the Rakosi regime, had tortured political prisoners and opponents of the pro-Soviet government. The Hungarian rebels showed them no mercy

Exercise 8

Map work: Source Two

Study the map of Eastern Europe after 1945 (page 172) and then answer these questions:

a Copy the map into your exercise book.

b Devise some shading to indicate:
  i   those Communist countries under Soviet domination;
  ii the Communist country independent of the Soviet Union.

c Under the name of the following countries write the name of the Communist leader who first took control: Poland; Hungary; Bulgaria; Czechoslovakia; Albania; Yugoslavia.

d In 1946 Churchill made a speech in which he talked of an 'Iron Curtain' descending across Europe from 'Stettin in the Baltic to Trieste in the Adriatic'. The 'Iron Curtain' divided Europe into Communist and non-Communist parts. But Churchill was inaccurate. Why was Stettin the wrong choice of Baltic port to mark one end of the curtain? Which port should he have chosen?

e Mark onto your map the correct line of the Iron Curtain at the end of the 1940s. Be sure to include Zone D of Austria. Why?

f By the end of October 1955 all Allied troops (including Russian) had withdrawn from Austria. Austria, it was agreed, would not be a Communist state but a capitalist one like the rest of Western Europe but it would have to remain a neutral one. Why were the Hungarian rebels later grateful for this change?

Rumania: a measure of independence

Moscow's hold on the Warsaw Pact countries remained generally firm after the lesson handed out to the Hungarians in 1956. However, Albania and, to a lesser extent, Rumania did manage to achieve some independence. Enver Hoxha in Albania was a fervent admirer of Stalin and he disapproved of Khrushchev's attack on Stalin in 1956 – as did China. Relations between these two followers of Stalinism rapidly grew closer until in 1961 diplomatic relations between Moscow and Albania were cut. In 1968 Albania left the Warsaw Pact. Hoxha was able to get away with this because he had a powerful ally in China, and Russia did not want to make worse what were already bad relations with the Chinese by taking military action against Albania. Hoxha's death in 1985 seems unlikely to bring about any major change in Albania's policies.

The Rumanians under Ceaucescu have not gone as far as Albania. Rumania is still a loyal member of the Warsaw Pact and a strictly Communist regime in the Soviet mould. It is in the area of foreign affairs that the Rumanians in the early 1960s began to develop a policy very different from the Soviet Union. Russian was dropped as a compulsory school subject in 1962 and Rumania was the only Warsaw Pact country not to support the Russian invasion of Czechoslovakia. It is also the only one to have full relations with Israel. The Russians, while not pleased with these developments or with Rumania's close relations with China, have not intervened because under Ceaucescu the Rumanians have not threatened Russia's security. The fact that the Rumanians are the only Warsaw Pact nation with their own oil supplies has been very important. The remaining nations in the Soviet Bloc are totally dependent on cheap Russian oil supplies to keep their economies afloat.

The Berlin Wall 1961

In 1961 Berlin once again became the focus of East–West tension. Walter Ulbricht, the Communist leader of East Germany, had for a long while been concerned at the steady flow of East Germans leaving the country for the West through East Berlin. Most of these refugees from Communism were well qualified and young – half the 2 600 000 emigrants between 1949 and 1961 were under 24. In the early hours of Sunday morning, 13 August 1961 a 30 mile barrier was erected across the city of Berlin, sealing off the Eastern sector from the West. In most places the barrier consisted of a high brick wall, topped with barbed wire and guarded by machine guns in towers. There would be no more people leaving East Berlin for life in the West. The West Berliners were suddenly cut off from friends and relatives in the East. Relations between the United States and Russia, already strained because of the U-2 incident, got sharply worse. (In May 1960 a high-altitude American spy plane, a U-2, was shot down over Soviet territory. Its pilot, Gary Powers, was taken prisoner. Khrushchev demanded an apology from Eisenhower at the Paris Summit meeting two weeks later. The incident led to the break-up of the Summit. Powers was exchanged in February 1962 for a Soviet spy held by the Americans.) But Western action did not go beyond protests and speeches. Khrushchev had taught the new, young American President Kennedy, a sharp lesson in power politics. Since the building of the Wall another lesson has been taught to the 74 East Germans that have died trying to cross the Wall.

The Prague Spring 1968

Unlike the other East European Communist states, Czechoslovakia had been a **democracy** between 1918 and 1938. The Czechs and Slovaks felt more bitter about their loss of freedoms. A

The Berlin Wall. Hastily built three months earlier, a section of the wall collapsed in November 1961 during the first frost. Note the wooden barrier behind the wall

Czechs inspecting a burnt-out Soviet tank in Prague

promise of change was in the air when, in January 1968, Alexander Dubcek took over from Novotny as Secretary of the Communist Party and leader of Czechoslovakia. Dubcek planned only limited reforms. His policy was called 'Socialism with a human face'. Czechoslovakia was to become less repressive, its government was to be more efficient and living standards raised. Co-operatives would be encouraged and workers given a bigger say in the running of their factories. Travel to the West would be open to all and not just a few trusted Communists. The Russians might have tolerated some or even all of these changes. However, they did advise Dubcek to slow things down.

Dubcek then promised that the Czechs would remain part of the Warsaw Pact, but in July he was swept along in the tremendous burst of popular feeling for greater change. He announced that free elections would be held and that opposition political parties would be set up. The probability that Communism would be voted out of power was too much for Brezhnev and his colleagues. On 22 August 500 000 Warsaw Pact troops invaded Czechoslovakia. Unlike in Hungary 12 years earlier, this time there was no organised resistance. Dubcek was removed from office but not executed. He was given a job in the Forestry Commission. In January 1969 a 21 year old Czech student, Jan Palac, burnt himself to death in Prague as a protest against the Russian occupation of his country.

Poland: Solidarity

The Russian action in Prague did not seem to be as effective a lesson as the crushing of the Hungarian Rising had been. Two years later Polish workers again took to the streets in protests against steep increases in food prices. The riots forced the resignation of Gomulka and his replacement by Gierek. The whole process was repeated 10 years later in Gdansk over the same issue, this time led by shipyard workers and their leader, Lech Walesa. This time the workers also set up their independent trade union, Solidarity, and demanded the right to strike and to be consulted on all major decisions affecting their living and working conditions. The new Leader, Kania, agreed. The Russians were not pleased but waited until December 1981. Then the Polish army leader, General Jaruselski, with Soviet backing, seized control of the country. Solidarity was banned and its leader, Walesa, arrested. Prices were increased 400% in basic foods and Poland was now under military rule.

The West did not intervene to help the Poles in 1981. It had not come to the aid of Czechoslovakia in 1968 nor Hungary in 1956. Eastern Europe forms part of the Soviet Bloc and the Soviet Union has a free hand there to ensure Soviet domination or **hegemony**. In much the same way, the United States can overthrow unfriendly governments in its own sphere of influence, whether that government is in Chile (1973) or in Grenada (1983). There is no room for sentiment in 'superpower' politics of the twentieth century.

Exercise  **9**

a Why did Enver Hoxha disapprove of Khrushchev's speech in 1956?
b In what area of policy have the Rumanians taken a very different line to the Russians?
c Why is the fact that the Rumanians have their own oil supplies so important?
d Why was the Berlin Wall erected?
e Which Dubcek policy provoked the Russians to send in troops in August 1968?
f Explain what you think the author means by the last sentence in the text above – 'There is no room for sentiment in 'superpower' politics . . .'

Exercise 10

a What posts in the Soviet government were occupied by the two men in hats?
b What sort of people is the cartoonist trying to make the Russian leaders look like?
c Why was Dubcek likely to find it difficult to go surfing?
d What is the cartoon implying was the Russians' real intention of dealing with Dubcek? Did subsequent events prove the cartoonist right?
e Do you think this cartoon was typical of American reaction to the events in Prague in August 1968 and why?

Source Four

American cartoon 'Someone is taking Dubcek surfing'

Exercise 11

Study the cartoon on page 178

a Identify the 'bear trainer' in the ring.
b What did the six 'bears' in the ring all have in common?
c What point of view is the cartoonist trying to get across by having some of the bears sitting upright on their stools and others getting off them?
d According to the cartoon, which of the bears was the most rebellious? What evidence can you find in the text to support this view?
e Name the two bears absent from the cartoon that also belonged to this 'family'.

Source Five

Punch *cartoon'*
31 October 1956

f Describe the events immediately before this cartoon (31 October 1956) that led to the Hungarian bear attempting to leave its stool. What action did the ringmaster take to get it back under control?

g Describe the way in which two of the three obedient bears later attempted to escape the control of the bear trainer. Which one of them succeeded?

h The bear is the symbol of Russia. Why do you think it was appropriate for the cartoonist to show these nations as bears as well? What is your opinion of this cartoon as a method of getting across a political view about Russia and its relations with these 'bears'?

Chapter 15

China this century

China before 1911

For many hundreds of years China had been a closed country, visited by few foreigners and largely ignored. But in the nineteenth century this began to change. China was an area of some 400 million people who would provide an excellent market for European goods. The problem was that the Chinese distrusted foreigners and very quickly came to hate them. The ruling family of China, the Manchu Dynasty, would only allow Europeans to trade through the port of Canton. This was not enough for European nations eager to expand their commerce and power. So they simply seized control of parts of China and established exclusive trading rights in those areas. The British seized Hong Kong and Shanghai; the French, Germans and Russians also helped themselves to chunks of Chinese territory. The weak Manchu Government could do nothing about it and had little real control over most of the huge country.

Many Chinese were unhappy with this situation. In 1900 an anti-foreigner and nationalist group called the Righteous Harmony Fists, nicknamed 'the Boxers', staged what became known as the Boxer Rebellion. They launched an attack in Peking against the Western community which was put down after 55 days by Russian and Japanese troops. After this, the Western powers increased their influence and control over China. The Japanese were also becoming more involved in the 'scramble for China' and by 1910 they had seized Formosa (1895), Manchuria (1905) and Korea (1910). Another country interested in the area was the United States. The Americans objected to the European powers seizing control of China's main trading cities because these were then barred to American goods. The United States favoured what they called an 'Open Door' policy in which all nations had equal rights to trade with China. European powers were very unwilling to give up their monopolies.

Opposition to both foreigners and the Manchu Government continued to grow rapidly. One man who worked very hard to organise a **revolution** to overthrow the Manchus was Sun Yat-sen. He was a lawyer who had travelled a great deal abroad. He was determined that China should become a modern, democratic and independent nation. He set up a secret society dedicated to his 'Three Principles': **Nationalism, Democracy, Socialism'**. The

Foreign spheres of influence in and around China in 1910

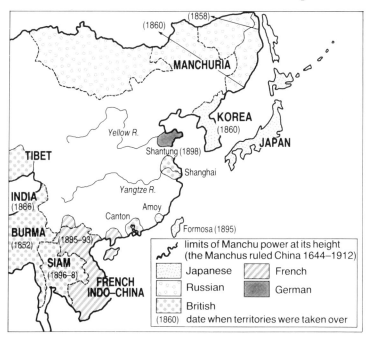

(1858)

(1860)

MANCHURIA

Yellow R.

KOREA (1860)

Shantung (1898)

JAPAN

TIBET

Shanghai

Yangtze R.

INDIA (1886)

Amoy

Canton

BURMA (1852)

(1885–93)

Formosa (1895)

SIAM (1896–8)

FRENCH INDO-CHINA

limits of Manchu power at its height (the Manchus ruled China 1644–1912)

Japanese	French
Russian	German
British	
(1860)	date when territories were taken over

first of these principles would bring about the expulsion of foreign domination from China. Then China would develop a democratic, parliamentary system of government which would modernise the country by improving the standard of living – especially for the peasants.

The 'Revolution of the Double Tenth'

On the tenth day of the tenth month of 1911 Sun finally managed, on his eleventh attempt, to stage a successful rebellion against the Manchu Dynasty, whose emperor was five year old Pu Yi. The general sent to put down the rebellion was Yuan Shi-kai, but instead of suppressing the rising he joined it. In 1912 Sun set up his People's Nationalist Party, the Kuomintang, and China was declared to be a democratic republic. Yuan Shi-kai insisted on becoming its first president and Sun gave way. But Yuan was interested only in power for himself and cared nothing for Sun's 'Principles'. Within a few months the Kuomintang (KMT) was made illegal and Yuan was **dictator** of China.

The First World War further complicated matters. Japan declared war on Germany in 1914 in return for a promise that they would be given the German controlled province of Shantung when the war was over. The Japanese defeated the Germans in Shantung and went on to list 'Twenty-one Demands' which extended Japanese influence in China. Yuan was forced to give in to most of the Demands. He died the following year in 1916. China was by now split into several quarrelling factions, each of which claimed to be the legal government of China. The two most powerful were the Kuomintang who controlled the south and the warlord successor to Yuan, based in the north in Peking. The Peking government also declared war on Germany in 1917, hoping that foreign interference in China would be ended after victory. In fact, the situation was made worse as the Treaty of Versailles handed over all Germany's Chinese spheres of influence to Japan. Only Bolshevik Russia of the Western powers won favour in China by giving up all Russian interests in the country. Once the terms of the Versailles Treaty became known they sparked off huge violent demonstrations in Peking and elsewhere against Allied 'treachery'. These demonstrations became known as the 'May the Fourth Movement' following a nationwide demonstration on 4 May, and won many new supporters for the Kuomintang.

Exercise 1

a Why did the Western powers become so interested in China in the nineteenth century?
b How did these powers establish their influence in China?
c How did Sun Yat-sen's 'Revolution of the Double Tenth' go wrong?
d Why could the Chinese feel cheated by the Allies after Germany's defeat?
e What evidence is there in the text that relations between Russia and China were likely to improve?

Exercise 2

Study the cartoon on page 181

The figure of war (*Krieg*) stands over the pack of European powers scrambling over China. The caption reads: 'When everything there is devoured I will be forced to set these beasts onto each other, otherwise they will end up tearing me to pieces'.

Der Krieg.

Source One
German cartoon

a What are the main nations involved in 'devouring' China?

b Which of these powers had been most active in 'devouring' China before 1918? Give reasons for your answer.

c Explain why the United States is sitting in the background, not taking part in the attack.

d How would you describe the cartoonist's attitude to the behaviour of these powers?

e Why would this cartoon be approved of by Sun Yat-sen?

f How good a prophecy did the cartoon prove to be as regards 'War' setting the beasts onto each other?

The Civil War, part one: 1927–37

The Chinese **Communist** Party was set up in 1921, inspired by the revolution of 1917 in Russia – a country similar to China in its vastness, backwardness and mainly peasant population. Among its nine founder members was a 28-year-old library assistant, Mao Tse-tung. In 1923 the Russian Communists sent military and political experts to assist the Kuomintang build up its popularity and its own army. The Chinese Communists and Kuomintang joined together in a fruitful alliance to defeat the northern warlords and so establish a single government for China. The Northern Expedition was planned against the warlords but Sun Yat-sen was never to see it as he died in 1925. The expedition was led by the Kuomintang's new leader, Chiang Kai-shek, and set off in 1926. By March 1927 they controlled all of China south of the Yangtze river. It was then that Chiang turned on his Communist allies. Chiang was basically a military man whose chief ambition was to become sole ruler of all China. To do this he needed the backing of powerful landowners and businessmen who disapproved of the Communists.

Chiang turns on the Communists

In April 1927 Chiang's forces were ordered to turn on their former Communist allies in Shanghai and elsewhere. Thousands were slaughtered in the streets. One method used to identify Communists was to check the neck of suspects for the red stain left by red scarves worn by Communists in the fighting against the warlords. In wet weather the dye ran. An American eye-witness described this scene in Canton, where 6000 'Communists' perished:

> Execution squads patrolled the streets, and on finding a suspect, they questioned him, examining his neck for the tell-tale stain. If found, they ordered the victim to open his mouth, thrust a revolver into it, and another coolie came to the end of

A Kuomintang execution squad in search of Communists in Shanghai: 6000 Communist suspects were executed without trial in the streets of Shanghai

his Communist venture . . . I myself saw a rickshaw stopped, the coolie grabbed by the police, his shirt jerked from his neck disclosing the red stain . . . He was rushed to the side of the road, compelled to kneel down, and unceremoniously shot while the crowd of people in the street applauded.

(R. North, *Chinese Communism*)

The Communists were forced to abandon the cities which had been their strong-holds and escape southwards to the remote provinces of Kiangsi and Hunan. Here Mao Tse-tung and a Communist general in the Kuomintang, Chu Teh, began to reorganise what was left of the Red Army and the Communist Party. Mao soon realised that a party which based its appeal only on the support of industrial workers – as Communist parties were supposed to do – would have little chance of success in a country where 97% of the population were peasants. So Communist policy was changed. The Communists promised to lead the peasants in a revolution in which they would seize the land from the landowners and which would belong to them. In Kiangsi they taught peasants new farming methods and how to fight. A 'People's Liberation

Army' (PLA) was organised which, at first, numbered just 10 000. But they were well trained in a new method of **guerrilla** war which was suited to the terrain:

> The enemy attacks, we retreat:
> The enemy camps, we harass:
> The enemy tires, we attack:
> The enemy retreats, we pursue.

The Long March

The PLA fighters behaved very well towards the peasants, never stealing, always paying for what they took or damaged and treating prisoners well. After capturing Peking in 1928 and the rest of China, except for Manchuria, Chiang turned his attention to the Communists in the south in 1930. His first three campaigns were dismal failures. The PLA grew to 300 000 men. Finally in 1934 Chiang came up with a more effective scheme of surrounding the Communist base and cutting off their food supplies. The PLA forces soon dwindled to 100 000 and Mao and Chu Teh realised that they had to break out of Chiang's encirclement. In October 1934 they set off on what became known as the Long March – a 6000 mile, year-long journey to a mountainous northern province called Shensi. On their way the Communists fought over a dozen battles, crossed 24 rivers and 18 mountain ranges, covering on average 24 miles a day. When they reached their new base at Yenan in October 1935 there were just 20 000 survivors of the original 100 000.

Japanese invasion of China

The province of Shensi became the base from which the Communists could organise and spread their ideas. Throughout the Long March the PLA had behaved well and had dealt with wicked landlords, spreading their ideas and winning peasant support. In Shensi the peasants were educated and benefited from the low rents that the Communists made the landowners charge the peasants. Any new land that was cultivated was shared among the landless peasants. But the Communists and Kuomintang were not the only people fighting over China. In 1931 the Japanese had conquered China's most northern province, Manchuria. Chiang seemed to have little enthusiasm for a war against the Japanese, preferring to destroy Mao instead. But one of Chiang's commanders thought differently and in December 1936 he kidnapped Chiang and forced him to agree to Mao's suggestion for an alliance against the Japanese. It did not come a moment too soon, for in July 1937 the Japanese launched an attack on the rest of China. (See the map below.)

Exercise ▬ 3

a Why did Chiang turn on the Communists in 1927?

b Why did Mao decide to change Party policy and base its appeal on the peasants?

c How did the Communists win over peasant support?

d What evidence is there in the American eye-witness report that Communists had little support in Canton?

e Do you think Mao was wise to forget about trying to build up Communist support in the cities? Explain your answer. (Mention the following points: the small number of workers in China, 2 million in fact; the strength of the Kuomingtang (KMT) in the towns and cities; the remoteness of the rural areas; the huge numbers of peasants in China.)

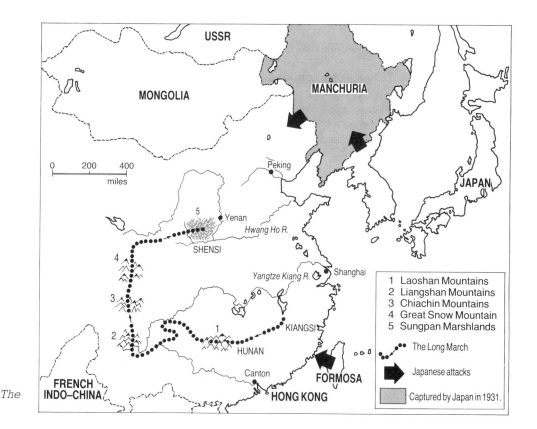

1 Laoshan Mountains
2 Liangshan Mountains
3 Chiachin Mountains
4 Great Snow Mountain
5 Sungpan Marshlands

●●● The Long March

➡ Japanese attacks

▨ Captured by Japan in 1931.

Source Two   *The*
Long March

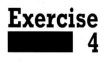

Exercise 4

a Where, according to Source Two, did the Long March begin and end?
b Describe the geographical features that the Communists had to deal with on the March.
c Why do you think the Communists chose this more difficult route to reach their destination?
d Why were Mao and his supporters now more likely to face the Japanese in Yenan than they had been in Kiangsi?
e What qualities do you think the Communists displayed in making this march?

The Civil War, part two: 1945–49

The alliance between Chiang Kai-shek and the Communists was fragile at best. The Japanese soon occupied all of lowland China and its ports. Mao's guerrilla forces staged an effective campaign against the Japanese while Chiang largely kept his forces in reserve for the day when the war against Mao would start again. Japan's attack on the United States in 1941 brought the Americans and Britain into the war, and China's struggle against the Japanese became part of the Second World War. The Red Army stepped up its actions against the Japanese whose 'three alls' campaign did little to win them support: 'burn all, slay all, loot all'. By 1945 the Communists had won back most of the territory occupied by Japan. After Japan's defeat the Kuomintang, thanks to American help, were able to seize hold of most of south China and the cities of the north. The Communists controlled the northern countryside. The Russians had declared war on Japan as well in 1945 and had occupied Manchuria. They did little to ensure that Mao's forces took over the province when they left – indeed, they helped themselves to $2000 million of industrial machinery on their way out. At this stage, the odds favoured a Kuomintang victory. They outnumbered the Communists three to one, had complete control of the air and were well supplied with weapons by the United States.

When Chiang captured Yenan it seemed as though the Kuomintang would indeed win, but Mao was no longer interested in defending remote provinces. He was now committed to a conventional war against Chiang. By 1948 Mao's army, roughly 3 million strong, was as large as Chiang's and much better trained and motivated. The decisive battle was fought in Central China at the end of 1948. Chiang's defeat there meant the loss of Peking in January 1949. In October, after Chiang and the remains of his army, some 1.5 million, had fled to the island of Taiwan, Mao declared the existence of the People's Republic of China.

Why did Mao win?

Perhaps the most important factor in the Communist's victory against Chiang was their role in the war against Japan between 1937 and 1945. The fact that Chiang mounted a half-hearted and ineffective war against the Japanese invaders allowed Mao to put himself forward as the real defender of China's independence and freedom. This not only won huge backing from the peasants but also much of the middle class who, though not Communists, recognised that Mao was fighting to defend China's national interests. United States' backing for Chiang also lost him support since it appeared, correctly, that he was little more than the puppet of US interests. Those areas under the Kuomintang were harshly and badly governed. Corruption ruled and the needs of the landowners and business-men dominated at the expense of the peasants and workers. In the Communist areas the opposite was true. It comes as no surprise to learn that in 1937 Mao controlled an area covering just $1\frac{1}{2}$ million people. By 1945 the num-ber had grown to 100 million. In many areas the Communists did not hand over all the landowners' land to the peasants. Often they simply reduced the rent and this encouraged smaller landowners to back Mao and so only the rich landlords suffered.

Exercise 5

Two views of the rival armies

In the first of two extracts an American journalist, Jack Belden, describes how one sector of Chiang's forces went over to the Communists in 1948:

Extract One

'Brothers', the voices called across No Man's Land, 'Lay down your arms which you never wanted to take up. Did you join the KMT army? No, you were dragged into it at the end of a rope. Come over to us. If you want, we will send you home. Better still, you can join us and fight to free your
5   homes, as we have ours.'

A barrage of rifles greeted these demands ... Pretty soon, at scattered places along the front, the rifles ceased firing. At last a squad of seven men led by a soldier named Tang Kuo-Lua crossed the line. The KMT commander was frightened ... Squad Commander Tang himself called
10   across the 75 yards separating the two forces and begged his old comrades to follow him into the New China ... Within a few weeks 13 000 officers and men – over one tenth of Chiang's forces in the emerald city – crept over to the Communist side. Among them were 16 colonels and 282 officers of the rank of lieutenant or above. All brought rifles ...
15   Throughout the Japanese War and the Civil War that followed, this army was continually beaten because it had no soul. Its commanding staff was distinguished by a scorn of the common solider ... The rank and file, submitting to corruption, tyranny and death, was characterised by a philosophy of despair, by a necessity to loot, and by a hatred of their own
20   officers and of the common people, who pitied but despised them.

(J. Belden, *China Shakes the World*, 1949)

Extract Two

This extract comes from a German stationed at Tientsin in 1948, describing Mao's army.

All were armed, with Japanese rifles or automatic weapons of American make. In every group of half a dozen or so there would be one with a scrap of paper in his hand. These, we discovered, bore the addresses of the private houses on which the squads were to be billeted. Several times I
5   saw a soldier approaching a knot of by-standers ... and ... with a polite bow and a wide smile ask directions ... These must have been some of the first occasions in Tientsin's history of uniformed soldiers using all the forms of Chinese courtesy to ordinary civilians. On the civilians, at first astounded, and in the end mightily pleased, the effect was enormous.

10   As the weeks passed, standards of politeness, modesty, honesty and
          high discipline showed no signs of falling off. There was no looting, no
          pilfering.

          (J. Ch'en, *Mao and the Chinese Revolution*, 1965)

a What are the soldiers of the KMT being asked to do in the first paragraph of
Extract One?

b What evidence does the second paragraph provide that the Communist
message did not appeal only to the lower ranks?

c What do you think the journalist means by saying that the KMT was
continually beaten 'because it had no soul'?

d How did the civilians react to the Red Army soldiers? (Extract Two.)

e Where do you suppose the Communist soldiers acquired their Japanese
rifles and American automatic weapons mentioned in Extract Two?

f Contrast the image of the soldiers of each side that these two extracts
provide. How important do you think were the points that the extracts make
in deciding the outcome of the Civil War and why?

China under Mao: problems in 1949

The problems that faced Mao after the defeat of Chiang Kai-shek were enormous. China's most industrialised region, Manchuria, had been occupied by the Japanese and looted by the Russians. Industrial production was 50% down on the best pre-war figure and food production was 25% down. Inflation was a serious problem as was the devastated railway and road network. The corrupt local government of Chiang Kai-shek had to be replaced by honest Communists, and a stable currency and national taxation system introduced. Mao set about tackling these problems in whatever way suited China best. He was not a dogmatic or inflexible Communist and was prepared to adapt or even abandon some Marxist ideas if they were not the right solution to China's difficulties. Mao decided to proceed slowly in both agriculture and industry. Though a great admirer of Stalin, Mao believed that he had made a mistake in the way he had ruthlessly collectivised Soviet farms in the 1930s.

The Chinese peasants were to be encouraged and persuaded to join the State-run **collective farms** – not forced. The first priority was to change the old, traditional attitudes of the peasantry. Landlords were brought before 'speak bitterness' meetings throughout the country in which peasants were urged to list the crimes and acts of greed of their former masters. One landlord, Ning, was accused of having beaten one man's son to death because the family had fallen behind with the rent:

A weeping girl took up the story: 'You took our plough, chains, everything, because we could not pay the rent. The list of Ning's crimes was very long and at last he broke down 'I'm to blame . . . wholly to blame. You can divide up my houses and land.' A year later, Ning was tried for his crimes and shot.

(P. Townsend, *China Phoenix*)

By 1952 over 115 million acres of land had been handed over from 4 million landlords to some 300 million peasants. The peasants were encouraged to pool

their farms together in co-operatives of 30 to 40 families in which they still owned their land privately but shared out its produce. The next stage was the collective farms which would consist of the land of between 80 to 100 families. The difference here was that the peasants no longer owned the land but, unlike in Stalin's Russia, they had given it up freely.

Death of a landlord. A bound landlord awaits a bullet in the back, having been found guilty by a People's Court, 1953

Assignment unit

A People's Court

An unknown number of landlords perished as a result of trials before People's Courts like the one shown in the photograph above. How guilty of 'crimes' these landlords were is difficult to say. Not all of them were very wealthy. The one in the photograph, Huang, owned two-thirds of an acre – about the equivalent of the land occupied by three modern houses in Britain! In this unit you are to write a report for a Western newspaper of such a trial. (You can, if you wish, use the case of Huang and the photograph as the basis for your article). In addition to your eye-witness account of the trial before the People's Court, you must also 'fill in' the background detail for your readers as to how the Communists had taken control of China. Describe the new policy of the government towards land and why trials like these are occurring. What are the crimes the landlord is accused of and what is his defence and fate? (Note: it is very unlikely that any Western reporters would have been allowed to witness such a trial. The photograph of Huang's trial was taken by an official Communist photographer but was then smuggled out to the West. For the purposes of this assignment unit, though, we shall have to 'bend' the facts.)

Industry: the Five Year Plan

Mao also moved gradually as regards industry. At first, only foreign trade, the banks and heavy industries were **nationalised**. The rest were left in private hands. When the smaller factories and firms were taken over their former owners were often given well paid jobs as managers so that the business would benefit from their skills and their experience. For a while non-Communist parties were tolerated and their representatives sat in the People's Consultative Conference, or Parliament, until 1954 when the new Soviet style constitution came into effect. Another feature of the Soviet system adopted in China was the Five Year Plan. The first of these appeared in 1953. Like the Russian model, the First Five Year Plan concentrated on heavy industries like steel, coal, electric power, oil and cement. Output was set to double but in fact it increased by 120% and in some cases rather more – coal production increased from 16.5 million tons in 1952 to nearly 131 million in 1957; oil from 400 000 tons to 1.5 million and steel from 1.3 million to 5.3 million tons. But these increases, spectacular as they were, did little to improve the standard of living of the Chinese who were desperate for consumer goods such as bicycles.

The Hundred Flowers Campaign

Mao also tried various methods of encouraging the acceptance of Communist ideas – especially among China's 5 million intellectuals who distrusted Communism. China was also beginning to produce many technical experts and engineers. Did it matter whether they believed in Communist ideas as long as they were good at their jobs? Some Chinese Communists did not think it

was important but Mao did. He decided that China's intellectuals – the professors, writers and scientists – should be encouraged to give their views about the Communist system and perhaps be won over to **Marxism** by debate. 'Let a hundred flowers bloom and a hundred schools of thought compete' declared Mao in 1957. For a brief period during the 'Hundred Flowers' campaign criticism of the system did indeed blossom. The Communist Party was described as 'a party of new aristocrats', its daily paper 'a Great Wall blockading Truth' and the official news agency 'a machine manufacturing poison'. The criticism was fast and furious, so much so that Mao decided that what were blooming were not 'fragrant flowers' but 'poisonous weeds'. By the middle of 1957 the campaign came to an end. Despite its rather hasty termination, the campaign did double the number of intellectuals in the Party and its overall membership increased by 30% by 1961.

Exercise 6

a What problems faced Mao in industry and agriculture in 1949?
b How was Mao's approach to the peasants different to that of Stalin?
c What two features of Soviet rule did Mao copy?
d Why did Mao quickly end the 'Hundred Flowers' campaign?
e Was the campaign worthwhile from the Communists' point of view?

The Great Leap Forward

In 1958 Mao decided that China was ready to press ahead towards full-blooded Communism with a 'Great Leap Forward' – the Second Five Year Plan (1958–62). It was an extremely ambitious plan in which industrial output was again set to double and agricultural output due to increase by 35%. Central planning was abandoned in favour of local organisation and the absence of advanced machinery was to be made up for by hard, manual labour. China was set the target of overtaking British

steel production levels. This was to be partly achieved with the campaign for 'Little Steel' in which each village and household, school or factory was to have its own small steel furnace. The biggest change was to occur in agriculture. New, large communes were to replace the smaller co-operative and collective farms. The average size of a collective farm contained 169 families. They were about the size of a traditional village which was a unit the Chinese peasant could understand. By the end of 1958, 99% of all peasant farms were part of communes, which numbered over 4600 families. The communes took on the responsibilities of local government, building roads, hospitals and schools. The idea may have been sound in principle but in practice it failed because the peasants found the commune as a unit too large and one in which family life was no longer central. The Russians had warned of failure, of trying to do too much too quickly. There was no substitute for expert advice and experience, they argued. Mao believed China could make up for what she lacked in advanced technology by superhuman effort. He was wrong.

The Great Leap Forward was a failure but not caused only by Mao's ambitious hopes. There were three years of disastrous harvests, caused by floods and drought. After 1960 the Russians began to withdraw their technicians and advisers as a result of a quarrel between the Russians and the Chinese. This deprived the Chinese of much needed expertise and cash. In 1961 more traditional solutions to China's problems were adopted. The communes were cut down to about a third of their 1958 size and decision making was returned to the village-sized collective farm units. Professional managers were put back to run the factories in place of enthusiastic but unskilled Communists and bonus schemes were introduced to boost output. Men like Teng Hsiao-ping were the main force behind these changes. They were practical minded men who were not really concerned about a man's political suitability – in other words, how good a Communist he was – as long as he did his job. As Teng Hsiao-ping put it, 'What does it matter if the cat is black or white, as long as it catches mice?'

Exercise 7

Two views on the not so great leap

This exercise contains two extracts on the Great Leap Forward. The first is an extract from a Russian publication of 1969 and the second is by Edgar Snow, an American journalist.

Extract Three

From 1949 to 1957 the Communist Party of China pursued a realistic course in the main ... Peking leaders put forth a 'new program' of economic development whereby gross industrial output was to be increased not twice but 6.5 times in five years. Farming was expected now to cover a
5   twelve year programme in three years ...

Deceit and self-delusion, these unfailing attributes of the autocratic regime, had a sorry effect on the plans ... The idea of rapid industrialisation via the 'big leap' in so-called small-scale metallurgy was also an utter failure. Hundreds of thousands of primitive pig-iron and steel
10   furnaces ... were abandoned after a year and left scattered all over China.

(F. Burlatsky, *The True Face of Maoism*, 1969)

Extract Four

[The communes suffered because of] the incredible haste with which they were established; the lack of preparation; ... the lack of incentives; the threat to home life before a broad community life had been fully established to replace it; the enormous technical responsibility and
5   initiative demanded from inexperienced and poorly trained cadres (leading Party members); ... When unbelievably bad weather added its powerfully negative vote, the communes were rapidly driven back ...

(E. Snow, *The Other Side of the River*, 1963)

a What did the Peking leaders 'new program' contain?

b What reason does the author of Extract Three give for the failure of 'the plans'? (line 7)

c Given what you know of the relations between China and the Soviet Union after 1960, why do you think Extract Three was likely to be critical of Chinese policies?

d How does the author of Extract Four imply that the policies of the Great Leap Forward were no longer realistic?

e Which of these two extracts would be of more use to a student of Chinese history and why?

The Cultural Revolution 1966–69

Mao was not likely to stay in the shadows for long. He became increasingly concerned that the ideas of Teng Hsiao-ping and his followers were leading China towards 'revisionism', that is revising the ideas of Marx and Lenin to make China less revolutionary and more like the Soviet Union or the **capitalist** countries. To combat revisionism Mao launched the 'Cultural Revolution' which would restore the energy and passion of the Chinese for revolution and get rid of revisionist elements who called for more moderate and cautious change. In effect, Mao was launching an attack on rivals within the Communist Party. The army Chief of Staff was purged and all symbols of rank abolished by the Minister of Defence, Lin Piao. Massive student demonstrations were organised in Peking in support of Mao's policies and his ideas were published in a little red book containing the 'Thoughts of Chairman Mao'. These 'Red Guard' students, numbering tens of thousands, marched across China attacking anything and anyone considered revisionist. They broke into schools and universities, shut them down and sent the teachers to work in the fields and learn the life of the peasants. They were lucky to escape with their lives as this extract makes clear:

On the athletic field, I saw rows of teachers, about 40 or 50 in all, with black ink poured over their heads and faces. Hanging on their necks were placards with such words as ... 'class enemy so and so' ... They all wore dunce caps. Hanging from their necks were pails filled with rocks. I saw the principal, the pail round his neck was so heavy that the wire had cut deep into his neck and he was staggering. ... Beatings and tortures followed ... eating nightsoil and insects; being subjected to electric shocks; forced to kneel on broken glass.

(Ken Ling, *The Red Guard*, 1972)

When red meant go!

The Red Guards did not limit their activities to schools and universities. They disrupted factories to hold meetings

Mao's Red Guards. The Red Guards were used by Mao to defeat his opponents inside the Communist Party

and sacked factory managers whose views were not correct – no matter how good they were at their jobs. The Guards even called for a change in the traffic-light system – red should mean 'go' and not 'stop'! Mao had said before that 'Revolution is not a dinner party' and the Cultural Revolution was a violent affair in which several thousands probably perished at the hands of the Red Guards. Teng Hsiao-ping was removed from his post as General Secretary of the Party and the President of the Republic was sacked as well. From late 1967 the People's Liberation Army (PLA) was able to exercise more control over the activities of the Red Guards and schools and universities began to reopen. It was about this time that Chou En-lai began to emerge as a major figure, trying to bring the Maoists and their opponents in the Party together. In 1969 Mao's official successor, Lin Piao announced that the violence was over and that the country was once again united. However, two years later Lin Piao, was killed in a plane crash trying to escape to the Soviet Union after attempting to overthrow Mao. The new successor was Chou En-lai who was 73 in 1971, just five years younger than Mao.

In 1973 Teng Hsiao-ping was brought from disgrace as China prepared for life after Mao. Things did not go as smoothly as planned. Chou died in January 1976 and the power struggle to succeed Mao began all over again. Teng was dismissed once more from posts under Mao's orders and a compromise candidate, Hua Kuo-feng, was agreed as the successor. In September 1976 Mao Tse-tung died, aged 83.

Mao's achievement

Mao's most significant achievement was, perhaps, that he created a unified country and provided strong, efficient government for a people unused to such things. **Industrial output** in 1976 was ten times what it was in 1949. Oil production in 1974 stood at 50 million tons compared to 0.4 million in 1952. Agriculture, as in the Soviet Union, has been less of a success for Mao but the commune system, in which 80% of the population are organised, has provided the Chinese with an important measure of control over their own lives. Education also saw real progress during Mao's time. The percentage of people able to read and write in 1949 stood at about 20% but by the time of Mao's death it was 75% and there were four times as many children and students in education. China also became a major military power with an army in the mid 1970s of 2.8 million men, just behind the United States and the Soviet Union. There has been a price for these benefits. There is no freedom of expression in China. Mao left a country in which the 12 million Party members – out of some 800 million people – had a firm grip on the nation and much of the old China had disappeared. Some of that old China – respect for the elderly, loyalty to family and ancestors – was perhaps good but much of it was not. Young girls no longer have their feet bound, and the practice of killing new born baby girls, common in the China of the Manchus, is firmly opposed by the government – though it still does happen.

Exercise 8

a What was 'revisionism' according to Mao?
b Who were the 'Red Guards'?
c How can we tell from the text that divisions inside China did not end with the winding down of the Cultural Revolution in 1969?

   d What do you suppose was meant by the phrase 'class enemy' quoted in the extract on the Red Guard activities?
   e Write a 20 line obituary on the life of Mao Tse-tung from his days as a Communist leader during the Civil War until his death. Try to make your own judgement as to whether he will be remembered as a good ruler for China or as a tyrant (or perhaps both)!

China since Mao

Immediately after Mao's death conflict within the Party broke out again. The Maoists, who wanted a return to the principles of the Cultural Revolution, were led by Mao's widow, Chiang Ching and three others. It was not just a war of words but deeds as well, and the fighting was especially severe around Shanghai, the centre of support for the 'Gang of Four', as the Maoist leaders were called. The Gang of Four were arrested in October and later put on trial. Mao's widow was too important a figure to execute and she was sentenced to a period of house arrest. Hua Kuo-feng became the new leader of China, determined to do away with the remnants of the Cultural Revolution and its chaos. But it soon became clear that the real power in China was the Vice-Chairman of the party, Teng Hsiao-ping. Mao was still treated with respect, and the blame for the effects of the Cultural Revolution was placed, not on Mao, but the Gang of Four. At her trial in 1980 Chiang Ching was accused of a host of crimes – including watching *The Sound of Music* and playing poker. Teng described her as a 'very, very evil woman. She is so evil that anything you can say about her can't be evil enough'. Hua was eased out of power by Teng in 1981 and was replaced by one of Teng's supporters.

Beethoven and Shakespeare

Teng has brought about a deep change in China's way of life since 1976. Experts now dominate China – not the Cultural Revolutionaries with the correct line in Communist thinking who often had little idea of how to run an efficient economy. Workers are once again paid bonuses and managers encouraged to produce profits in their factories.

Under Mao, students were admitted to university if they had a good political record. Teng restored tough examinations for university places. Beethoven could be heard for the first time in years and Shakespeare read and performed. Some measure of private trade was introduced. In 1983 China had as many as 44 000 markets where farmers could sell their produce privately with the result that the income of agricultural workers tripled between 1977 and 1983. Private businesses were encouraged on a small scale and there are now over 3 million private companies. But there are difficulties. A television set costs two years' wages and a bicycle a month's pay. Unemployment, according to Western estimates, stood at 12% in 1983 and this turn to modernisation along Western capitalist lines has also brought Western-style problems such as a rising crime rate and football hooliganism.

China's foreign policy since 1949

Relations between China and the West were never going to be easy from the moment Mao took power in 1949. The Chinese had long and bitter memories of the conduct of 'foreign devils' in the country from the last century. The United States, with its military and political support for Chiang Kai-shek during

'Johnson: ''Anway out of this fix?''
McNamara: ''Bring in another 100000 flies! How about it?''
A sharp Chinese comment on President Johnson's involvement in Vietnam. China's support for North Vietnam during the war soon ended after the war was over

the Civil War, made no secret of its hostility to the Communist Government. Indeed, the US 6th Fleet patrolled the waters around Taiwan, where Chiang had fled in 1949, to prevent Mao from finishing him off. The Americans refused to recognise the Peking Communist Government as the rightful government of China. They preferred to view Chiang's dictatorship in Taiwan as the legal government of all China. As a result, the United States used its veto in the United Nations to forbid the entry of Red China into the UN.

China's invasion of Tibet – which had been a Chinese province up to 1911 when it declared itself independent – in 1950 and its military involvement with the North Korean Communists during the Korean War (1950–53) convinced the United States that China was an aggressive power. However, the reconquest of Tibet was something that Chiang Kai-shek would have attempted had he been in a position to do so as it was regarded by both Nationalists and Communists as part of China. In 1965 the area was given the status of a self-governing region of China. China's war with India over a disputed border in 1962 was a brief affair and the Chinese gave up territory conquered during the campaign to which they felt they had no right. China's lack of real aggression is reflected in the fact that they made no moves to force the British out of Hong Kong. Negotiations were started in 1983

with a British delegation in Peking led by Sir Geoffrey Howe, the Foreign Secretary, over the fate of the colony and its lease which was due to end in 1997. It was agreed that China should regain Hong Kong at the end of the lease but that the port would keep its **capitalist** economy for 50 years.

The Sino–Soviet split

China's foreign policy over the last 25 years has been dominated by two major developments: the break with Russia and the improvement in relations with the United States. The Sino–Soviet split, as the break in relations with Russia is known, did not occur suddenly. Relations became strained after Khrushchev's attack on Stalin in 1956. Mao felt that he should have been consulted over such an important shift in Communist thinking and that he had not been treated as an equal by the Russians. Russia's refusal to help the Chinese develop an atomic bomb and the visit by Khrushchev to the United States in 1959 all helped to worsen relations between the two countries. In addition, the Russians refused to assist the Chinese during their brief border war with India in 1962. The Russians were keen to establish good relations with India. Russia's policy of **'peaceful co-existence'** with the capitalist world seemed to Mao a betrayal of Communist principles which required hostility and the eventual overthrow of non-Communist systems. Towards the end of the 1960s there were regular armed clashes between Chinese and Russian border patrols along the frontier dividing the two nations.

Improved relations with the US

China could not afford to be the enemy of both superpowers at the same time and so from 1971 serious efforts were made to improve relations with the United States. This was particularly surprising as US forces were still fighting

Improved relations with the United States: President Nixon and Chairman Mao, 1972

Americans also gave up their veto on China's entry to the UN Security Council in place of Taiwan. Events got a little out of control, however, and Taiwan was also expelled from the UN.

China has also been careful to establish good relations with the **Third World** nations with whom China had identified herself. Substantial aid has been given to African nations, like Tanzania, attempting to develop an African form of **socialism**. One Third World nation that China does not get on with at present is her neighbour, Vietnam. Vietnam has earned China's displeasure by establishing ever closer relations with the Soviet Union and in the late 1970s and early 1980s frequent clashes and a small-scale invasion (1979) by China have soured relations between these two, at one time friendly, nations.

in Vietnam against Vietnamese Communists who were heavily backed by the Chinese. Nonetheless, in 1971 President Nixon lifted a ban on trade with China and within two years US–Chinese trade had increased a hundred times to $500 million. In that year the

Exercise 9

a What sort of policies did the Gang of Four favour?
b Who gradually emerged as the real power in China after Mao?
c What changes has Teng introduced to China's economy?
d Why were relations between the Communist government and the US bad from the start?
e What two major developments have dominated Chinese foreign policy in the last 25 years?

Exercise 10

Source Three is an American cartoon on President Nixon's visit to China in 1972. Source Four is also an American cartoon from 1979.

Source Three
(left)

Source Four
(right)

a To whom is Nixon seen bowing in Source Three? Why are these two men portrayed as behaving so politely towards one another?
b What is the full name of the Chinese leader shown in Source Four?

c What decision by the US in the previous year had led to this improvement in relations?

d What does the cartoonist show as the consequence of Nixon's bow to Mao's China? What, in reality, did this mean?

e What up until then had been the relationship between the United States and Chiang?

f What point of view is the cartoonist trying to get across by showing Teng prodding the bear with the flag?

g What incident in 1979 would have made relations between Teng and the bear still worse?

h Which of these adjectives, in your opinion, best sums up the attitude of these two cartoons to 'Red' China:

i   insulting;

ii friendly;

iii hostile;

iv bitter?

Explain why you have chosen the adjective that you have and find evidence in the text to show that your choice is justified. For example, if you have chosen (iii) 'hostile' then find some references in the text to the hostile relations between the USA and China in recent years.

i Look at the cartoon on page 193. What do you think the American response would have been to such a cartoon? How does it compare to the attitude in Source Four and how could you explain the difference in attitude?

Chapter 16

The United States since 1945

The Second World War was a major boost for the American economy. The amount of war material produced was staggering: 87 000 tanks, 296 000 planes, 6500 warships. In 1944 the United States' war production was twice that of all the enemy nations put together. There was full employment and, once the war was over, people's expectations were that living standards would improve even more sharply. Generally speaking, living standards did improve still further but there were problems. Sugar, clothing, meat and housing were in short supply and in 1946 prices rose by 32%. These problems could be overcome and they were. But some, more serious, difficulties that were just below the surface also existed. The most serious was the issue of race, and the rights and hopes of the American Negroes who had fought in large numbers for their country during the war. The fact that they had had to fight in segregated units of black and white soldiers indicated how much of a struggle they would have. Poverty was also a problem and has remained one. Even as late as 1966 some 30 million Americans out of a population of 200 million were said to be living below the poverty line. However the poor in 1945 were in a worse situation than in 1966 because they had only limited welfare benefits and no health system.

Harry S. Truman, 1945–52 (Democrat)

Truman was determined to tackle some of these problems. As a Democrat he believed, like Roosevelt before him, that the state had a responsibility to help the poor, control big business and generally improve the standard of living of ordinary Americans at the expense, if necessary, of the rich. But Truman faced a major obstacle in achieving these aims – **Congress**. Truman, like all Presidents, had to put his policies before the elected representatives of the people in Congress for approval. Sometimes the majority of those representatives in the House of Representatives or the Senate belong to the same political party as the President. When this is the case, the President usually has no trouble in getting his policies approved and made in to law. Quite often, though, Congress is dominated by an opposing party which votes against the President. This happened to Truman. Truman's programme, known as the 'Fair Deal', planned to spend some $2700 million on slum clearance and to introduce a national health system paid for by the government as well as a national old age pension and child and maternity benefits. Until 1948 Congress was controlled by Truman's opponents, the conservative Republican Party, and they threw out his 'Fair Deal' programme.

The Republicans used their majority in Congress to force through the anti-trade union Taft–Hartley Act (1947). This act made it illegal for a union to force a worker to join a trade union ('the closed shop') and forced all unions to wait 60 days in a 'cooling off' period before striking. Truman tried to **veto** or forbid this becoming law but a President's veto can be defeated by a two-thirds majority in Congress and Truman's veto was rejected. In domestic affairs, Truman's three years in office had not been a sparkling success but he had made a strong impression in foreign affairs with his determined stand against the expansion of Soviet Communism. Against all expectations Truman won the 1948 Presidential election against his Republican opponent, Thomas Dewey, by 24 million votes to 22 million for Dewey. What made his victory more surprising was the fact that there were also two other Democratic candidates standing against him. The more conservative-minded Democrats from the South disliked Truman's pro-Negro attitude and they put up their own candidate and became known as the 'Dixiecrats'.

The year 1948 also saw a Democrat majority elected to Congress and this meant that some of Truman's 'Fair Deal' programme could now be approved – but not all of it. Social security benefits were extended and the minimum hourly wage was increased from 40 cents an hour to 75 cents but Congress still rejected his national health scheme and his suggestions to guarantee Negroes their civil rights. Truman's opponents here were not the Republicans, who were in a minority, but his Democrats from the south who often voted with the Republicans. However, some progress was made towards desegregating the army, finally achieved in 1954.

McCarthyism

Truman had made a firm stand against **Communism** as a foreign policy issue and it was a popular position with the voters. From 1949 until 1954 a Republican senator called Joseph McCarthy made anti-Communism a major issue for domestic policy as well. The Alger Hiss case of 1948 was the background to the McCarthy campaign to expose 'Communists' in high places. Hiss, a State Department official, was accused by an American Communist of handing over 200 secret documents to him. He also claimed that Hiss was a Communist as well. Hiss denied these accusations but he was found guilty of perjury (lying under oath) and was sentenced to five years in gaol. The late 1940s was a bad time to fall victim to anti-Communist hysteria. The **Cold War** in Europe and the crisis over Berlin (see Chapter 13) especially helped to pave the way for 'McCarthyism'. In February 1950 McCarthy announced that there were 205 Communists working in the State Department – the government department responsible for foreign affairs. McCarthy was never able to prove his claim but it was daring enough to whip up an hysterical campaign of anti-Communism which McCarthy was able to lead. The outbreak of the Korean War in June 1950 made it seem all the more urgent to hunt down these Communists and the thousands of others that McCarthy claimed were plotting to destroy the American way of life. Suspected Communists were brought before McCarthy's investigating Senate Com-

Senator McCarthy displaying 'evidence' before the Senate Investigating Committee

mittee and were ruthlessly bullied and threatened.

McCarthy's witch-hunt led to the investigation of over 9 million people. Many decent people had their lives ruined by McCarthyism: 9500 civil servants were sacked and another 15 000 resigned; 600 teachers lost their jobs and the careers of several fine actors were ended when they were put on McCarthy's 'blacklist' for being Communists or sympathisers. Charlie Chaplin was one such victim and he never worked in America again. Eventually McCarthy's obsession with Communists led him to accuse the army of shielding Communists and even hinted that the President at this time,

Eisenhower, knew of it. McCarthy's sordid campaign came to an abrupt end in 1954 when the Senate passed an official motion of criticism. McCarthy sank without trace. Nonetheless, McCarthy had left his mark on American law and two new laws were passed to deal with the Communist 'menace': the 1950 McCarran Act forced Communist organisations to send a list of members to the government, and eventually in 1954 the Communist Control Act banned the Communist Party altogether for 'conspiracy to overthrow the government of the United States'. One of the proposers of this attack on political freedom was a certain Senator, John F. Kennedy.

a What sort of policies did Democrats believe in?
b Why was Truman unable to see his 'Fair Deal' made law before 1948?
c Why was much of Truman's programme still blocked after 1948?
d Why do you think McCarthy was so popular for a time in America?
e Truman did not like McCarthy but to what extent, if any, can Truman be blamed for helping McCarthyism to develop?

a What are the political views of the man taking the oath? How can you tell?
b To which country's constitution is he swearing loyalty?
c Of what is this man accused and who is the likely accuser?
d What is the cartoonist's view of this man? How does the cartoonist get this across?
e Look at the opinion poll results in Exercise 3. In which year, and why, would this cartoon have been most popular?

Source One
*American cartoon,
1950s*

American public opinion

A sample of Americans was asked the following question in 1945, 1948, 1954 and 1956: 'Do you think members of the Communist Party in this country should be allowed to speak on the radio?' The results of the poll are given below:

	Yes	No	Undecided
1945	48	39	13
1948	36	57	7
1954	22	73	5
1956	24	76	3

a What is the overall trend in the poll from 1945 to 1956;

b What developments in general do you think might have accounted for the change in opinion between:
  i 1945 and 1948 (clue: events in Europe);
  ii 1948 and 1954 (clues: McCarthy; Korea).

c Can you suggest any reason why almost half the people questioned in 1945 did not object to Communists on the radio?

Eisenhower's presidency 1952–60

Franklin Roosevelt was the last American President to be re-elected more than twice. In fact, he won four elections for the Democratic Party. However, after Roosevelt Congress decided Presidents should only be allowed to have a maximum of eight years as President – in other words, to be elected twice. So for the election in November 1952 the Democrats had to find a new candidate to replace Truman. The Republicans also found a new candidate – General Eisenhower, the Supreme Commander of the Allied Forces in the Second World War. Nobody knew what Eisenhower's political views were and it did not seem to matter. He would probably have stood for the Democrats if they had asked first! It seems that after 20 years of Democrat rule, the strains of the Korean War and Truman's constant battles with Congress, the American people wanted a Republican in control. Eisenhower defeated Adlai Stevenson by a convincing majority of 6.5 million votes. Eisenhower kept a 'low profile' as President, preferring to leave the running of the country to his ministers or assistants like John Foster Dulles who managed Foreign Affairs until his death in 1959. Dulles was a firm anti-Communist but he would not be drawn into reckless action. He was prepared to defend Chiang Kai-shek in Formosa against Red China but would not commit America to defend Chiang beyond the island. Like Truman he was determined to contain Communism by a system of alliances and in 1954 the South East Asia Treaty Organisation (SEATO) was set up, and in 1955 it was followed by the Baghdad Pact, later the Central Treaty Organisation (CENTO).

Eisenhower and civil rights

Eisenhower faced a similar problem to Truman in that Congress was generally controlled by the Democrats and hostile to him. But Eisenhower did not have much in the way of new ideas anyway and his record in domestic affairs is not startling. Some help was given to people over 65 to pay their medical bills and the education budget was expanded in science and mathematics after the shock to American prestige with the launch of the first (Russian) space satellite in 1957. He paid farmers massive subsidies to produce less so that the income of poorer farmers would increase as prices rose. Prices rose but incomes did not. The minimum wage did increase to $1 an hour. All in all, Eisenhower was content to leave things as they were and this was seen as a betrayal by the more right-wing Republicans who wanted to see the 'New' and 'Fair Deal' laws repealed (or cancelled).

One area where Eisenhower did involve himself more effectively was civil rights for Negroes. He made two efforts in 1957 and 1960 to make it easier for blacks to vote and he acted firmly to ensure that the decision of the Supreme Court was carried out in one state at least. In 1954 the Supreme Court ruled that separate schools for black and white children were illegal and contrary to the **Constitution**, and in 1955 declared that schools must be desegregated or made open to children of all colours and races. This did not go down at all well in the South where the 'Jim Crow' laws forced blacks to use different facilities in many areas – different restaurants, fountains, seats in buses and hotels. One governor, among many others, refused to allow nine black teenagers into Little Rock School, Arkansas. Eisenhower sent 1000 paratroopers to Little Rock to ensure that the black children got in to the all-white school. But it was really a token gesture. In 1961 there were no black children in white schools at all in Mississippi, Alabama or South Carolina and just nine in Georgia. The law was slow to act and blacks were taking matters more and more into their own hands.

Exercise 4

a How many elections did Roosevelt win?

b What sort of role did Eisenhower adopt as President?

c In which area of domestic affairs did Eisenhower involve himself more decisively?

d Why do you think the Republicans chose Eisenhower to be their presidential candidate?

e What does the choice of Eisenhower as a Presidential candidate tell you about America's political system?

America's 'white problem'

Though slavery had been abolished in the United States in 1864 freedom did not bring equality for the American Negro. Indeed, the Supreme Court in 1896 ruled that the 'Jim Crow' laws in the South that forced blacks to use separate facilities were legal, provided that these separate facilities were equal to those used by the whites. It was not until 1954 that such laws were declared illegal. Having equal rights in theory was one thing, being able to enjoy them in practice was another. In 1955 a black woman refused to give up her seat to a white man on the bus, as the law in Montgomery, Alabama said she should. She was arrested and blacks in Montgomery staged a year-long boycott of the bus service until the company gave in and abandoned the policy. The campaign had been led by a 26 year old Baptist minister, Martin Luther King. He preached non-violence and passive resistance, following the ideas of Gandhi in India. The Civil Rights Movement organised similar campaigns in the states of the deep South where other segregation laws still discriminated against blacks. Black 'Freedom Riders' toured southern cities in buses organising sit-ins in hotels and cafes reserved for whites. These non-violent forms of protest provoked brutal attacks by gangs of white racists in the South and television film of mass arrests and beatings of these protesters by the police brought the issue of black rights into every living room in the country. The

Martin Luther King, seventh from the right in the front line, with civil rights marchers in Washington, August 1963. Note the demands on the placards

year 1963 was perhaps a turning point for the campaign for black rights. In that year Martin Luther King staged a march on Washington of 250 000 people to present a petition to a sympathetic President Kennedy. The response of some whites was not slow. Before the year was out four black children had died in a church bombing in Birmingham, Alabama, and Kennedy had been shot.

The black backlash

The more militant blacks who believed King's non-violent tactics to be ineffective decided that the time had come for militant tactics. Stokely Carmichael led

the 'Black Power' movement and urged blacks to 'Stop begging and take power – black power'. Some groups, like the Black Muslims, wanted a separate black state within America's borders for black people only. From the mid 1960s onwards black anger exploded into violence after riots shook black ghettoes in Watts (Los Angeles) in 1965 in which 34 died. During the next three years there were 150 major riots, and two major eruptions in 1967 in Newark and Detroit alone caused 69 deaths. The basic cause was the economic plight blacks found themselves in. The Supreme Court may have given them equal political rights and ended discrimination, but who was going to give them jobs in areas like Watts where unemployment was 30%? Even by the mid 1970s one in every three black families lived below the poverty line and earned just 58% of the average white family. The murder of Martin Luther King in April 1968 by a white assassin in Texas seemed to indicate that his efforts to integrate the white and black communities of America had a long way to go.

Exercise ▪ 5

a What was the Montgomery boycott campaign about?
b What was the response of some whites to the Civil Rights Movement?
c What was the aim of the 'Black Muslims'?
d What do you think Carmichael meant by 'Stop begging and take power – black power'?
e The previous section is sub-headed 'America's "white problem"'. What point is the author trying to make about the problem of race relations in the US?

Exercise ▪ 6

Extract One: 'Civil Rights in the Deep South'

This is the text of a radio broadcast by a BBC correspondent, Charles Wheeler, in 1965:

> Outside the Sheriff's office, a recruiting poster for the Ku Klux Klan. Next to it a drinking fountain, curtly marked 'White'. The door opens and there appears a tall figure in a Texan hat and cowboy boots, with a star on his chest and a pistol in an open holster . . .
> 5   No, it's not a film; it's last Wednesday at the County Court House in Philadelphia, Mississippi, and the man in the doorway is Deputy-Sheriff

Price, who, with his chief, Sheriff Rainey, and seventeen other citizens, faces charges in connection with last summer's murder of three young Civil Rights workers, two of them white New Yorkers and the third, a local
10 Negro.

The three were arrested for speeding; were held in the local jail until night time, and then, according to Price, were released. Forty-four days later, after a search by hundreds of Federal agents and troops, their bodies were found eighteen feet below the surface of a newly-constructed
15 dam.

Price, Rainey and the rest are on bail pending the resumption of the trial . . . In the meantime, life in Philadelphia goes on much as before. I called on the Deputy-Sheriff. 'I wonder who killed those men', he said, and grinned . . . A local doctor, who suggested they be suspended from their law-
20 enforcement duties until the trial is over, lost too many patients and has moved his practice to another county.

I went to see the Mayor. 'I never hear anybody talking about that case', he said. 'Do the Negroes talk about it?' I asked. 'Oh we never have trouble with the niggers here', he said, 'not now.'

(*From Our Own Correspondent*, Ed. R. Lazar)

a With what crime were the Sheriff and his Deputy charged?
b What sort of work do you think the murdered civil rights campaigners were involved in?
c What sort of organisation is the Ku Klux Klan? What is so surprising about where the Ku Klux Klan poster was displayed? (Line 1)?
d Why do you think it was necessary to use Federal troops (line 13) and not local state troops to search for the men?
e What evidence is there in the text that locals sympathised with the accused?
f What evidence is there in the text that other highly placed local officials were unsympathetic to the blacks?
g What does this report tell you of the progress that had been made since the Supreme Court decision of 1954 towards civil rights for blacks?

Exercise ▉▉▉▉ 7

Separation or integration: a black debate

In 1962 two leading black activists debated the merits of integration with the whites of America and the merits of creating a separate black state. Malcolm X was a leading member of the Black Muslims. He called himself 'X' because his surname was his white slave name and because he did not know his real African surname which dated back to the time his ancestors were brought from Africa to the United States as slaves. The other speaker was James Farmer of the Congress of Racial Equality (CORE).

Extract Two: Malcolm X on black separatism

And despite the fact that 20 million black people here don't yet have freedom, justice and equality, Adlai Stevenson has the nerve enough to stand up in the United Nations and point the finger at South Africa . . . All we say is that South Africa preaches what it practises and practises what it
5 preaches; America preaches one thing and practises another. And we

don't want to integrate with hypocrites who preach one thing and practise another . . .

10

So we think this, that when whites talk integration they are being hypocrites, and we think the Negroes who accept token integration are also being hypocrites, because they are the only ones who benefit from it, the handful of hand-picked high-class, middle-class Uncle Tom Negroes . . . But if all the black people went into the white community, over night you would have a race war. If four or five little black students going to school in New Orleans bring about the race riots that we saw down there,

15

what do you think would happen if all of the black people tried to go to any school that they want, they would have a race war . . . we feel that it is more sensible than running around waiting for the whites to allow us inside their attic or inside their basement . . .

Extract Three: *Farmer on integration*

We can't wait for the law. The Supreme Court decision in 1954 banning segregated schools has had almost eight years of existence, yet less than eight per cent of the Negro kids are in integrated schools . . . As a result of one year of the student sit-ins, the lunch counters were desegregated in

5

more than 150 cities . . . In Lexington, Kentucky, the theatres were opened up by CORE as a result of picketing and boycotting. Some of the theatres refused to admit Negroes, others would let Negroes sit up in the balcony. They boycotted that one, picketed the others . . . All of the theatres there are open now. . . .

10

What are our objectives; segregation, separation? Absolutely not! The disease and the evils that we have pointed to in our American culture have grown out of segregation and its partner, prejudice . . .

(*Documents of American History*, Ed. H.S. Commager)

a What do you think Malcolm X meant by the sentence: 'America preaches one thing and practises another' (Extract Two, line 5)?

b How fair do you think the comparison was between the polices of South Africa towards its blacks and the United States' policy in 1962?

c Why does he accuse the blacks who favour integration of being hypocrites?

d What does Malcolm X (Extract Two) suggest would be the best blacks could expect from whites by trying to integrate with white society in lines 15–20?

e What does Farmer (Extract Three) claim have been the benefits of the integration campaign for American Negroes?

f Why does he reject separation (the creation of a separate black state in the US)?

g With which of these extracts would Luther King have been in agreement and why?

h Which of these two speakers would you say had the more idealistic policy and which the more practical? Explain your answer.

Exercise 8

Write a television or newspaper interview with Martin Luther King. Question him on his non-violent campaign to secure civil rights and the tactics involved. What is his view of Malcolm X's separate state idea and Carmichael's Black Power movement?

Kennedy and Johnson 1960–68 (Democrats)

The election of John Fitzgerald Kennedy to the presidency in November 1960 marked two firsts: he was the first Catholic President, and the youngest, aged just 43. His victory over the Republican candidate, Richard Nixon, was a very narrow one. He won by just 118 000 votes out of 69 million cast. Kennedy had much in his favour. He came from a very wealthy family and was married to a young and attractive woman. His war record had been distinguished. He symbolised a new, eager generation determined to tackle the poverty and ignorance still apparent in the nation. 'We stand today on the edge of a new frontier', he declared. The 'frontiers' to be crossed included a medical scheme for the old and poor, increased benefits for the unemployed and more spending on housing and education.

The 'New Frontier' was a bold and ambitious programme but to many in Congress, among both the Republicans and Southern Democrats, the programme smacked of 'creeping **socialism**'. Though Congress was dominated by the Democrats Kennedy found much of his programme was either rejected or watered down by a hostile Congress. His 'New Frontier' promised much more than it ever achieved. No extra money was allowed for education and his 'Medicare' scheme for old people was rejected. However, there was some extension of welfare benefits for the children of unemployed fathers and the minimum wage was raised to $1.25. Loans were made available to buy houses and there was some extension in the period of time for which unemployment benefit could be paid.

Kennedy's New Frontier

Kennedy's New Frontier also extended to blacks and Kennedy tried to establish, once and for all, equality of rights and opportunity for the Negro. In 1962 he sent the army to Mississippi to ensure that a black student could enrol in the university. He appointed the first Negro ambassador and black warship commander. These gestures could have been dismissed as paying lip-service to the idea of equality but Kennedy also drew up a wide-ranging Civil Rights Bill. The bill planned to make illegal racial discrimination in housing, education, public facilities (such as hotels, stores and restaurants) and voting. Many blacks were denied their right to vote by tough literacy tests in which blacks had to prove their ability to read and write before they could vote. The bill would have ensured that the tests for whites would now be the same for blacks. The bill was rejected by Congress. It was only passed, along with much of the New Frontier programme, after his death during the presidency of his former Vice-President, Lyndon Johnson. Kennedy's assassination in November 1963 brought to an end a promising career after just two years and ten months of the four year term served. The measure of his popularity and the affection in which he was held by the people is clear from events after his death. A wave of public sympathy swept a conservative Congress along to approve the very same policies it had so fiercely rejected while Kennedy was alive.

Kennedy's handling of foreign affairs had also helped to strengthen his reputation. Caught by surprise over the Berlin Crisis in 1961 (see Chapter 14, page 175) and humiliated by the Bay of Pigs fiasco over Cuba (Chapter 17, pages 223–27), Kennedy soon learnt how to deal with Khrushchev and Russia's ambitions. The Cuban Missile Crisis (Chapter 17) established him as a firm and skilful defender of American interests. The establishment of the Moscow–Washington telephone link and the Nuclear Test Ban Treaty in 1963 also showed him as someone keen to move away from traditional Cold War positions with the Soviet Union. The involvement of first Kennedy and later Johnson in Vietnam is dealt with in another chapter. The expenditure on Vietnam wrecked much of Johnson's ambitious programme for 'the Great Society' but he did get Kennedy's Civil Rights Bill through Congress (1964) and followed it with another in 1968 which made it illegal to discriminate in selling property or letting accommodation. He also introduced the Social Security Amendment Act (1965) which provided medical care for the over 65s.

Who shot Kennedy?

The problems raised by the assassination of President Kennedy on 22 November 1963 are typical of the difficulties historians face in putting together the past. Reconstructing the past can be difficult enough but then conclusions and opinions have to be based on the evidence. Sometimes that evidence is incomplete, sometimes it is inaccurate. After Kennedy's murder a commission was set up under Chief Justice Warren to examine the evidence. This first extract is taken from the report in 1964:

Extract Four: The Warren Commission

1. The shots which killed President Kennedy and wounded Governor Connally were fired from the sixth floor window . . . of the Texas School Book Depository. This determination is based upon the following:

5

  a Witnesses at the scene of the assassination saw a rifle being fired from the sixth floor window of the Depository Building.

  b The nearly whole bullet found on Governor Connally's stretcher . . . and the two bullet fragments found in the front seat . . . were fired from the 6.5 Mannlicher-Carcano rifle found on the sixth floor of the Depository building . . .

10

  c The three used cartridge cases found near the window of the sixth floor . . . were fired from the same rifle which fired the above-described bullet . . .

  d The windshield in the Presidential limousine was struck by a bullet fragment on the inside surface of the glass, but was not penetrated.

15

  e The nature of the bullet wounds suffered by President Kennedy and Governor Connally and the location of the car . . . establish that the bullets were fired from above and behind the Presidential limousine, striking the President and the Governor as follows:

   1 President Kennedy was first struck by a bullet which entered at the

20

   back of his neck and exited through the lower front portion of his neck, causing a wound which would not necessarily have been lethal. The President was struck a second time by a bullet which entered the right rear portion of his head, causing a massive and fatal wound.

2. Governor Connally was struck by a bullet which entered on the right

25

   side of his back and travelled downward through the right side of his chest, exiting below his right nipple. This bullet then passed through his right wrist and entered his left thigh . . .

(*Documents of American History*, Ed. H.S. Commager)

The Mannlicher–Carcano rifle. It was made in Italy in 1940. Each time it was fired the bolt had to be pulled back and the eye moved from the telescopic sight. Tests later showed it to be a rather poor rifle, and ammunition for it was often faulty and liable not to work because of its age. According to the Warren Report, this rifle fired three shots in 7.6 seconds, two of them striking Kennedy

Source Two

Scene of the assassination according to the Warren Report

Extract Five: 1979 Select Committee Report

Congress set up another investigation into the assassination in 1976. This is a summary of its key findings:

> Lee Harvey Oswald fired three shots at President . . . Kennedy. The second and third shots he fired struck the President. The third shot he fired killed the President. The shots that struck President Kennedy from behind were fired from the sixth floor window . . . of the Texas School Book Depository
> 5 Building. [The Committee also stated that there was a 'high probability' that two gunmen fired at the President. A newly-found tape recording of a policeman's motor-cycle radio transmission showed that there were four shots fired and not three. Further analysis indicated that one of those shots was fired from a small grassy mound in front of the President's car. The
> 10 report further stated:] The Committee believes . . . that President Kennedy was probably assassinated as a result of a conspiracy. The Committee is unable to identify the other gunmen or the extent of the conspiracy.

(Report of the Select Committee on Assassinations, 1979)

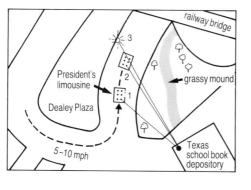

a What pieces of evidence can you find in Extract Four (apart from witnesses' statements) that the shots that struck Kennedy were fired from behind him?

b Which of these shots, according to Extract Four, was fatal?

c According to the map in Source Two which of the shots missed?

d Does Extract Five agree with the Warren Report on the number of shots fired *from the Texas Book Depository*?

e In what way does Extract Five differ from Source Two (the map) on the order in which these shots were fired?

f What are the two most serious differences between Extract Five (the Select Committee) and Extract Four (the Warren Report)?

Conspiracy?

Lee Harvey Oswald is a puzzling figure. He claimed to be a Communist and, indeed, he did live in the USSR for some thirty months. He married a Russian woman but decided to return to the USA in June 1962. He was given back his United States passport without any difficulty – even though he had given up his American citizenship. In the USA Oswald became involved in the 'Fair Play for Cuba Committee', an organisation which supported the left-wing leader and ally of the Soviet Union, Fidel Castro. Oswald had been a US Marine and was trained in radar electronics, serving in Japan, Taiwan and the Philippines. He left the Marines, of course, before leaving for the Soviet Union. It is worth asking the question whether the CIA would have been keeping a close watch on a man who called himself a Communist, had lived in the Soviet Union and given them all the information he had about his work in the Marines and had now returned. Would the CIA not have known that his wife was the niece of an officer in the MVD, part of the Soviet KGB?

Oswald was never given an opportunity to defend himself. He was shot dead by Jack Ruby on 24 November 1963 – just two days after Kennedy's assassination. Oswald denied any involvement in the murder. Ruby claimed he shot Oswald out of anger but Ruby was known to have connections with the Mafia and had been involved in criminal activities. Organised crime had good cause for complaint against the Kennedy Administration. Kennedy had increased by eight times the number of convictions of members of organised crime gangs. Ruby died in prison. All he ever said was that the people 'who put me in the position I'm in, will never let the true facts come overboard to the world'.

It is unlikely that we will ever know the true facts either. The next time someone tells you that history is about a 'load of boring old facts', ask one question: 'Who shot Kennedy – and why?'

Nixon 1968–74 (Republican)

The 1968 presidential election campaign is remembered for the assassination of Robert Kennedy, John Kennedy's younger brother, in June of that year. Two months earlier Martin Luther King had been shot dead. The war in Vietnam had drained much support as well as money from Johnson's Democratic administration and Johnson decided not to stand for re-election The Republicans put forward a strong conservative in the form of Richard Nixon who stood as a defender of law and order. He avoided making any definite statement about the Vietnam war but spoke of a secret plan to deal with it. His victory over the Democrat, Hubert Humphrey, though narrow, indicated that Americans wanted an end to the liberal policies of Johnson with his concern for the under-privileged.

Nixon's America: white, middle-aged and wealthy

Nixon pitched his appeal to 'Middle America', the 'non-young, non-black, non-poor'. He was anxious to reduce spending on Johnson's poverty programme and cut back sharply on money spent by the government. Unemployment increased steadily to over 4 million (6% of the working population) and was twice its 1967 level. Nixon responded by introducing a prices and wages freeze in 1971 which checked inflation. Medical care was extended to the disabled under 65. Nixon's first term of office as President is largely remembered for some important developments in the foreign affairs field. China was admitted to the United Nations in 1971 after the US dropped its veto on China's entry, and in the next year Nixon made an historic visit to Peking. At the same time he was able to improve relations with Russia by visiting Moscow in the same year as the China visit. Nixon's search for '**détente**' or easing of tension between the superpowers was a policy in which he was ably assisted by Henry Kissinger, his Special Adviser on National Security. The visit to Moscow also saw the signing of SALT 1 (the Strategic Arms Limitation Talks) which set limits on nuclear missile development. Nixon's plan to gradually withdraw from the war in Vietnam by 'Vietnamisation' (in which the South Vietnamese were being made more and more responsible for their own defence) promised an end to American involvement. Nixon's victory in the 1972 election campaign was overwhelming, winning 61% of the votes. His second term of office was marked by the signing of a cease-fire with North Vietnam in January 1973 and by the middle of February the last American combat troops had left the country. At about the same time, a news story that had started in 1972 began to attract serious attention.

Nixon (right) grasps the hand of Brezhnev, the Soviet leader, in June 1973 during Brezhnev's visit to the United States

Watergate

During the 1972 election campaign a group of rather amateurish burglars had been arrested while trying to 'bug' the Democratic Party Headquarters in Washington, known as the Watergate building. They had been sent by members of the 'Campaign to Re-elect the President' (CREEP). The arrested men kept quiet at first but one eventually revealed that CREEP had been involved as well as key White House figures. Two of Nixon's top advisers, Bob Haldeman and John Ehrlichman, resigned, and a third, John Dean, was dismissed. Throughout all this Nixon claimed he had known nothing of the break-in and its planning. 'There will be no white-wash at the White House', he promised the nation on television. In mid July 1973 it was revealed that Nixon had tapes of all conversations held in his White House office but refused to hand them over. Eventually a Senate Committee prepared to impeach him. Impeachment is the legal process by which a President can be put on trial and removed from office if found guilty. Nixon handed over the tapes rather than face impeachment and probable imprisonment. The tapes revealed that Nixon had for a long time been involved in the 'cover-up' over the Watergate break-in. On 9 August 1974 Nixon resigned, a disgraced and broken man. His Vice-President, Gerald Ford, took over and immediately granted Nixon a pardon so that he could not be tried for his crime.

Exercise 10

a What two acts of violence marked the 1968 presidential election campaign?
b What did Nixon do to encourage détente?
c Why do you think he won the 1972 campaign so convincingly?
d What do you think Nixon meant by the phrase 'There will be no whitewash at the White House'?
e What does the Watergate scandal tell you about the kind of man Nixon was?

Exercise 11

Source Three (left) *'Vandalism',* and **Source Four** (right) *American cartoons*

Write 20 lines describing each of the cartoons, Sources Three and Four, and the message each is trying to get across about the 'Watergate' scandal. When you have described them individually compare them, explaining which, in your view, is making the more serious comment about the scandal.

Carter 1977–80 (Democrat)

Gerald Ford narrowly beat a former film star, Ronald Reagan, to become the Republican candidate for the presidential election of November 1976. Gerald Ford had been an uninspiring President, often ridiculed by the media for his occasional blunders.

In August 1974 *The Guardian* said of him when he became President: 'A year ago Gerald Ford was unknown throughout America, now he is unknown throughout the world'. The fact that he narrowly lost to the Democratic candidate, Jimmy Carter, and that only 55% of the voters bothered to turn out to vote says a great deal about the interest the campaign aroused and the weakness of Carter's popular appeal.

Camp David

Carter's main and perhaps only attraction to American voters was that he had not been involved in any scandals and had solemnly promised never to tell a lie. Carter's commitment to human rights throughout the world – especially in the Soviet Bloc – was a definite

Carter and Sadat at Camp David

change from previous Republican administrations. He made serious efforts to negotiate another agreement with the Soviet Union over strategic nuclear weapons and an agreement was signed in June 1979 with Brezhnev. Of more lasting success was his part in bringing together the leaders of Israel (Begin) and Egypt (Sadat) at the President's retreat, Camp David. A treaty was signed in 1979 between Egypt and Israel, finally bringing to an end the state of war between them.

Events towards the end of 1979, however, were later to wreck any hopes Carter may have had of being re-elected President. The most serious, from Carter's point of view, was the seizure of 50 American hostages in the American embassy in Iran by supporters of Iran's new religious ruler, the Ayatollah Khomeini. This humiliation for Carter and Americans was made worse when a rescue mission in April 1980 ended in disaster and death when two US helicopters collided whilst on their way to rescue the Americans in Tehran. The invasion of Afghanistan in the last week of December 1979 by 50 000 Soviet troops seemed a further insult to American prestige. All that was left for the Americans to do was to boycott the 1980 Olympic Games in Moscow. Carter's election had seemed to promise well for détente and better relations with Russia. Even the agreement with Brezhnev, SALT 2, fell victim to the new climate of tension and the Senate refused to approve it. By the time the elections for President in 1980 took place, Carter's administration was in tatters and was easily swept aside by a Republican candidate, Ronald Reagan, skilled at handling the US press and television.

Reagan (Republican)

With a cruel sense of timing the hostages in Iran were handed over to American officials on the same day that Carter handed over the presidency to Ronald Reagan. Reagan's election in 1980 marked a strong shift to the right in American opinion. He was committed to a tough line against Communism, especially its spread in Central America, and to economic policies which would keep inflation down and the dollar strong. He called his approach the 'New Federalism' in which the central, or Federal, government would hand over its responsibility for social programmes to the individual states. He also promised cuts in government spending in all areas except defence. Spending on defence in 1982 stood at $187 billion and by 1984 it had risen to $242 billion with a further increase of 18% predicted for 1984–85. His commitment to halt the spread of Communism – especially where it threatened, in Reagan's view, American security – was made clear in October 1983. In that month 5000 US troops invaded the tiny island of Grenada in the Caribbean to overthrow a Communist government which had just seized control of the island. Reagan claimed the island was being used as a base by the Cubans to spread Communism and train the Grenadan army for acts of aggression. Less than 600 Cubans were found on the island and most of these were construction workers building an airport. During the invasion 18 Americans and 27 Cubans died in the fighting.

Further strains on US–Soviet relations

American troops had been active elsewhere. In August 1982, 800 Marines were sent to the Lebanon to supervise the evacuation of the Palestine Liberation Organisation from Beirut. However Reagan found it difficult to get the Marines out. Soon there were 1600 based in the city and in October 1983 suicide bombers struck at the bases of the Marine and French forces in Beirut: 219 Marines died and 58 French troops. The Marines were withdrawn four months later. It was a bitter defeat for Reagan and Shultz, chief of the State Department.

Relations with the USSR were also very difficult at this time. In September 1983 a South Korean airliner was shot inside Soviet airspace by Russian jets. All 269 on board perished. To nobody's surprise the nuclear arms limitation talks in Geneva soon broke up with both sides already increasing missile numbers in Europe. The Soviet Union's continued occupation of Afghanistan (until its withdrawal in 1989) added further tension to East-West relations. Military aid worth $300 million to the Afghan rebels from the United States did not make a serious impact on the Russian grip on the country.

Nicaragua

Future developments elsewhere did not promise well. Central America and Nicaragua in particular were to become a source of major conflict. Ever since the overthrow of the right-wing **dictatorship** of Somoza in 1979 by the left-wing forces of the Sandinista army, some Americans felt their security under threat. Carter

US Marines in Beirut searching for survivors among the ruins of their base. The four storey building was demolished by a suicide bomber driving a truck packed with explosives

"NOW BE A GOOD FASCIST LIKE THE REST OF CENTRAL AMERICA"

Guardian *cartoon, 30 June 1986*

1986. The response was instant. At least four Libyan patrol boats were sunk and one missile base destroyed by US aircraft. Within three weeks Reagan had launched an even bigger attack by 33 fighter-bombers which attacked targets in Tripoli and Benghazi. Of the planes used 18 flew from US bases in Britain. Many of the dead were civilians. One political commentator said of Reagan: 'Since the last war, America has frequently faced the choice of being either loved or feared. In the Middle East, Reagan has clearly made his decision'.

However mixed Reagan's successes between January 1981 and November 1984 may have appeared to outsiders, to Americans he was doing a fine job. In November 1984 he was re-elected with a massive majority (59% of the vote) against the Democrat candidate, Walter Mondale. Mondale, having won majorities in just two of the 51 states, retired from politics. Reagan, though 73 years old when re-elected, promised a vigorous bout of activity to simplify the tax system, to reduce the national debt and balance the budget and cut government spending. These last three targets had been declared in 1980 also and had not been achieved. He had cut inflation from 12% in 1980 to 4% in 1984 but at the cost of another 3 million unemployed. Though the Senate had a narrow Republican majority Reagan faced more opposition from a firmly Democratic House of Representatives. Of the 435 Congressmen in the House of Representatives there were just 19 blacks. Civil rights, an issue raised at the beginning of this chapter, clearly still have a long way to go.

did not take a hostile position towards the Sandinistas but Reagan did.

Reagan gave substantial military aid to anti-Sandinista forces operating in Nicaragua but Congress became increasingly concerned that America was becoming too involved in the area, and in April 1985 refused to allow any further help for the anti-government forces. This set-back for Reagan, however, was partly reversed in June when Congress decided that $27 million of 'humanitarian' aid would be allowed. Such aid would include food, clothing and medicine but not weapons.

Unable to make a big impression over Nicaragua, Reagan decided to strike a blow against Colonel Gadafy's Libya instead. The Americans, believing Gadafy to be behind many of the world's terrorist incidents, provoked an attack by Libyan missiles on the US fleet near the Libyan coast in March

Exercise 12

a What was Carter's main attraction to voters?
b What success did Carter achieve in the Middle East?
c What two developments ruined Carter's hopes of re-election?
d How did Reagan prove his commitment to halt the spread of Communism in October 1983?
e Why do you think Reagan was re-elected with such a big majority in 1984?

Exercise ▋▋▋13

Source Five

American cartoon: détente and Ronald Reagan

a What is the meaning of the word 'détente'?

b What point is the cartoonist making by displaying détente as an exhibit in that particular building?

c What developments since Reagan became President led to the policy of détente ending up in this situation?

d Have recent events in Eastern Europe, Afghanistan and Nicaragua (where the Sandinistas gave up power after free elections in 1990) supported the view of détente illustrated above? Explain your answer.

Chapter 17

East and West in conflict: Korea, Cuba and Vietnam

Korea: 1950–53

The tension and hostility that developed between the Soviet Union and the Western powers in Europe after the Second World War have been dealt with in another chapter (Chapter 13). As far as Europe is concerned, that conflict was largely one of words and threats between rival political systems. But outside Europe the threats went beyond an exchange of words. In Korea the situation had been tense since the Japanese defeat in 1945. Russian troops occupied the north of the country and American troops the south. It had been agreed at Yalta that elections would be held in the whole country to decide what form of government it should have. The problem was that neither side could agree on how the elections should be organised. Truman declared that Korea had become a 'testing ground' in the conflict between **Communism** and **democracy**. When American and Russian troops pulled out of Korea in 1949 North Korean forces seized their opportunity to spread Soviet-style Communism south of the 38th parallel which divided north from south. In June 1950 the North Korean army of Kim Il-sung invaded the South across the 38th parallel.

It was a clear act of aggression and for once the United Nations was able to act swiftly and with some effect. A resolution was passed calling for the sending of United Nations forces to assist the South Korean government of Syngman Rhee. Russia, as a member of the UN Security Council, could have opposed that resolution. The Russian **veto** would have been enough to prevent a single UN soldier setting foot in Korea. Unfortunately for the Russians the Soviet delegation at that time was boycotting the UN in protest at the refusal of the UN to admit Communist China. The resolution was passed without opposition. The vast majority of the troops came from the United States but 15 other countries, including Britain, sent forces as well.

The Truman Doctrine in action

At first the North Korean troops had made rapid progress and had occupied the whole of South Korea except for the south-east around the port of Pusan. But the UN reinforcements quickly turned the tables and drove the North Koreans back over the 38th parallel by the end of September 1950. Truman then decided to let the UN commander, MacArthur, launch an invasion of the North. This seriously concerned China, which borders North Korea along the Yalu River. In November, the Chinese, fearing an invasion of Manchuria, launched a 300 000 strong offensive against the UN troops in North Korea. Within three months the UN forces had been driven back over the 38th parallel and Seoul, the South's capital, had been captured again. MacArthur advised Truman to launch an attack on China – with nuclear bombs if necessary. Truman wisely decided that such a policy could well lead to a full-scale war and settled instead on an offensive to drive the North Koreans

Land occupied by
North Korea up to
1 August 1950

USSR

CHINA

25 Nov. 1950 UN line
(after MacArthur's advance)

NORTH KOREA

Pyongyang

eventual cease-fire line

38th parallel

Seoul
Inchon

UN line 31 Dec. 1950
(after Chinese offensive)

UN troops
land
15 Sept, 1950

SOUTH KOREA

Pusan

limit of
North Korean
advance

Five phases of the Korean War

and Chinese back over the 38th parallel. He also decided to remove MacArthur from his post.

By June 1951 Truman's objective had been achieved and talks began at Panmunjom to settle a peace agreement. It took two years to finally end the war and the new frontier between the two states was established – roughly along the 38th parallel. One of the more significant results of the war was that now China was also drawn into **Cold War** confrontation with the United States. The Chinese stepped up their aid to fellow Communists waging a war to free Indo-China from French colonial rule. In many respects American confidence had been boosted by the Korean War – even though over 40 000 US troops had died. A bid to break through the Truman Doctrine had been beaten off and the UN had actually put a stop to an aggressor nation's efforts to seize control of another country – as South Korea now was. The Americans now turned their attention to another Far Eastern country where the Truman Doctrine seemed under attack: Vietnam. American involvement here was to prove much more costly in every respect, and to end in failure.

Exercise 1

a Why did Korea become a focal point for tension between Russia and the United States after the Second World War?

b What response did the United Nations make to the attack by the North in June 1950?

c Why was the UN able for the first (and so far only) time able to send in combat troops to settle a dispute?

d Why do you think Truman decided to replace MacArthur?

e To what extent do you think Truman had defended the principle of the Truman Doctrine in fighting the Korean War?

The Vietnam wars: 1946–54 and 1961–75

The South East Asian countries of Vietnam, Laos and Cambodia (now Kampuchea), were colonised by the French in the last 50 years of the nineteenth century. The area became known as French Indo-China. During the Second World War the colonies were occupied by the Japanese. Vietnamese nationalists found Japanese rule no more to their liking than French rule. An independence movement, the League for Vietnamese Independence or Vietminh, was set up with the aim of driving the Japanese out of Vietnam. It was led by an experienced Communist called Ho Chi Minh. It was not his real name but it gave a good idea of his ambition, 'Ho, the Seeker of Light'. The man who had worked in the kitchens of the Carlton Hotel in London was eventually to humble first the French and then the most powerful nation in the world, the United States. With the defeat of Japan in 1945 Ho declared the independence of the Democratic Republic of Vietnam. But the French were not prepared to give up their colony without a struggle, and from 1946 a bitter war raged between the Vietminh and the French.

The French defeated: 1946–54

The French seriously underestimated the strength and determination of the Vietminh. By the time they realised that they had a real war on their hands it was too late. As in China the independence movement had massive support among the peasants, but also the backing of non-Communists who were keen to see Vietnam free of foreign control. From 1950 onwards Ho Chi Minh had crucial and decisive support from Mao's China. The United States was also heavily involved in keeping the French well stocked with weapons and supplies. In 1954 they gave $1000 million dollars of military aid. Despite this overwhelming advantage in war material the French suffered a crushing defeat at the battle of Dien Bien Phu. Dien Bien Phu was a fortified camp held by the French deep in Vietminh territory. It was besieged for two months from March to May in 1954 by General Giap's peasant Vietminh army. Of the 16 500 French defenders only 3000 survived the battle and captivity. The defeat broke the French will to fight on, and within two months a cease-fire had been agreed.

The Geneva Agreements of 1954 set up Laos and Cambodia as independent states and divided Vietnam along the 17th parallel. The division was only to be a temporary one. Ho Chi Minh's Vietminh government in the north was recognised. South Vietnam's government was backed by the Americans but in 1956 there would be elections throughout the country to create a united government for all Vietnam. The government of the south was in the hands of Ngo Dinh Diem. His rule was corrupt and tyrannical. The elections in the south were never held and the United States did not press Diem to hold them. They were afraid that Ho Chi Minh would win them and Communism would spread south of the 17th parallel. Diem refused to carry out any reforms in the south. He was a Catholic and his policies angered the Buddhist majority of the people. He did nothing to help the peasants own land which remained firmly in the hands of the landlords. Soon a Communist guerrilla army, the National Liberation Front (NLF), was operating in the south against Diem. It won widespread support from peasants, Buddhists and those who did not like American influence in their country any more than French. As in China these guerrillas behaved well towards the peasants and worked with them. The peasants sheltered them and provided them with food. The strength of the NLF greatly concerned President Eisenhower. His 'domino theory' stated that if one domino in a row of dominoes was knocked over the rest of the row would all fall quickly as well. Eisenhower's dominoes were the coun-

French parachutist dropped over Dien Bien Phu in November 1953

tries of Asia. The Chinese domino had already fallen to Communism; so had the North Korean and the North Vietnamese dominoes. He was determined to prevent the South Vietnamese from falling as well.

Exercise 2

a By what name did the countries of Vietnam, Laos and Cambodia used to be known?

b Who replaced the Japanese as the enemy of the Vietminh in 1945?

c Why was Dien Bien Phu such an important battle?

d Do you think American fears about the result of an election in Vietnam in 1956 were justified? Explain your answer with evidence from the text.

e Can you suggest any reasons why the countries of South East Asia had fallen like dominoes under Communist rule since 1945?

Exercise 3

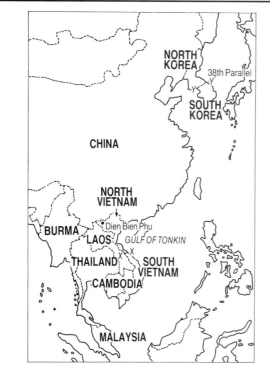

Source One
South East Asia

a Copy the map (Source One) into your exercise book. Shade all those countries which had Communist governments by the end of 1954.

b Identify the two lines X–X and Y–Y on the map.

c What took place at Dien Bien Phu in 1954? From the map can you say why the French faced a difficult task in trying to hold their fortress there?

d From the map why was China ideally placed to encourage the spread of Communism in South East Asia?

e Name the next three countries which Eisenhower may have had in mind when he made his 'domino theory' speech in 1954 about the spread of Communism from North Vietnam.

America's war in Vietnam 1961–73

The removal of Diem

Eisenhower first began American involvement in Vietnam, sending not just huge supplies of military aid but also military advisers. When John F. Kennedy took over as President in 1961 the number of advisers was increased rapidly to 16 000. He also encouraged the development of the 'safe village' policy in which villagers were removed from areas in which the NLF were strong to fortified settlements. These 'safe villages' were heavily 'protected' and guarded to keep out Communist agents. They were a failure because in many cases the NLF were already inside the villages anyway. The

Americans found it impossible to tell who was an NLF fighter and who was not, as in a **guerrilla** war like this the NLF wore no uniform. By 1964 it was estimated that the Vietnamese Communists, assisted by regular troops from North Vietnam, controlled 40% of South Vietnam's villages. More seriously from the United States' point of view was the realisation that the peasants increasingly supported the Vietcong, or VC, as the Communists became known. Kennedy realised that the South Vietnamese government had to win not just a military war but a war also for the 'hearts and minds' of the people. Diem was a major obstacle to this because of his unpopularity. His overthrow and execution by a South Vietnamese army coup in 1963 was welcomed by the United States and was probably helped by the American Central Intelligence Agency. Diem's departure did nothing to bring about popular support for the South Vietnamese government because the men that succeeded him were no more honest or efficient.

America's first defeat

Kennedy restricted US involvement to advisers and military supplies but after his assassination in 1963 American policy changed sharply. Lyndon Johnson believed that the war could be won quickly with a big increase in American involvement. Johnson used a minor incident in the Gulf of Tonkin in 1964 to justify the increase. An American ship in North Vietnamese waters was attacked by a North Vietnamese torpedo boat. It provided Johnson with the excuse to ask Congress for a massive increase in America's role in Vietnam. At the end of 1964 there were just 23 000 US servicemen in Vietnam. By November 1965 there were 165 000 combat troops and two years later the number was 500 000. The Americans also began a huge bombing campaign of North Vietnam – despite the fact that America was never officially at war with its Communist government. During the next seven years the US air force dropped more bombs on the North than all the bombs dropped by both sides in the Second World War. The American commander in Vietnam, General Westmoreland claimed the war would soon be won. Indeed, 1967 was a bad year for the Vietcong as they were forced to yield some ground to US and South Viet-

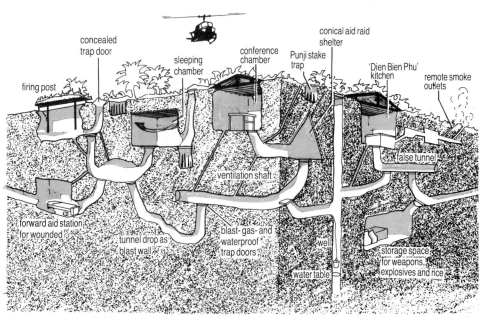

Vietcong tunnel system. Such tunnels as these stretched for 200 miles around Saigon. They enabled the Vietcong to reach the outskirts of the city during the Tet Offensive undetected. The narrow size of the tunnels (sometimes only 3 × 3 feet or 1 × 1 metre) made it difficult for the big US troops to crawl into. Only direct hits from B52 bombers could destroy them

concealed trap door

conference chamber

conical aid raid shelter

Punji stake trap

sleeping chamber

'Dien Bien Phu' kitchen

remote smoke outlets

firing post

false tunnel

ventilation shaft

forward aid station for wounded

tunnel drop as blast wall

blast- gas- and waterproof trap doors

well

storage space for weapons, explosives and rice

water table

US soldiers fighting in the grounds of their own embassy in January 1968 during the Tet Offensive

namese forces. Vietcong supply lines from the North, known as the Ho Chi Minh trail, were bombed repeatedly.

Suddenly, at the end of January 1968, the Vietcong launched a large scale offensive, the Tet Offensive. It lasted a month and though much ground was gained at first the Communist guerrilla fighters proved to be less effective in conventional fighting. The VC were quickly beaten back, leaving some 40 000 dead compared to just over 4000 US and South Vietnamese killed in action. Nonetheless, the Tet Offensive played a major role in turning US public opinion against the war. Americans at home saw on their television screens this 'beaten' army fighting in the grounds of the US embassy in Saigon. Americans realised that even if the war could be won it would take years of bitter and costly war. The war was costly both in terms of men and money. In 1969 14 000 Americans were killed, and the war was costing $2000 million a month. In order to halt the offensive many troops had had to be withdrawn from the countryside to fight to save the towns. The VC were then able to regain control of parts of the rural South.

Nixon and 'Vietnamisation'

Johnson decided not to stand for re-election as President in 1968. He knew he had no chance of winning because of

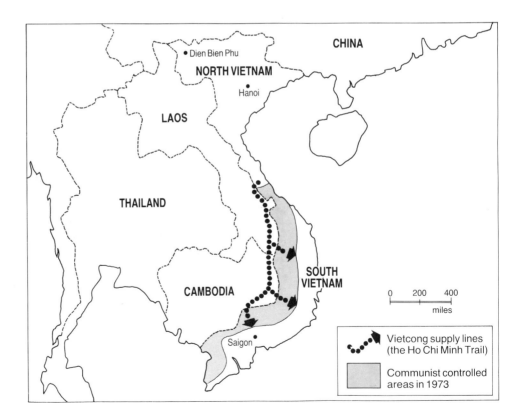

The Vietnam War 1961–73

the way the war was going. The war had also wrecked his ambitious welfare policies, the 'Great Society', because huge sums were spent on the war and taken away from slum clearance or health programmes. The Democrat Party could not recover the ground that Johnson had lost and Nixon, a Republican, won the election. Nixon did not promise to end the war but his policy of 'Vietnamisation' later proved a vote winner. 'Vietnamisation' meant that more would be spent to arm and train the South Vietnamese army to fight the Vietcong.

Gradually all the US troops would be withdrawn to allow the South Vietnamese to take on a bigger and bigger share of the fighting until there were no more American combat troops left. In the meantime Nixon started bombing the North again – Johnson had ordered a halt in March 1968. In 1970 Nixon also ordered the bombing of neutral Cambodia in an effort to destroy the Ho Chi Minh trail. He believed that the North Vietnamese could be bombed into a peace agreement which would let the United States get out of Vietnam without looking beaten.

Exercise 4

Extract: Johnson's message to Congress, August 1964

... The threat to the free nations of south-east Asia has long been clear. The North Vietnamese regime has constantly sought to take over South Vietnam and Laos. This Communist regime has violated the Geneva accords for Vietnam. It has systematically conducted a campaign of
5 subversion, which includes the direction, training, and supply of personnel and arms for the conduct of guerrilla warfare in South Vietnamese territory ...

As President of the United States I have concluded that I should now ask the Congress, on its part, to join in affirming the national determination that
10 all such attacks will be met, and that the United States will continue in its basic policy of assisting the free nations of the area to defend their freedom.

(*Documents of American History Vol. 2*, Ed. H.S. Commager)

a What incident earlier in 1964 led President Johnson to make this appeal to Congress?
b What was the name of the organisation for which North Vietnam, according to Johnson, provided 'arms for the conduct of guerrilla warfare in South Vietnamese territory'?
c To what extent do you think Johnson was justified in describing South Vietnam as one of 'the free nations of the area'? Explain your answer.
d Johnson accused North Vietnam of violating the Geneva accords of 1954. What do you think the response of Ho Chi Minh would have been to this?
e How did Johnson show America's 'national determination' to assist the 'free nations' of the area in his policy towards the war?

Exercise 5

Study the cartoon on page 220

a Name the American shown here wielding the axe at the rear of the train at the time this cartoon was drawn.

Source Two Punch *cartoon, 1967: 'The Train Robbery'*

b Explain briefly to what the phrase 'Great Society' on the side of the carriages refers?

c What is the message the cartoonist is trying to convey in the cartoon as regards this President's Vietnam policy?

d What was the consequence for this President of his involvement with this problem in 1968?

e Contrast the view of the Vietnam War expressed in this cartoon with the view expressed by Johnson in Exercise 4.

f Would the protesters in the photograph below have supported the view expressed in the extract in Exercise 4 or Source Two? Give reasons.

'Peace with honour' 1973

By 1972 American troops remaining in Vietnam numbered just 47 000. Nixon had continued with this 'Vietnamisation' policy despite the fact that South Vietnamese forces were clearly unable to wage war against the Vietcong and North Vietnamese on their own. The year 1972 was election year and withdrawing US troops from the war was a popular vote-winner. Nixon was re-elected with a massive majority. In January 1973 a cease-fire was agreed with the VC and North Vietnamese. American troops and personnel would be totally withdrawn from Vietnam. Communist forces were not to extend their control beyond areas already occupied by them. President Thieu of South Vietnam considered America's withdrawal a betrayal of her promise. Few people believed that the war would end there and then. Soon Communist forces began their final push on Saigon. The South Vietnamese army collapsed and its men threw away their uniforms and melted back into civilian life. Saigon was captured on 30 April 1975 and was later renamed Ho Chi Minh City in honour of the North's leader who had died in 1969. Perhaps a million Vietcong, North Vietnamese soldiers and civilians died in the war. South Vietnamese soldiers and civilians killed probably numbered some 600 000. Over 50 000 American troops lost their lives. North Vietnam had suf-

Anti-Vietnam War demonstration in New York. Many Vietnam veterans joined in. Such demonstrations helped to turn public opinion against the war

A North Vietnamese militia unit manning an anti-aircraft gun. Note the presence of women in the gun crew – the North Vietnamese mobilised all their people in the war. This photograph was taken by an official East German photographer

fered widespread destruction from bombing and much of Vietnam's jungle had been poisoned by chemicals to strip away the foliage which concealed VC troops.

Why did the United States lose the war?

The Americans realised too late that the real war in Vietnam was not a military one but a political one – for the 'hearts and minds' of the peasants of South Vietnam. The NLF from the start set about winning the support of the peasants. In areas under its control the peasants were given land and were well treated. The American response to the presence of VC guerrilla fighters in an area was all too often to call in air strikes which killed countless thousands of innocent civilians. In 1968 over 300 old men, women and children were gunned down by US troops at My Lai – a village suspected of having sheltered Communist fighters. On the military level the VC and North Vietnamese regulars proved much more skilled guerrilla fighters who were at home in the dense jungles. To Americans the environment itself was hostile and they never succeeded in learning how to cope with it. The Communists also had vital military backing from China and the Soviet Union. Russian anti-aircraft guns and missiles played a key role in defending the North from air attacks and Russian tanks were important in bringing about the collapse of the Saigon regime in 1975. The Communist forces were convinced from the start of the justice of their cause and their morale was high. The average US 'grunt' or soldier never wanted to do anything more than finish his year tour in one piece and get home. Over-keen American officers were sometimes 'fragged' or shot by their own men if they issued orders that seemed too dangerous.

Exercise 6

a Why was Kennedy's 'safe village' policy a failure?
b How did Johnson step up American involvement in the war?
c Why was the Tet Offensive so important for the outcome of the war?
d Why do you think Nixon adopted his 'Vietnamisation' policy?
e In what ways was America's defeat one of morale and politics rather than simply a military defeat?

Exercise 7

Study the cartoon on page 222

a Identify the figure on the right in the dug-out.
b Explain what was meant by the word on the back of the soldier.
c What is the cartoonist suggesting about the effectiveness of the policy?

Source Three

Guardian *cartoon, May 1972: "If this boy of yours is real, how come we gotta wind him up all the time?"*

Vietnam since 1975

American officials had predicted that there would be a bloodbath in Saigon once the North took over the country, but it never happened. The two halves of Vietnam were finally united in 1976 – some 20 years and nearly 2 million lives later. Many thousands of South Vietnamese who helped and co-operated with the Americans fled for their lives. Over 600 000 refugees made their way out of Vietnam, 250 000 of them as 'boat-people'. Vietnam joined Comecon, the Russian economic group, in 1978 and this close alliance with the Soviet Union concerned China. Relations with China rapidly got worse, between 1978 and 1981 violent clashes took place between Chinese and Vietnamese forces along the border. The Vietnamese invasion of Kampuchea (Cambodia) in 1979 and the overthrow of its pro-Chinese Communist government showed just how quickly relations between China and Vietnam had turned sour. It also showed how out-dated the domino theory really was. Communist governments in South East Asia were more likely to go to war with each other than they were to plot the overthrow of other non-Communist governments.

At first the new rulers of a united Vietnam tried to move quickly to establish a Communist system in the south of the country by taking over the factories and **collectivising** the land into state farms. This policy, similar to China's Great Leap Forward of the late 1950s, was not a success. In 1979 the government called a halt to collectivisation. More co-operatives were encouraged and slowly rice output began to rise. In 1976 output stood at 12 million tons. By 1984 it had increased by nearly 50% to 17.2 million tons – just about enough to feed the population. The shortage of rice, however, means that the price of a kilo on the open market is 100 times the government subsidised ration price. Massive Soviet aid (in exchange for naval bases on the Vietnamese coast) is helping to keep the country afloat. There is little aid available from the West as the United States follows a hostile policy towards the Communist government in Hanoi. Washington has consistently refused to pay any of the reparations demanded by Hanoi for the tremendous damage caused by seven years of saturation bombing.

Ho Chi Minh City is in many respects still the Saigon of the 1960s. The prostitutes and gambling dens have gone but the southerners' flamboyant style of

Life goes on in the New Vietnam although relics of the recent past, in this case a rusting US tank, are never far away

dress and life style have had an effect on the capital Hanoi in the north. After 30 years of war, self-denial and hardship the people of Hanoi have begun to change. In 1976 the BBC correspondent had this to say:

> In Hanoi, women's hair styles are more frivolous; girls can be seen with lipstick; blouses are brighter; there are more cars and motorcycles – all rather superficial but exciting. After the years of self-denial, then victory, the expectations of the Northerners have been aroused. To a very limited extent these are starting to be met.

The Cuban Missile Crisis: showdown in Havana

Castro's revolution

A glance at the map on page 225 will show you that the island of Cuba is about 100 miles from the coast of Florida in the United States. It has always been a vital part of American foreign policy to ensure that countries in that part of the world do not fall into 'unfriendly' hands. This is known as the 'Monroe Doctrine'. Since 1940 Cuba had been under the control of a military **dictator**, Batista. He allowed US businessmen and the Mafia to make big profits in Cuba. Prostitution and gambling were large money earners for criminal elements in the United States and Cuba. The vast majority of Cubans lived in miserable squalor. This situation of extreme poverty and wealth was bound to lead to violence and **revolution**.

The man who was to organise that revolution was Fidel Castro. Like many revolutionaries, Castro came from a comfortable middle-class background. But he was a man determined to improve the lot of the ordinary Cubans. An attempt to overthrow Batista in 1956 was a failure but he, and a bare dozen followers, retreated to the mountains of the Sierra Madre. In January 1959 Castro and 800 guerrillas marched into the capital, Havana. Batista and his detested government disintegrated. The Cuban **revolution** had begun.

Castro's political views at this time were basically nationalist. All he really wanted to do was free Cuba from US influence and improve the welfare of the people. He shut down the gambling casinos and the brothels. Cuba's main export was sugar and the mills were American owned. Castro **nationalised** them. The USA replied by refusing to buy any more of Cuba's sugar and so Castro seized 1 000 million dollars' worth of American property. Not surprisingly, diplomatic relations between Cuba and the new administration of John F. Kennedy were broken off in January 1961. Castro had been forced into a corner and the only country willing to help was the Soviet Union. The Soviets offered to buy Cuba's sugar and supply her with oil. Castro's views became steadily Communist and Cuba, having shaken off American interference in her affairs, gradually fell under Soviet 'influence'.

Exercise 8

a What was the Monroe Doctrine?
b Why do you think the Americans were happy with Batista's rule in Cuba?
c What evidence is there in the text that Batista had little popular support?
d What evidence can you find in the text that small countries find it very difficult to survive without the support of one of the superpowers?

The Missile Crisis

When Castro took over in 1959 some Cubans fled to the United States and soon began planning an invasion of Cuba to overthrow Castro. President Eisenhower approved the scheme and the US government's secret activities organisation, the Central Intelligence Agency or CIA, trained the 1500 rebels for the attack. President Kennedy also approved the scheme when he took over the Presidency from Eisenhower in January 1961. In April 1961 the anti-Castro forces, backed by fighter aircraft, landed in the Bay of Pigs in Cuba. The exiles were routed and the 'invasion' easily crushed. The whole affair was badly planned. Many of the landing craft had their bottoms ripped out by reefs which the CIA had mistaken for seaweed! The few rebels that did get ashore faced a hostile population who would not support them against Castro. One result of the fiasco was that Kennedy developed a low opinion of the CIA.

The Bay of Pigs attack convinced Castro that Cuba needed increased military assistance from Russia. Shortly, Soviet nuclear missiles began arriving in Cuba by ship. The United States stepped up U-2 high altitude reconnaissance flights over the island. By the middle of October Kennedy had photographic evidence that the Russians were installing nuclear missile sites in Cuba.

(Below) *Castro (left) is welcomed by Khrushchev, (right) in Moscow*

Source Four
(right) *Missile sites in Cuba*

Source Five *A Soviet freighter is shadowed by the* USS Barry *(foreground) during the Missile Crisis*

Exercise ◼ 9

a Do you think the photographs of the missile sites and the Soviet freighter were taken by the same type of aircraft? Explain your answer.

b What evidence is there of missiles on the Soviet ship?

c How do you think the American intelligence experts were able to identify the features labelled on the photograph of missile sites?

d What does the photograph of the freighters tell us about the Soviet attitude to secrecy in the affair?

e If we assume that the Soviet Union wanted the Americans to know about the presence of these missiles, can you think of any reason behind the Soviet action?

For the very first time every major American city was within striking distance of a Soviet Medium Range Ballistic Missile (MRBM). The United States felt very threatened. Kennedy was determined that Khrushchev, the Soviet leader, would back down and withdraw the missiles. But if Khrushchev refused to back down then the world was on the brink of a Third World War.

Kennedy had three options open to him. He could order an air strike against the missile sites or he could authorise an invasion with the 14 000 troops now on stand-by. He opted for the third option – negotiation. To strengthen his position, Kennedy ordered a naval blockade of Cuba. All Soviet ships approaching the island were to be stopped and searched to prevent any more missiles or their support systems from reaching Cuba. But what if the Soviets refused to allow their ships to be searched and 'taken into custody'?

Khrushchev wrote to Kennedy in

Blockade of Cuba

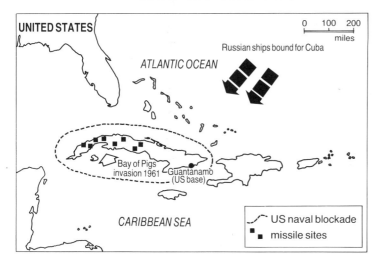

October 1962, suggesting a way out of the crisis:

I have learned with great pleasure of your reply to Mr. U. Thant (Secretary General of the UN) to the effect that steps will be taken to avoid contact between our ships and thus avoid fateful irremediable consequences.

You have been worried concerning the fact that we have helped Cuba with weapons, with the aim to strengthen its defensive capacities – yes, precisely its defensive capacities because no matter what weapons it possesses Cuba cannot equal you . . .

Our aim has been, and still is, to help Cuba . . . to enable Cuba to live in peace and develop in the way its people desires . . . All countries want to make themselves safe. But how are we, the Soviet Union, to assess your actions which are expressed in the fact that you have surrounded the Soviet Union with military bases . . . Your rockets are situated in Britain, in Italy and are directly aimed at us. Your rockets are situated in Turkey. You are worried by Cuba. You say it worries you because it is a distance of 90 miles from the coast of America but Turkey is next to us. Our sentries walk up and down and look at each other. Do you then consider that you have the right to demand security for your country and the removal of weapons which you call offensive and do not acknowledge the same right for us?

I therefore make this proposal: we agree to remove from Cuba those means which you regard as offensive means . . . and make a pledge in the United Nations. Your representative will make a declaration to the effect that the United States . . . will remove its similar means from Turkey.

Exercise ▮▮▮▮10

a Why was contact likely between Soviet and American ships?
b What do you think Khrushchev meant by 'fateful irremediable consequences'?
c What issue especially concerned the Russians?
d On what grounds could the Soviet Union accuse the United States of operating a double standard over its missiles in Europe?
e Do you consider Khrushchev's proposal to be a reasonable one? Give your reasons.
f What risks do you think Kennedy might have run if he had agreed with Khrushchev?

Kennedy replied to the Russian leader's letter with counter-proposals of his own: firstly, the Russians would dismantle their nuclear missile bases in Cuba and undertake 'to halt the further introduction of such weapons systems to Cuba'; secondly, the Americans on their part would end the quarantine measures then in effect and 'give assurances against the invasion of Cuba'. For a week the world waited as the Soviet vessels approached Cuba. The two super powers seemed on the brink of a nuclear war. Then Khrushchev ordered the ships to turn around and agreed to remove the missiles. It was a massive defeat for the Soviets. Two years later Khrushchev was removed from office in disgrace.

There were, though, some benefits from the crisis. A direct telephone link was installed between the White House and the Kremlin. The following year the two leaders signed the Nuclear Test Ban Treaty by which they and Great Britain agreed not to test nuclear weapons in the atmosphere. It seemed as though Kennedy and Khrushchev had realised just how close they had come to a terrible war and had both decided to work that much harder for 'peaceful co-existence'. Unfortunately the new understanding between the two leaders ended abruptly in November 1963 with President Kennedy's assassination.

Exercise 11

Now study the cartoons in Sources Six (*top*) and Seven (*bottom*) published at the time of the crisis.

But those behind cried 'forward'
And those before cried 'back'
And backward now and forward
Wavers the deep array

Source Six *How the* New Statesman *saw the crisis,
5 October 1962*

Source Seven *The* Daily Mail
view of the missile crisis

a *Time* is a magazine widely read by American businessmen. How else does the cartoonist suggest that Kennedy is being pushed by big business interests into a confrontation with Castro?

b Does the cartoonist show Kennedy as a willing partner in the confrontation with Cuba? Give your reason.

c What reasons did American business interests have for wanting this confrontation and what do you think they hoped to gain from it?

d How does the *New Statesman* show its sympathy for Cuba in the cartoon?

a Suggest a title for this cartoon.

b Name the characters from left to right.

c Would you say that the cartoonist's attitude towards Castro is:
i angry, ii mocking; iii fearful;
iv respectful?
Support your opinion with evidence from the cartoon.

d How would you describe the cartoonist's attitude towards Khrushchev? In what ways does he show the Soviet leader as a menacing figure? (Look at his expression, his clothes and gestures.)

e How can we tell that the cartoonist has a much friendlier opinion of Kennedy?

f Do you think the portrayal of Castro in the cartoon is a fair one? Explain your answer.

Exercise 12

Comparing the sources

a Contrast the two views of events concerning Cuba expressed by Sources Six and Seven.

b Which of the two cartoons is more effective in putting across its point of view and why?

c Which of the two cartoons provides a better understanding of the causes of the crisis over Cuba? Explain your answer.

Assignment unit

Kennedy's reply to Khrushchev

In the letter from Khrushchev to Kennedy quoted on page 226, the Soviet leader demanded the withdrawal of US missiles from Turkey in exchange for the withdrawl of Soviet missiles from Cuba. In a second letter Khruschev dropped the idea of the exchange and merely asked for a US assurance not to launch an invasion of Cuba – a reference to the Bay of Pigs. In his reply to this letter Kennedy agreed to end the blockade around Cuba under United Nations supervision and gave an assurance not to invade Cuba. In exchange, the Soviet Union was to withdraw its missiles from Cuba under UN supervision and ensure that no further missiles were ever installed in the country again. This letter also made references to a US interest in 'reducing tensions and halting the arms race' and the possibility of a 'détente affecting NATO and the Warsaw Pact'. Your task is to write the text of Kennedy's reply on the following lines:

1 Comment, first of all, on the welcome change of approach between Chairman Khrushchev's first letter and the second.

2 Describe the background to the crisis from the American point of view, beginning with Castro's actions as leader of Cuba.

3 Explain in detail the proposal outlined above to settle the crisis.

4 Expand on the possibilities of 'reducing tensions' and achieving a 'détente affecting NATO and the Warsaw Pact'. To do this, it will be necessary to discuss world issues which are causing tension between the two powers. Here are some examples: the Berlin Wall; Soviet influence in Vietnam; the recent failure of the Paris Peace Summit (see Chapter 14, page 175) – though the release of Gary Powers in February 1962 is an encouraging development. You may be able to think of others. Finally, suggest a nuclear test ban agreement and the setting up of a 'hot-line' between Moscow and Washington as two positive steps that could be agreed (as indeed they were).

Chapter 18

Southern Africa in transition

Africa after 1945

Towards the end of the nineteenth century, European powers anxious to acquire the prestige and markets associated with big **empires** seized almost all of Africa. This 'scramble for Africa' left only Abyssinia and Liberia free of European rule in 1919. The Second World War, though, was to bring about a tremendous change in the map of Africa within twenty years of its end. The movement towards independence first scored major success in the Far East and India. India ceased to be a British colony in 1947. Burma and Ceylon followed in the next year. The French abandoned Indo-China in 1954. The Dutch East Indies became Indonesia in 1949. In most cases there was bloodshed before the old imperial

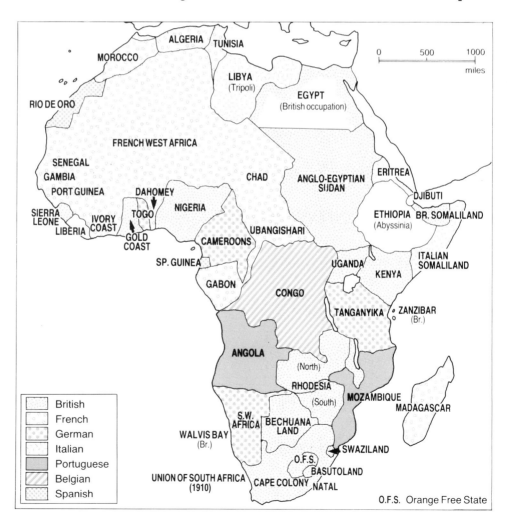

Africa in 1914

Africa in 1980 (with dates of independence)

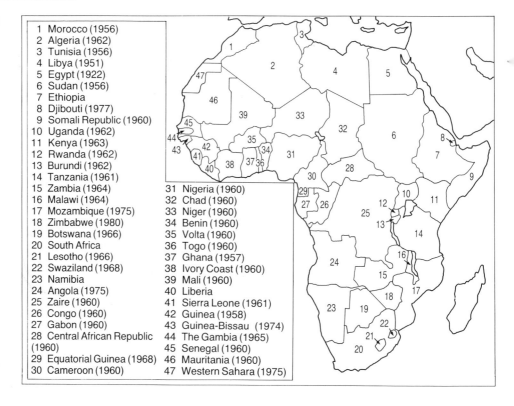

1 Morocco (1956)
2 Algeria (1962)
3 Tunisia (1956)
4 Libya (1951)
5 Egypt (1922)
6 Sudan (1956)
7 Ethiopia
8 Djibouti (1977)
9 Somali Republic (1960)
10 Uganda (1962)
11 Kenya (1963)
12 Rwanda (1962)
13 Burundi (1962)
14 Tanzania (1961)
15 Zambia (1964)
16 Malawi (1964)
17 Mozambique (1975)
18 Zimbabwe (1980)
19 Botswana (1966)
20 South Africa
21 Lesotho (1966)
22 Swaziland (1968)
23 Namibia
24 Angola (1975)
25 Zaire (1960)
26 Congo (1960)
27 Gabon (1960)
28 Central African Republic (1960)
29 Equatorial Guinea (1968)
30 Cameroon (1960)
31 Nigeria (1960)
32 Chad (1960)
33 Niger (1960)
34 Benin (1960)
35 Volta (1960)
36 Togo (1960)
37 Ghana (1957)
38 Ivory Coast (1960)
39 Mali (1960)
40 Liberia
41 Sierra Leone (1961)
42 Guinea (1958)
43 Guinea-Bissau (1974)
44 The Gambia (1965)
45 Senegal (1960)
46 Mauritania (1960)
47 Western Sahara (1975)

powers realised that it was pointless trying to hold on to their colonies in face of bitter opposition. The Second World War had opened up the eyes of the colonised peoples to the fact that their masters were not invincible. After stubbornly resisting the Japanese during the war, the peoples of Asia had no intention of meekly allowing their European masters to regain control. It was not long before the colonies in Africa decided that their time had come for independence.

Britain gave up her colonies in Africa without too much trouble: the Gold Coast became Ghana in 1957; Nigeria achieved independence in 1960; Tanganyika and Zanzibar formed Tanzania in 1961 and this was followed by independence for Uganda (1962) and Kenya (1963). In Tanzania, Uganda and Kenya a complicating factor was the presence of white settlers. For a time the British insisted that whites be represented in multi-racial governments after independence. In Kenya

throughout the 1950s there was bloodshed and anti-British rioting by blacks who insisted on black majority rule. Eventually the British Prime Minister of the day, Harold MacMillan, gave in and the principle of total black control of the newly independent states was established. In Rhodesia the 250 000 whites in a country of 4 million Africans refused to accept the idea of black majority rule and took steps to prevent it.

From Rhodesia to Zimbabwe

In 1953 the British government drew up plans to create an independent state consisting of Northern Rhodesia, Southern Rhodesia and Nyasaland. The state would be known as the Central African Federation. The Federation was unstable from the start and by 1964 had

Two Africans reading about the banning of ZAPU in September 1962

not content with this. One such group, the Zimbabwe African People's Union, (ZAPU) led by Joshua Nkomo was banned in 1962 by Whitehead.

In the 1962 elections Whitehead's party was defeated by the racialist Rhodesia Front party which believed that Whitehead had made too many concessions already to the blacks. The new Prime Minister was Winston Field. He represented a patient approach and sought a negotiated solution with Britain. When it was announced in 1963 that Northern Rhodesia and Nyasaland would be granted full independence, Field applied for the same treatment for Southern Rhodesia. He was told that independence would only be granted by the Conservative Government on the basis of black majority rule. The hardline whites in the Rhodesia Front lost patience with Field and in 1964 he was replaced by Ian Smith. Smith was prepared to act without the approval of the British government. A general election in May 1965 gave Smith all 50 of the seats allocated to the white voters under Whitehead's constitution. Urgent talks between Smith and Britain's new Labour Prime Minister, Harold Wilson, went on throughout that summer but no agreement could be reached. On 11 November Smith made his Unilateral Declaration of Independence (UDI) in which Rhodesia was to be an independent state without British approval.

broken up. Northern Rhodesia achieved independence as Zambia under Kenneth Kaunda, and Nyasaland as Malawi under Hastings Banda. In both these states majority black rule was established. But the situation in Southern Rhodesia, known as Rhodesia, was becoming very complex. Garfield Todd, the Prime Minister between 1953 and 1958 and Sir Edgar Whitehead (1958–62) had tried to follow progressive policies. Whitehead's plan was to gradually draw the Africans into a partnership with the white settlers and eventually to hand over power to them. But in the meantime the blacks, 96% of the population, would have to make do with just 15 out of 65 MPs in the Rhodesian Parliament. Not surprisingly, Rhodesia's black nationalists were

Exercise 1

a What was the 'scramble for Africa'?
b Where did the movement against the old empires first begin?
c Why was the end of British colonial rule in Southern Rhodesia always likely to be difficult?
d Why were black Rhodesians unimpressed by Whitehead's new constitution of 1961?
e What do you think would have been the response of black Rhodesians to Smith's illegal white government?

Smith's Rhodesia

Immediately there was pressure on Wilson from some Commonwealth states, notably Nigeria and Ghana, to use armed force to remove Smith's illegal government. Wilson rejected this, partly because the loyalty of British troops against white Rhodesians could not be guaranteed and partly because he believed that Smith's government could be brought to its knees through economic **sanctions** without bloodshed. Britain forbade the sale of oil to Rhodesia in 1965 and stopped buying tobacco and sugar. The United Nations backed this policy and called on its members not to buy anything from or sell anything to Smith's government – a total trade embargo was imposed. If these sanctions had been enforced then perhaps Smith's government might have collapsed. But British oil companies continued to sell oil to Rhodesia in defiance of the order. South Africa and neighbouring Portuguese-run Mozambique also defied the trade embargo. Efforts to negotiate with Smith proved no more successful in bringing about majority rule. Wilson twice met Smith – in 1966 on *HMS Tiger* and in 1968 on *HMS Fearless*. On each occasion Smith's refusal to move in the direction of majority rule led to a breakdown in the talks.

In 1970 the racist thinking behind Smith's government was made more obvious with a new **constitution** in which a white majority of seats in Parliament was to be guaranteed. Black Rhodesians were forcibly evicted from more territory allocated to the whites under the Land Tenure Act. The activities of black **guerrilla** groups were being largely controlled by Smith's well trained and white-led army. In 1971 Smith reached an agreement with the Tory Foreign Minister, Sir Alec Douglas-Home. One condition of the agreement was that it had to be approved by Rhodesia's blacks. A commission from Britain was sent to Rhodesia under Lord Pearce to sound out black opinion. The message from Rhodesia's black population was very clear: 'no to the agreement' and 'majority rule now!'

1974, the turning of the tide: Portugal's empire collapses

From 1974 onwards things began to go badly wrong for Ian Smith. The most serious blow was the collapse of Portugal's African empire. In 1974 the 50 year old right-wing dictatorship in Portugal was overthrown by a military coup led by young army officers. Many of these officers had served in Mozambique and Angola, fighting a colonial war against black guerrilla independence movements. In 1974 they decided that the wars could not be won and had to be ended along with Caetano's dictatorship. Its overthrow in April 1974 meant the end of support from a friendly Portuguese government for Smith. It also meant that Robert Mugabe's guerrilla forces, the Zimbabwe African National Union (ZANU), could now use Mozambique as a base for strikes against Rhodesia; and it meant that the oil pipeline from the port of Beira in Mozambique to Rhodesia was now cut off by Mozambique's black **Marxist** government. Smith continued to get oil from Oman and Brunei but the supplies were harder to come by and ZANU's military effectiveness was much increased. The activities of Joshua Nkomo's guerrilla army, the Zimbabwe African People's Union (ZAPU), based in Zambia, were causing further problems for Smith.

South Africa, Smith's most reliable ally, also began to realise that some agreement would have to be reached with the Zimbabwe guerrilla forces. South Africa felt her own security threatened by the victory of the Marxist MPLA (Popular Movement for the Liberation of Angola) in Angola against Portugal. The South Africans were becoming increasingly involved in efforts to bring about the victory of a rival pro-Western guerrilla group in Angola, the FNLA (National Front for the Liberation of Angola).

Exercise 2

a What steps did Britain take to bring about the collapse of Smith's illegal government?

b Why did these steps prove ineffective?

c Why did Smith's agreement with Douglas-Home in 1971 fail?

d Why did South Africa have less time to devote to assisting Smith after 1974?

e The text above suggests that Wilson was reluctant to use troops against Smith because 'the loyalty of British troops against white Rhodesians could not be guaranteed'. What do you think the author means by this?

Exercise 3

Source One

Punch, *cartoon:*
'White Supremacy in Rhodesia

a Identify the figure originally in the middle of the three, holding the roof of 'white supremacy'.

b Identify the ruler of Portugal shown walking away from the other two.

c Why is he shown walking away? What year do you suppose this cartoon was drawn?

d What is meant by the phrase 'white supremacy in Rhodesia'?

e How much had the other two countries done to ensure the survival of this supremacy in Rhodesia?

f How much of a blow to the man in the middle of the cartoon was the loss of the support of the man walking away?

Exercise 4

Source Two

'Black Samson'

a What is meant by the heading 'colonialism'?

b Which two countries are referred to in Source Two as colonial powers?

c In what sense, from the point of view of black Africans, is South Africa a colonial power?

d In what way does Source Two support the view of Source One on the importance of events in Portugal in 1974?

e In what way is the emphasis of Source Two different as to the cause of those events?

f How appropriate do you think 'Black Samson' is as a title for this cartoon? Explain why.

1976–80: the end of UDI

Under pressure from South Africa Ian Smith agreed to the principle of majority rule. It was announced that a meeting would be held in Geneva in October 1976. Britain, the Smith government, Nkomo, Mugabe and two other black Rhodesian leaders (Bishop Muzorewa and the Reverend Sithole) would all be represented. Smith, however, would make no firm commitment. The conference broke up in failure. Mugabe and Nkomo, despite serious political differences, agreed to set up a united military structure for their armies – the Patriotic Front. The Patriotic Front stepped up its campaign of guerrilla war, backed by the five 'frontline states' of Mozambique, Angola, Zambia, Botswana and Tanzania.

Smith decided to create his own internal settlement. He reached an agreement with Muzorewa and Sithole in which new elections would be held with 72 of the 100 seats allocated to blacks. The catch was that the remaining white MPs would control the army and police forces and could **veto** any law of which they disapproved. The Patriotic Front refused to have anything to do with Smith's rather undemocratic set-up.

In April 1979 Smith stepped down as Prime Minister in favour of the winner of the election, Bishop Muzorewa. The new Zimbabwe–Rhodesia failed to convince Britain or the USA and only South Africa recognised the government. Neither Muzorewa or Sithole had armed fighters behind them in the bush against Smith's regime. They knew that their only chance of power was to come to terms with the white Rhodesians in unequal partnership. When genuine elections did finally take place in 1980 black voters turned their backs on Muzorewa and Sithole for their betrayal of the black cause of majority rule.

The Lancaster House talks

In 1979 the Patriotic Front (PF) had some

15 000 guerrilla fighters in the war against Smith's government. The biggest of the two groups that made up the PF was Robert Mugabe's ZANU. Mugabe was a Marxist and his army was based in Marxist Mozambique. The heaviest fighting of the war was therefore around north-east Rhodesia, along the border with Mozambique. By 1979 some 400 Rhodesian troops and 3300 guerrillas as well as over 100 white civilians had died in the war. The war was having a bad effect on white morale. Many began to emigrate, mostly to South Africa. Smith soon realised that his 'Zimbabwe–Rhodesia' settlement was not going to work. In September 1979 he agreed to attend real talks with Mugabe and Nkomo at Lancaster House in London, chaired by the Foreign Secretary, Lord Carrington. To considerable surprise the negotiations reached an agreement by December. Muzorewa was to step down as Prime Minister; the guerrillas were to lay down their arms at cease-fire assembly points; Lord Soames was to take over as governor of Rhodesia until new and democratic elections could be held.

A Patriotic Front guerrilla at a cease-fire assembly point in January 1980

Mugabe's Zimbabwe

The elections took place in February 1980 and all the parties were represented. To the great disappointment of Margaret Thatcher's Conservative government the Marxist Mugabe easily beat the pro-Western Joshua Nkomo. Mugabe's ZANU won 57 of the 80 seats reserved for blacks. Nkomo picked up 20 seats and the remaining 3 went to a heavily defeated Muzorewa. The remaining 20 white seats went to Smith's Rhodesia Front. The victory of Mugabe caused white Rhodesians and Western governments much concern. Mugabe was expected to call in Soviet military and economic aid and turn Zimbabwe (as Rhodesia officially became in April 1980) into a Russian satellite. But Mugabe surprised many by his cautious actions. Several whites were included in his first government and he publicly called for an end to past bitterness.

But Mugabe could not afford to disap-point his own supporters either. Diplomatic relations with South Africa were broken off in September 1980 but Zimbabwe continued to trade with the South African government and the South Africans are Zimbabwe's biggest trading partners. Relations between Mugabe and his minister for Home Affairs, Joshua Nkomo, were always strained. One reason was that Mugabe and Nkomo represent different tribes, each hostile to the other. Some of Nkomo's men refused to accept Mugabe's government and continued to stage terrorist attacks on government supporters among Mugabe's Shona tribe. Mugabe has replied with similar acts of murder among Nkomo's Ndebele tribe. In 1982 Nkomo was removed from the government and in 1983 he fled from Zimbabwe to London, claiming his life was at risk – though he returned within six months. Zimbabwe's white population has fallen sharply from 200 000 to 100 000 since 1980. But white emigration has not been as severe as many expected and most whites seem prepared to give Mugabe a chance. Even Ian Smith continues to farm in Zimbabwe – though he also has a home in South Africa.

Political problems

Zimbabwe's economy relies heavily on tobacco and maize exports to earn foreign currency. But the maize crop has fallen steadily since 1981 from its total of 2.8 million tons then to just 600 000 in 1983. Adult unemployment is probably in the region of 40%. Despite these serious problems Zimbabwe is without doubt one of the most wealthy states in Africa and Mugabe has made determined efforts to improve the standard of living of the black majority – especially in education. In 1983 there were twice as many primary school pupils as in 1979 and secondary school pupils numbered 316 000 compared to 73 000 in 1979. The number of secondary school teachers in 1984 was 15 000 – up

Robert Mugabe (left) and Joshua Nkomo at Lancaster House in 1979

babwe's future is not economic but political. The 1985 election has split Zimbabwe into three very separate and hostile camps. Ian Smith's party won 15 out of 20 seats allocated to the whites and Smith had made no secret of his hostility to Mugabe and his plans for the country. Mugabe's ZANU swept the board among the black voters increasing its 1980 total of seats from 57 to 63 while Nkomo's ZAPU fell from 20 to 15 seats. Mugabe will probably abolish the right of white voters to their guaranteed 20 seats in 1987 and the evidence is that he still plans to introduce a one-party state eventually – though with parliament's approval.

from 3500 in 1979. Generally, the most difficult problem threatening Zim-

Exercise 5

a What was the Patriotic Front?
b Why was Ian Smith's internal settlement really a fraud?
c Why were many Westerners disappointed and concerned by the 1980 election result?
d What has been one source of conflict between Mugabe and Nkomo?
e Why could the July 1985 election seriously threaten the unity of Zimbabwe?

South Africa since 1945

In 1910 South Africa became a self-governing Dominion within the British Empire. Its population was then, and still is, racially mixed. Some 70% of the population are black Africans, 20% are white and the remainder are described as 'coloured' – mixed race, Chinese and Asians. Of the 4 million whites in South Africa's population of 22 million most are of Dutch descent. The Boers, as they are called, have always had an uneasy relationship with those whites of British origin. It is the Boers who have dominated South Africa since 1910 with their language (Afrikaans) and their policies, providing all of South Africa's Prime Ministers. The Boers became particularly concerned after the Second World War at the break-up of

(Right) An early black anti-apartheid poster. Note the demands of the African National Congress which put up the poster

the British Empire. This was not because they were admirers of Britain and her empire – in fact they disliked

Black demonstrators killed at Sharpeville, 1960

that empire heartily. They were worried at the spread of ideas of racial equality that Britain had accepted. The Boers, led by the Afrikaaner Nationalist Party, were determined that such ideas would never take root in white South Africa. In 1948 the Nationalist Party, under Dr Malan, won the elections – in which, of course, Africans could not vote. That victory saw the beginning of South Africa's official policy of '**apartheid**'. Apartheid is an Afrikaans word meaning 'apartness'. It has come to mean 'separate development' in which blacks have been rigorously forbidden to mix with whites. In theory they have been provided with 'separate but equal' facilities. In practice, South Africa's black and coloured population have been allocated the worst of everything in terms of schools, hospitals and jobs.

Apartheid in practice

It would be a mistake to assume that apartheid started after 1948. In fact, Dr Malan merely speeded up and intensified policies of racial discrimination which were already in existence. As early as 1936 the South African government had passed a law allocating $12\frac{1}{2}\%$ of South Africa's land to the blacks and $87\frac{1}{2}\%$ to the whites, who were outnumbered four to one. Discrimination in

jobs against blacks had been legal since 1911 and sexual relations between whites and blacks illegal since 1927. In 1956 coloureds were removed from the voting list. The pre-war 'pass laws' were tightened up. Blacks were required to carry a pass book with them wherever they went. It showed their occupation and which area they had permission to be in. To be stopped without being in possession of the pass meant a hefty fine and probably a beating. In 1976, 250 000 blacks were fined for not having their pass with them. The fine was $115 – nearly eight times the average black monthly wage then. In 1960 a meeting held in Sharpeville to protest at the hated pass laws led to 69 African deaths when police opened fire to disperse the crowd.

In 1959 the government decided that blacks should not be entitled to South African citizenship. It created the Bantu Self-Government Act in which eight regions of South Africa would be handed over to the Africans as independent states. These bantustans or tribal trustlands would be reponsible for the welfare of their African citizens. The fact that these tiny areas contained the poorest soil and no industry meant that they would be totally dependent on South Africa for any income as cheap labour. The Transkei was the first of the bantustans to become 'independent' in 1976. The Transkei is recognised only by South Africa as an independent nation. The bantustan policy will mean eventually that some 70% of the population will be allocated just 14% of the territory in which to live.

Apartheid affects every aspect of daily life in South Africa, from separate toilets and picnic areas to jobs reserved only for whites. The start made by Malan was enthusiastically continued by Verwoerd (1958–66) until his assassination and by his successor, Vorster (1966–78). But there has been opposition from within South Africa. Much of this has been ruthlessly dealt with

Black schoolchildren rioting in Soweto, 1976

under the Suppression of Communism Act (1950). This act gave the government wide powers to deal with anyone suspected of opposing apartheid and anyone who, in the narrow minds of South Africa's white racists, opposes apartheid must be a Communist. Much of the opposition to the government has come from young Africans. In 1976 thousands of black teenagers rioted in Soweto against government policy to make them learn Afrikaans – the language of the Boers. Soweto (*South West Township*) is a shanty town on the outskirts of Johannesburg. The pass laws permit only a few blacks to live in Johannesburg. Blacks who work in the white city have to return to their slums in Soweto each day. The black children rioted for days against the government's education policy. The response was brutal. Over 500 were killed by the South African police in the space of three days. The death of Steve Biko, a moderate leader of black youth, while in police custody in September 1977 showed that hardline elements were prepared to do whatever they felt necessary to silence opposition.

External opposition to apartheid

In 1961 South Africa left the Commonwealth after a series of strong attacks on its policy of apartheid, and the United Nations followed this up with criticisms of its own. The UN also repeatedly called on South Africa to give up its illegal occupation of South West Africa – originally given to her as a **mandated** territory in 1919. In 1971 the UN recognised the South West Africa People's Organisation as the true representatives of Namibia, as South West Africa is now known. Efforts to organise trade and arms **boycotts** of South Africa have failed. For one thing, the West relies on South Africa for its gold and diamond supplies. Another reason why arms shipments have never been halted is that the West sees South Africa as a key element in the struggle to stop the spread of Communism in Africa. But South African sport has been badly hit by the boycott. South Africa is banned from the Olympic Games, and any teams visiting the country for friendly games, such as the British and New Zealand rugby teams, risk retaliation from most black African nations. As a result of this boycott some effort has been made to ease apartheid in sport and introduce multi-racial competition. Increasing hostility to South Africa in the United States may have an even more dramatic effect. In June 1985 the US Senate Foreign Relations Committee voted to apply immediate **sanctions** against South Africa. The Committee imposed a ban on all new bank loans and on trade in nuclear technology and military computers with South Africa. This move was not favoured by Reagan but the policy has a great deal of support in both the Republican and Democratic parties. If no major progress has been made towards ending apartheid by March 1987 then tougher sanctions will be imposed.

Recent trends

Vorster's successor as Prime Minister in 1978 was P. W. Botha. Botha was a man who realised that if the whites are to hang on to power then there had to be changes in the system. Some observers speak of Botha's 'liberalisation' of apartheid. It is true that some of the 'petty apartheid' restrictions have been ended. There is less obsession about sexual relations between the races and blacks have been given trade union rights. The decision to recognise black trade unions was inevitable as black workers had seized those rights anyway by organising themselves so efectively. Botha also had long-term plans to bring coloured (2.5 million in number) and Asians (800 000) into partnership with the whites by granting them political rights in a Parliament which will represent all three racial groups. How far Asian and coloured groups will go along with this scheme to isolate South Africa's black Africans remains to be seen but Botha achieved some success when white voters backed the constitution by two to one in 1983. The approval by whites came as no surprise in view of the fact that whites will continue to hold a decisive majority in the new parliament.

The period since August 1984 has proved to be the longest spell of unrest in the country's recent history. More than 1600 people died in two years of protest against apartheid. The response of Botha's government to this pressure for change was severe. A state of emergency was declared in July 1985 in those areas where the protests were strongest and the foreign press and media were forbidden to cover the riots. The execution of the black poet, Benjamin Moloise, in October 1985 for the murder of a policeman led to rioting in the centre of Johannesburg. The state of emergency was finally lifted in March 1986 and the following month Botha announced that 'pass' laws would be abolished. As the tenth anniversary of the Soweto riots approached in June 1986 the South African government became increasingly nervous. On 12 June a nationwide state of emergency was imposed, silencing the voice of opposition of whites as well as blacks. The response of the international community to these developments was varied. The Commonwealth called forcefully for a trade boycott of South Africa – a call supported by black opposition leaders, such as Bishop Desmond Tutu. Mrs Thatcher's Conservative government and President Reagan both rejected such a policy, with the result that Britain's relations with the Commonwealth became very strained. The XIII Commonwealth Games, held in Edinburgh in July 1986, were badly disrupted by a boycott of the leading black Commonwealth states. Their anger was directed against the British government's refusal to impose a trade boycott against President Botha's increasingly repressive regime.

In the meantime the harsh facts of life under apartheid remain unaltered. In 1981 there was one hospital bed for every 61 whites and one bed for every 337 blacks. In 1983, 30 000 black children died of malnutrition. There has been no improvement in that sad statistic since 1967.

Exercise 6

a What worried the Boers about the break up of the British Empire?

b What has 'apartheid' meant in practice for non-whites in South Africa?

c What do you think is the real idea behind the South African government's policy of creating bantustans?

d Why has South Africa been able to rely on considerable support from the West in economic and military terms?

e In what way do you think that Botha developed a more effective policy for maintaining white rule than previous Prime Ministers?

Exercise 7

In 1961 the South African Prime Minister described apartheid as 'a policy of good neighbourliness'. This was the *Daily Mirror*'s response:

Source Three

'"*Apartheid is better described as a policy of good neighbourliness*", Dr Verwoerd'
Daily Mirror *cartoon, 1961*

a Who was the South African Prime Minister at the time of the cartoon?
b Suggest two of the raw materials which might be said to make up the 'riches of South Africa'.
c In what way do you think the clothing that the Prime Minister is shown wearing is appropriate?
d What event in 1961 would have increased the hostility of a British paper like the *Daily Mirror* to the South African government?
e How does the cartoonist show that the blacks of South Africa are not given their fair share of these riches?

Exercise 8

a Copy the map on page 241 into your exercise book. Devise shading to show:
   i   former Portuguese colonies;
   ii former British colonies;
   iii countries still under white rule.
   In your book also write in brackets under the modern name the old colonial name (where appropriate) of the country.
b List the five 'frontline states' which supported the guerrillas against the white Rhodesian government. Why is it a geographically inappropriate term for two of the countries?

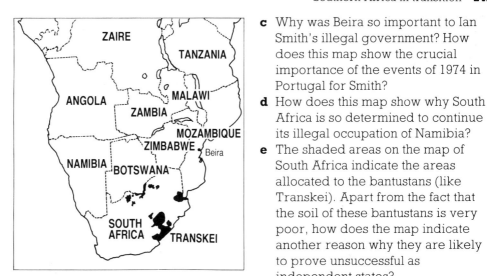

Source Four
Southern Africa

c Why was Beira so important to Ian Smith's illegal government? How does this map show the crucial importance of the events of 1974 in Portugal for Smith?

d How does this map show why South Africa is so determined to continue its illegal occupation of Namibia?

e The shaded areas on the map of South Africa indicate the areas allocated to the bantustans (like Transkei). Apart from the fact that the soil of these bantustans is very poor, how does the map indicate another reason why they are likely to prove unsuccessful as independent states?

South Africa After Botha

Botha's mixture of limited concessions to the non-white population and continued repression did not lessen the violence or bring about a more favourable attitude from the international community. Sanctions remained in force. As a result Botha was removed in 1989 from both his post as state president and leader of the National Party.

South Africa's new leader was FW de Klerk. De Klerk soon proved himself a man willing to take South Africa much further along the road towards reform than Botha. His most remarkable policy moves were to legalise the African National Congress and the South African Communist Party after nearly three decades as banned organisations. In February 1990 de Klerk ordered the release of Nelson Mandela, the leader of the ANC and imprisoned since 1963 for sabotage.

The release of Mandela opened up the possibility of genuine negotiations between the ANC and the whites about a peaceful transformation of South Africa.

Mandela revealed himself to be a man aware of the need to reassure whites about their future in a non-racial and democratic South Africa. But both men were threatened by more extreme elements among their own people. Militant blacks were not prepared to compromise with de Klerk and wanted the armed struggle waged by the ANC to continue. Equally, de Klerk faced the possibility of a violent backlash from whites in the strongly pro-apartheid Conservative Party and the neo-Nazi AWB who regarded de Klerk as a traitor.

South Africa prepared for its first-ever free elections in April 1994. The most serious threat to the stability of the country came from white racist groups like the AWB who refused to take part. They threatened a civil war if they were not given a separate white state of their own inside South Africa. Chief Buthelezi's Zulu Inkatha Freedom Party were also opposed to the elections because they feared only the views of the ANC would represent South Africa's blacks. South Africa's first steps towards democracy have left a bloody trail as township violence between the Zulus and the ANC claimed thousands of lives.

Chapter 19

The Arab–Israeli conflict: 1948–82

Origins of the conflict

Ever since AD 70, when the Romans destroyed the last independent Jewish state, the Jews have always hoped to return to their promised land of Israel. In 1897 the Zionist movement was created. Its basic aim was to set up the state of Israel in Palestine. In 1917 the British government sympathised with the Zionists and its Foreign Secretary, A.J. Balfour, made the Balfour Declaration. The government viewed 'with favour the establishment in Palestine of a national home for the Jewish people'.

After the First World War Palestine, a colony of defeated Turkey, was handed over to Britain by the San Remo Conference of 1920 as a **mandate** (see the map on page 35). This meant that Britain was to run the country until Palestine was in a position to run itself. The Arabs of Palestine felt cheated. They, along with all of Turkey's Arab subjects, had been promised in 1915 by Sir Henry MacMahon independence if they helped the British against Turkey. They did assist the British war effort and yet only Saudi Arabia became properly independent. What angered the Palestinians even more was the fact that now Jews were to be allowed into the country without any consultation with them.

In 1922 there were 84 000 Jews in Palestine and 590 000 Arabs. During the 1920s there was steady Jewish immigration into the country. They quickly bought up land and established themselves in business. Their prosperity caused resentment among the Arabs and anti-Jewish rioting frequently broke out. By 1932 the Jewish population had more than doubled to 180 000. The British tried to restrict immigration only to be faced by Jewish-led rioting. In 1937 the British-government-sponsored Peel Commission decided that the country should be partitioned or divided between Jews and Arabs but the decision was rejected by the Arabs.

Post-war Palestine

The outbreak of the Second World War temporarily led the matter to be shelved. But the effects of the 'Holocaust' in which 6 million Jews perished in Nazi death camps made the Zionists more determined than ever to establish their own state in Palestine. This time much of world opinion was behind them – especially the United States, where most of the world's Jews lived. In 1946 a Jewish terror group, led by Menachem Begin, blew up the British HQ in Jerusalem, killing nearly 100 people. Later the Irgun also hung two British undercover soldiers and booby-trapped their bodies. Ernest Bevin, the British Foreign Secretary, asked the United Nations to work out a solution to the crisis. The UN partition plan called for the division of Palestine into Arab and Jewish sectors. Britain prepared to withdraw its 100 000 troops even though the Arabs rejected partition – not least because more than half of the country was allocated to the Jews.

Britain's mandate was due to end in 1948 anyway and Bevin was anxious to see that it did. The partition plan, rejected by the Arabs, was put into effect

just the same because it had been approved by the United Nations' General Assembly. The new state of Israel was declared in May 1948. It was promptly invaded by the armies of Egypt, Syria, Jordan, Iraq and Lebanon. The Israelis won an astonishing victory and occupied more territory than even the UN had allocated them (see the maps on page 244). A million Palestinian Arabs fled from Israel to refugee camps in neighbouring Arab states. These embittered Palestinians have formed the backbone of the Palestine Liberation Organisation's often bloody and violent attempts to regain their 'homeland'.

The ruins of the King David Hotel, the British HQ, blown up in July 1946 by the Jewish terror group, the Irgun. Ninety-one people died

The British Navy, during the years of the mandate, patrolled the Palestinian Coast intercepting boat-loads of illegal Jewish immigrants heading for Palestine. This boat, in 1947, shows signs of the violence which resulted from the intervention of a Royal Navy boarding party

Exercise 1

a Why did both the Arabs and Jews have cause to be angry with Britain?

b Why did the British find themselves under even more pressure after the Second World War?

c Can you suggest any reason why the United States encouraged the Zionist movement?

d In what way do you think that the words 'anger' and 'helplessness' reflected British feelings at the time?

e Can you think of any other British 'trouble-spot' today where the same feelings might apply?

Exercise 2

a Identify the British Foreign Secretary seated on the donkey.
b Why has the cartoonist shown the road littered with skeletons?
c Identify the ways the cartoonist pokes fun at British policy in Palestine.

d How accurate was the cartoonist's prediction that the vulture of war would soon make an appearance? Explain your answer.
e In what ways do the photographs on page 243 support the view of the cartoonist?

Source One *'The Uncovered Wagon'*
28 April 1948

The Suez War 1956

The 1948–49 war left the Jews with more of Palestine than the UN partition plan had allocated them. All that was left to the Palestinian Arabs were the Gaza Strip (now under Egyptian control) and the West Bank (under Jordanian control). In 1952 the uneasy stability that had existed in the Middle East since the 1948–49 war was disturbed by a young Egyptian colonel, Gamal Nasser. He led a military coup or seizure of power against the corrupt and inefficient regime of King Farouk. Nasser was a nationalist, determined to rid Egypt of foreign influence, and keen to modernise the country. His ambition was to make Egypt the Arab world's leading state.

After unsuccessful efforts to buy arms

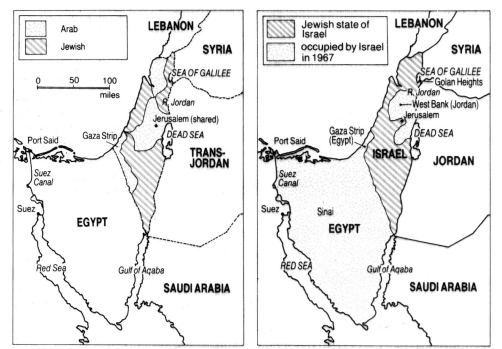

A comparison of the UN Partition Plan (left) and the actual boundaries of Israel in 1967 (right) show how quickly the State grew beyond the boundaries laid out in the plan

from the West, Nasser bought weapons from Czechoslovakia in 1955. This caused the Western powers to become concerned that Nasser was leading Egypt towards **Communism**. As a result Britain and the USA withdrew their offer to finance Nasser's ambitious scheme to build the Aswan Dam across the Nile. Nasser's response was daring. A week later, in July 1956, he ordered his troops to occupy the Anglo–French owned Suez Canal. Egypt would nationalise the canal and make it Egyptian. The tolls from the use of the canal would finance his dam project.

The secret plan of Britain, France and Israel

Israel also became concerned at developments when Egypt closed the Gulf of Aqaba (see the map below) to Israeli shipping. When the British and French suggested a secret plan to strike a blow against Nasser they were ready to listen. First, the Israelis would attack the Egyptians in the Sinai Desert. Once the Israelis had penetrated the Sinai the British and French would issue an ultimatum, ordering both sides to pull back 16 kilometres on either side of the canal. It was clear that the Egyptians would reject this demand as it would still leave Israeli forces on their territory. This would give the excuse for the Anglo–French forces to land by sea and air along the canal and seize it back. Anthony Eden, the British Prime Minister, had resigned in 1938 from Chamberlain's government over appeasement (see Chapter 10). He wrongly saw Nasser as another Hitler and was determined to make a firm stand against him. 'Nasser has a finger on our windpipe', he remarked. Nasser was going to be taught a lesson.

On 29 October the Israelis attacked across the Sinai Desert. The next day the Anglo–French **ultimatum** was delivered and, as expected, rejected by the Egyptians. On 31 October British and French aircraft destroyed the Egyptian airforce in a series of raids. On 5 November Anglo–French troops landed at the mouth of the canal at Port Said.

The United States' intervention

Britain and France had both expected that the United States would remain neutral during the conflict. They had both seriously miscalculated. President Eisenhower immediately condemned the invasion and threatened to cancel an important loan to Britain if the Anglo–French forces did not withdraw. The Soviet leader, Khrushchev, then threatened to use force to drive the 'aggressors' from the Middle East. The Suez Crisis came at just the right time for the Soviet Union. During the very same week Soviet tanks were crushing the Hungarian Rising in Budapest (see Chapter 14) and the attention of the world was distracted to events along the Suez Canal. On 6 November Eden lost his nerve and agreed to withdraw British forces. The French followed.

The Suez War

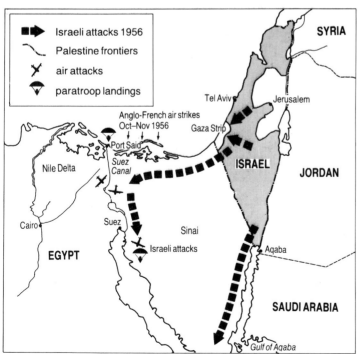

British troops inspecting Soviet and Czech-made weapons, taken from Egyptian prisoners

The results of the Crisis

Nasser emerged from the affair with credit. In the eyes of the Arab world he had stood up to the old imperial powers

Sunken ships blocking the Suez Canal, 1956

and defied them. His popularity at home and among the Arab states rose dramatically. Nonetheless, he had also miscalculated concerning the response of the British and French to his **nationalisation** of the canal and there would be no revenue from it for several months. Nasser had sunk several ships at the mouth of the canal to prevent its use. Israel was not happy at the outcome. She had nothing to show for the fighting in terms of land and vowed that the next time she would rely on no one else in a future confrontation with the Arab world. The Israelis could console themselves with the fact that, once again, they had bloodied Egypt's nose and the Gulf of Aqaba was open to their shipping. The United States had not done itself any harm in its firm handling of its Western allies. The Americans had shown themselves to be no friend of any modern day imperial adventures by the British and the French and this went down well in the poorer, developing Third World countries. At the same time, the US realised the importance of having influence in the area and began supplying the Israelis with modern weaponry. The Soviet Union had come to the same conclusion and so 'superpower' rivalry in the area grew quickly as some Arab states began receiving Soviet weapon supplies. Only Britain and France had nothing to feel pleased about. They had been humiliated by international opinion and made to look foolish. Eden, a sick and broken man, resigned in January 1957.

Exercise ▬ 3

a What evidence is there in the text that Nasser was not originally anti-Western in attitude?

b What do you think Eden meant by the phase 'Nasser has a finger on our windpipe'?

c In what sense did the British and French seriously miscalculate over their plan?

d How had both the Soviet Union and the United States benefited from the Crisis?

Exercise 4

Extract One: The Guardian

5

A telling part of the Prime Minister's broadcast was the echo of 1938. Many people in his audience may have said to themselves we must not again appease a dictator. But the parallel is misleading. By 1938 Hitler had broken international treaties not once but four times; Colonel Nasser has not yet broken any treaty, although he has dishonoured commercial agreements . . . Internally too, there is no parallel. Hitler had destroyed democratic government in a country where its roots went back to 1848. He had ruled by terror, with his storm troops and concentration camps . . . Colonel Nasser's government is arbitrary and military, but it has not gone to such excesses. It has substituted a measure of efficiency for corruption and incompetence, and it has undertaken essential land reform . . . until he turns against his neighbours or closes the canal there is no ground for military action against him.

10

Source Two

"Me too!"
Manchester
Guardian *cartoon,*
5 November 1956

(From the leading article of *The Guardian* 10 August, 1956.)

a The figure on the left in Source Two is Khrushchev. The other character depicted is Anthony Eden. Explain the significance of
  i   the tank;
  ii the aircraft.
b Do you think the phrase 'independent police action' is a fair description of Eden's action over Suez? Explain your opinion.
c What does the cartoon reveal about the cartoonist's view of the two actions depicted? How far was this view justified?

d Name the Prime Minister referred to in Extract One.
e What comparison was the Prime Minister trying to make in his speech?
f Does the author of the extract support the argument put forward by the Prime Minister? Use evidence from the passage to support your view.
g Both these sources are from *The Guardian*. Would you describe it as a supporter or opponent of the Conservative Government of the day on the issue of Suez? Explain your answer.

The Six Day War–June 1967

The end of the Suez War brought only a temporary lull in Arab–Israeli hostility. In 1959 Arab guerrilla raids into Israel began. The Syrians also began shelling Israel from the Golan Heights. In May 1967 Nasser ordered the United Nations' forces out of the Sinai and then shut the Gulf of Aqaba to Israeli shipping once more. Moshe Dayan, a hero of the Suez War, was the Israeli Defence Minister. He decided to strike first against the Arabs. On 5 June the Israelis bombed the air forces of Egypt, Syria and Jordan, destroying them all. Egypt

SAM (Surface to Air Missile). Egypt's Russian-made missiles proved very effective against Israeli aircraft in the October War of 1973

lost 300 of its 340 combat aircraft in three hours. The Israeli armies tore across the Sinai desert, into Jordan and through the Golan Heights in Syria. Deprived of air cover, the Arab tanks were helpless before the onslaught. Jordan surrendered on the 8th and finally Syria and Egypt capitulated on the 10th of June. Of Egypt's 935 tanks in the Sinai at the beginning of the war 820 were destroyed. Israel lost 122. The Israelis' crushing victory, obtained at the cost of just 750 dead, gave them control of the Sinai, the Gaza strip, the West Bank of the Jordan and the Golan Heights. Egypt was left to mourn its humiliation and 44 000 casualties.

The consequences of the war

Although a very brief war, the events of June 1967 have been decisive in shaping the Middle East as it is today. The Palestinians came to the conclusion that Israel could not be defeated in a conventional war. Instead the Palestine Liberation Organisation (PLO) and its Marxist splinter group, the Popular Front for the Liberation of Palestine, set out on a course of violent terrorist attacks on Israeli targets. Israeli responses to attacks such as the slaughter of passengers at Tel Aviv airport in 1972 and the deaths of Israeli athletes at the Munich Olympics in the same year have taken the form of air strikes against Palestinian refugee camps in which hundreds of civilians have died.

The overwhelming military success of the Israelis led them to ignore the call of the United Nations' resolution 242 to withdraw from the occupied territories even though it also recognised the right of the Israeli State to exist. They were confident of their military superiority. On the other hand, the Arab states – especially Egypt and Syria – were determined to reconquer their lost land.

There was also less sympathy for Israel within the world community. She had shown that she was more than able to defend herself, and the fact that Israel had struck first revealed a streak of deadly ruthlessness. France, under de Gaulle, moved towards the Arabs, and Britain adopted a more neutral position and became less pro-Israeli. The two superpowers, however, became more determined than ever to support their allies in the area and extend their influence.

The 1973 October War

After Nasser's death in 1970 Anwar Sadat became leader of Egypt. He was determined to avenge the humiliation of the 1967 war and this time the preparations were thorough. Russian advisers and weapons ensured that this time the Egyptians would give a very different account of themselves. The date picked, 6 October 1973, was Israel's Yom Kippur religious holiday. Many troops would be on leave. It was also, however, the middle of an Arab religious festival and the Egyptians hoped that the Israelis would not expect an attack for that reason. The attack was set for Saturday afternoon when Israeli soldiers on the Golan Heights would have the sun in their eyes. Nightfall would also give the Egyptians long hours to throw bridges across the canal free from air attacks.

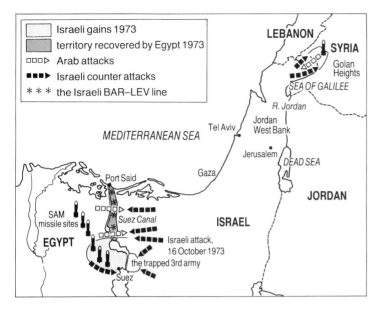

On 13 October the Syrians had been beaten back and the Israelis were able to transfer their forces against the Egyptians along the Suez Canal. Since their initial advance of some 20 miles into the Sinai the Egyptians had halted. They were reluctant to send their tanks outside the area covered by the SAM 3 sites on the west bank. By the time the Egyptian tanks did begin to move beyond the SAM 3 umbrella on 14 October the Israelis had prepared their counter-offensive. On 16 October the Israelis struck back and crossed the canal and established themselves on the west bank (see map of 1973 war). The Egyptian 3rd army was encircled but the fighting stopped on the 24th when the Russians and the Americans forced a ceasefire on the two sides. It had been a costly war. Israel had lost 2800 dead and 250 tanks; Egypt 11 000 dead and half its 1400 tanks destroyed. Syrian tank losses were even more severe: 1150 out of 1300. Nonetheless Arab pride had been restored and the east bank of the Suez Canal was once again under Egyptian control.

For Israel, the war had come as a bitter surprise. It was clear that there would be no more easy victories against the Arabs. Nearly 3000 dead in a country of just 3 million is a heavy price to pay. The Defence Minister, Moshe Dayan, the hero of 1967, and the Prime Minister, Golda Meir, both fell from office. When Anwar Sadat made peace moves towards the Israelis in 1977 they were ready to listen.

The 1973 October or Yom Kippur War. The Israeli Bar-Lev line consisted of about 30 isolated strong-points, overrun by the first Egyptian attacks

Despite the element of surprise and a massive superiority of tanks (1200–200) the Syrians could not make a decisive breakthrough in the Golan Heights. Once the Israeli reservists had been called up – greatly helped by the deserted roads of the holiday period – Syrians were driven back towards Damascus.

In the Sinai, things went very differently at first: the Israeli Bar-Lev line on the east bank of the Suez was overwhelmed by the Egyptians. The Russian-built tanks crossed the canal in large numbers and established a line 20 miles into the Sinai. The SAM (surface to air missile) sites on the west bank took a heavy toll of Israeli aircraft.

Exercise 5

a   What reasons can you give for the crushing defeat of the Arabs in the 1967 war?

b   How do you account for the much better performance of the Egyptian armies in 1973?

c   Dayan justified Israel's decision to strike first in 1967 on the grounds that Israel, being so small, could easily be overrun. What prevented Israeli territory from being overwhelmed in 1973? (Clue: the occupied territories.)

d On what grounds would Egypt have been pleased with the outcome of the October War?

Assignment unit ████████████

The October War

Write an article for an Egyptian newspaper on the October War. In addition to a description of the campaign and its careful preparations (from Egypt's point of view), you must justify the decision of the Egyptians and Syrians to strike first. How would you reply to the inevitable Israeli claims that the war was really an Israeli victory? What do you see as the effects of the war on future developments in the Middle East? (It might be worth commenting on the possibility of better US–Egyptian relations now that Egypt has broken with the Soviet Union.) Illustrate your article with the aid of maps and diagrams of the war.

The Camp David Agreement

The Arab states had another weapon that could be used against those Western states that continued to support Israel: oil. In 1973, after the Yom Kippur War, the Organisation of Petroleum Exporting Countries (OPEC) increased the price of oil by 400%. This caused tremendous problems for the Western economies. It also served as a reminder to the West that the Arab states should be listened to with more respect.

In 1975 President Sadat of Egypt and the Israelis reached an agreement in Geneva on new lines of separation along the Suez Canal which gave back to Egypt control of both banks of the canal. In November 1977 Sadat made a bold move, visiting Jerusalem in Israel. Sadat was desperate for peace. The Egyptian economy could no longer bear the crippling cost of the defence bill. Sadat was ready to recognise the right of the State of Israel to exist. Menachem Begin, the Israeli leader, agreed to hand back the Sinai to Egypt over a five year period. The final details were hammered out at Camp David in the United States after President Carter had become involved. However, no agreement could be reached over the Palestinians. They and the whole Arab world bitterly condemned the treaty. Sadat had hoped that the Israelis would agree to the creation of a Palestinian State on the West Bank of the Jordan. But Begin, despite strong American pressure, was inflexible. The anger of the Arab world left Sadat an isolated figure. In 1981 he was assassinated by religious fanatics during a military parade, but at last much needed money could now be spent to improve Egypt's desperate social problems.

Camp David, from left to right, Sadat, Carter and Begin, during the Middle East peace negotiations in June 1978

Exercise
◼◼◼ 6

Source Three
Guardian *cartoon*

a Name the figure in the cartoon seen making his way to Jerusalem.
b Name the month and year of his journey.
c Name the leader waiting to receive this man in Jerusalem.
d Explain why the Palestinians are depicted as sharks.
e What evidence is there in the cartoon that the figure in the foreground would not be entirely welcome in Israel?
f In what sense was the treaty between Egypt and Israel both a success and a failure for the man in the foreground?

The Middle East since 1977

During the period of the late 1970s and the early 1980s other dramatic events were occurring in the Middle East. The organisation representing the Palestinian people, the Palestine Liberation Organisation, continued to strike hard at Israel from its bases inside Lebanon. The repeated rocket attacks and guerrilla raids prompted Israel to invade Lebanon in 1978 and again, more decisively, in 1982. The aim was to destroy the PLO bases in south Lebanon and smash the organisation once and for all. The PLO put up stubborn resistance and the fighting was costly for the Israelis who lost over 500 men killed. Eventually the smaller and less well equipped Palestinian forces were driven out of the Lebanon – except for a few thousand around the northern town of Tripoli. Despite the casualties, Israel scored an important victory over the PLO. Yasser Arafat, the PLO leader for over 20 years, now found himself under attack from within the PLO itself. He was forced to abandon Lebanon with the remnants of his supporters. A Palestinian civil war was now added to the Lebanon's own long-standing civil war.

New problems for Egypt and Israel

The 1982 Israeli invasion of Lebanon was code-named 'Operation Peace for Galilee'. It seemed to succeed in that Arafat and 12 000 fighters were driven from the Lebanon. The Israelis hoped it was for good. By the beginning of 1986, though, it was clear that the vast majority of these PLO men had made their way back to Lebanon after further training in pro-Arafat Arab countries. Rocket attacks on Israeli villages from southern Lebanon have started again and once again the Israelis are launching air strikes against villages they claim contain Palestinian fighters. These Palestinian guerrillas are now better equipped – SAM-7 missiles were used against the Israeli planes – and have formed stronger alliances with their Lebanese supporters. The Israelis also face another serious problem on their southern border and it could soon lead to a major crisis in the Middle East.

Although the Sinai was handed back to Egypt by Israel as agreed at Camp David there has been no progress at all concerning the future of the Palestinians. The Israelis continue to refuse to negotiate with the PLO about the

Anti-Arafat PLO rebels man an anti-aircraft gun position in Tripoli, Lebanon

future of the West Bank and the Gaza Strip. Arafat, for his part, continues to refuse to accept UN Security Council resolutions 242 and 338, both of which recognise Israel's right to exist. Egypt, under Sadat's successor, Mubarak, faces continued hostility from the Arab world because of the agreement with Israel. At the same time, Mubarak is under great pressure from his own people to seek better relations with the Arab states by moving away from the close ties with the United States and Israel. Egypt's economy has been badly hit by the fall in the price of oil. In 1981, when Mubarak took over, each of Egypt's daily production of 700 000 barrels of oil was worth about $35. By April 1986 the price had fallen to just $10 a barrel. This has made Mubarak even more dependent on the $2.3 billion a year of United States' aid to Egypt. The Egyptians feel that Reagan took little interest in seeking a solution to the problems of the Middle East. One official in Egypt commented that, 'President Carter used to have a map of Sinai hanging in his bedroom – the Middle East was an obsession with him. That is the basic difference between the situation at the time of the peace treaty and the situation now'.

Glossary

anti-Semitic: a prejudiced attitude against Jews

apartheid: the policy of the white government of South Africa which separates the non-white races from the whites

appeasement: the policy of making concessions to people to win their favour; the policy followed by Great Britain towards Adolf Hitler in the late 1930s

armistice: a truce or ceasefire which is later followed by an official treaty

autocracy: a system of government in which one man (an autocrat) holds total power

blitzkrieg: German word for 'lightning war', a war of speed based on the rapid movement of tanks and aircraft

Bolshevik: member of Lenin's faction of the Social Democratic Party in Russia and believing in the need for violent revolution to create a Communist society

bourgeoisie: generally the middle classes; sometimes the owners of factories, and businessmen

boycott: refusal to trade or do business with a country or people

capitalism: the system in which businesses are privately owned and run for profit

Cheka: the first secret police organisation set up in Russia after the revolution

coalition: a government in which two or more political parties work together

collective farm: a government run and owned farm made up of a number of smaller farms put together

Cold War: a war of words and state of tension between the USSR and the USA and between their allies

colonialism: the taking-over of smaller and generally weaker countries by more powerful nations

Communism: the system in which all the industries are run and owned by the state on behalf of the people

Congress: the law-making body of the United States, made up of the Senate and the House of Representatives

constitution: the rules, usually written, by which countries are governed

coup d'état: seizure of power in a country, usually by an armed group

democracy: a system of government in which the people are able to choose by election those who should govern

depression: a situation in which business activity is low, leading to unemployment and lower living standards

détente: the easing of tension between the United States and the USSR

dictator: a ruler with total power over a country (similar to autocrat, above)

disarmament: a reduction or total removal of a country's armed forces

division: a large body of troops, usually 15 000–18 000 men

Duce: Italian word for 'leader', used to describe Mussolini

empire: a group of colonies under the rule of one nation

entente: an understanding or agreement between nations, similar but not as strong as an alliance, e.g. the Triple Entente of 1907 between Britain, France and Russia

Fascist: a member of Mussolini's Fascist Party, believing in violent overthrow of democratic government and in extreme patriotism

gold standard: a currency which, in theory, can be exchanged at any time for a fixed amount of gold

guerrilla: an unofficial soldier, fighting a war with hit-and-run tactics

hegemony: strong influence or domination of one country over another

industrial output: the level of goods produced by factories

inflation: rising prices

isolationism: used to describe US policy between the wars in which the US avoided contact with other countries

Kaiser: ('Emperor') title of Germany's rulers between 1870 and 1918

kulak: the richer peasants in the Soviet Union who employed other peasants

liberal: an attitude which, or a person who encourages tolerance of and freedom for the views of others

mandate: a mandated territory – an area placed under the control of a chosen power by the League of Nations until it was ready for self-rule

Marxist: a follower of the ideas of Karl Marx (1818–1883), the founder of Communism (see above)

mobilisation: the preparation of a country for war

nationalism: a strong feeling of support for one's country; it can take several forms – activity to free one's country from foreign control; to make the country united and strong; to assist it in dominating others

nationalisation: the government takeover of a privately owned business so that it can be run by the state

overproduction: the production of goods above the level needed

peaceful co-existence: policy of Soviet leader, Nikita Khrushchev, to improve relations with the United States and the West in general

plebiscite: a vote by the people on a special issue

primary evidence: historical evidence which is first-hand, coming from someone involved or present at the events described

proportional representation: a voting system in which a political party is given the same percentage of seats in parliament as it has of the vote, e.g. Party X with 10% of the votes, gets 10% of the seats in parliament

Putsch: German word for armed seizure of power by a small group

purge: to get rid of opponents by arrest or execution

rearmament: the building up of a country's armed forces

reparations: money paid by Germany after the First World War to the victorious powers to make up for the damage caused in the war

Resistance: organisation of men and women against the Nazis in countries under German occupation during the Second World War

revolution: a violent overthrow of a government, often involving large numbers of people – unlike a coup d'état (see above)

sanctions: methods used against a country to try and get it to change its policies, e.g. a trade boycott

secondary evidence: historical evidence which is not first-hand and does not come from direct involvement in the events described

segregation: the separation of people from one another, usually on the grounds of race as in apartheid (see above)

self-determination: the right of a people to decide to which country they belong or what type of government they will have

socialism: generally used to describe the system in which the major industries and businesses are run by the state

status quo: the present situation or way of running things

tariffs: a tax paid on goods imported into a country thereby increasing their price

Third World: the poorer countries of the world as opposed to the First World (the Capitalist countries) and the Second World (the Communist countries)

totalitarianism: the system of running a country in which a dictator or a single party has total control of the lives of all its citizens, with no opposition allowed

Tsar: Russian word for Emperor

ultimatum: demand made by one country against another, threatening war if the other does not agree to the demand

veto: the power to cancel or prevent a decision being made

Index